'The Killing Time'
The Morant Bay Rebellion in Jamaica

'The Killing Time'
The Morant Bay Rebellion in Jamaica

Gad Heuman

The University of Tennessee Press

Knoxville 37996-0325

First published 1994
Reprinted 2000

Published by
The University of Tennessee Press
Knoxville

ISBN 0–87049–852–5

Printed in China

Library of Congress Cataloging-in-Publication Data
Heuman, Gad J.
    The killing time: the Morant Bay rebellion in Jamaica/Gad Heuman.
        p.   cm.
        includes bibliographical references and index.
        ISBN 0–87049–852–5 (pbk: alk.paper)
        I. Jamaica–History–Insurrection, 1865.   1. Title
F1866.H48   1994
972.92'04–dc20   94–7057
                                                 CIP

Acknowledgements
The author and publishers wish to thank Blue Mountain Music Ltd. for permission to reproduce the words of the song '96 In The Shade' by William Clarke, Michael Cooper and Stephen Coore.

Photographs including front cover courtesy of the National Library of Jamaica.

Cover photo: Execution of Morant Bay rebels

To Daniel and Adam

Contents

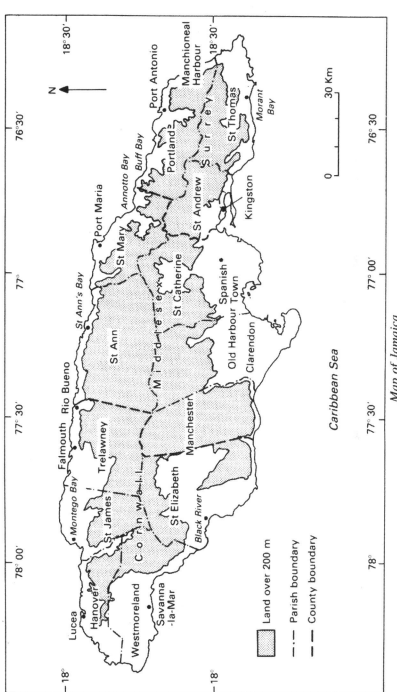

Map of Jamaica

Land over 200 m
—·—· Parish boundary
——— County boundary

Caribbean Sea

N

0   30 Km

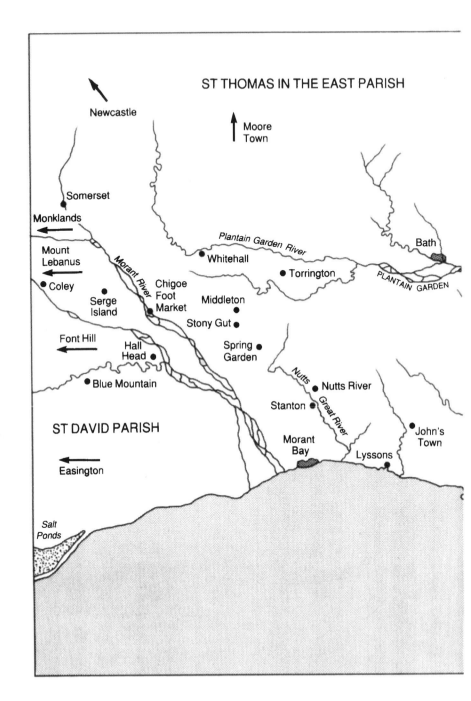

The Morant Bay area of Jamaica

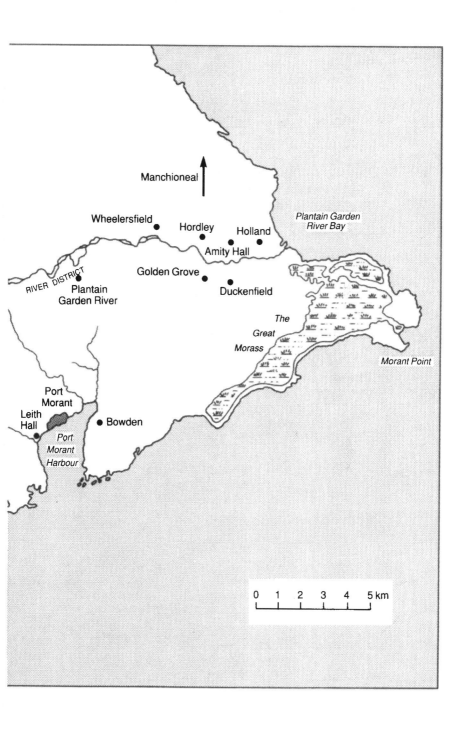

Manchioneal

Wheelersfield

Hordley

Holland

Amity Hall

Plantain Garden
River Bay

Golden Grove

RIVER DISTRICT

Plantain
Garden River

Duckenfield

The
Great
Morass

Morant Point

Port
Morant

Leith
Hall

Bowden

Port
Morant
Harbour

| 0 | 1 | 2 | 3 | 4 | 5 km |

Abbreviations

BMS   Baptist Missionary Society Records, London

CO   Colonial Office Records, Public Record Office, London

JRC   *British Parliamentary Papers*, 1866, [3683–1], XXXI, Report of the Jamaica Royal Commission, Part II, Minutes of Evidence and Appendix

MMS   Methodist Missionary Society Records, London

Papers   *British Parliamentary Papers*, 1866, [3682], XXX, Papers Laid before the Royal Commission of Inquiry by Governor Eyre

PP   British Parliamentary Papers

PRO   Public Record Office, London

Report   *British Parliamentary Papers*, 1866, [3683], XXX, Report of the Jamaica Royal Commission

Preface

The Morant Bay rebellion broke out in Jamaica on 11 October, 1865. On that day, several hundred black people marched into the town of Morant Bay, the capital of the predominately sugar-growing parish of St Thomas in the East. They pillaged the police station of its weapons and then confronted the volunteer militia which had been called up to protect the meeting of the vestry, the political body which administered the parish. Fighting erupted between the militia and the crowd and, by the end of the day, the crowd had killed eighteen people and wounded thirty-one others. Seven members of the crowd died. In the days which followed, bands of people in different parts of the parish killed two planters and threatened the lives of many others. The disturbances spread across the parish of St Thomas in the East, from its western border with St David to its northern boundary with Portland.

The response of the Jamaican authorities was swift and brutal. Making use of the army, Jamaican forces, and the Maroons (formerly a community of runaway slaves who were now an irregular but effective army of the colony), the government vigorously put down the rebellion. In the process, nearly 500 people were killed and hundreds of others seriously wounded. The nature of the suppression led to demands in England for an official inquiry, and a Royal Commission subsequently took evidence in Jamaica on the disturbances for nearly three months. Its conclusions were critical of the Governor, Edward John Eyre, and of the severe repression in the wake of the rebellion. As a result, the Governor was dismissed. More importantly, the political constitution of the colony was transformed and its 200-year-old Assembly abolished.

In the months which followed the outbreak and in the period since, there has been considerable debate about the origin and nature of the disturbances. The Governor and nearly all the whites and browns in the colony believed that tne island was faced with a rebellion. They saw it as part of an island-wide conspiracy to put blacks in power. This was not surprising in light of the Haitian revolution at the end of the eighteenth century and the massive 1831 slave revolt in Jamaica. Equally important, Jamaican society was demographically skewed: the overwhelming proportion of the population was black while whites and people of mixed race or coloureds formed a small segment of the population. For the whites and

Fig. 1   Governor John Eyre

browns of Jamaica, the Governor's actions in putting down the rebellion had saved the colony for Britain and preserved them from annihilation.

At the same time, there was a different perspective of the outbreak, especially in Britain. There, the humanitarian lobby perceived it as a spontaneous disturbance, a riot which did not warrant the repression which followed in its wake. John Stuart Mill and others formed the Jamaica Committee, hoping to bring the Governor to trial in England and thereby establish the limits of imperial authority.

This book seeks to show that the outbreak was a rebellion, characterized by advance planning and by a degree of organization. The leader of the rebellion was Paul Bogle, who, with other associates, organized secret meetings in advance of the outbreak. At these meetings oaths were taken and volunteers enlisted in expectation of a violent confrontation at Morant Bay. The meetings were often held in Native Baptist chapels or meeting houses; this was important since the Native Baptists provided a religious and political counterweight to the prevailing white norms of the colonial society.

Bogle was careful to take into account the forces which would be arrayed against him and attempted to win over the Jamaican Maroons. Moreover, Bogle's men were carefully drilled; when they marched into the town of Morant Bay to confront the vestry, their first target was the police station and the weaponry stored in the station.

It is significant that the rebellion took place in St Thomas in the East. One of the parish's representatives to the House of Assembly was George William Gordon, a brown man who had clashed with the local vestry and was ultimately ejected from it. Gordon had grown increasingly close to the Native Baptists in St Thomas in the East and to Paul Bogle, a deacon of the

Fig. 2   Paul Bogle

Fig. 3   George William Gordon

church. This identification with the Native Baptists marked Gordon out as a religious and political radical, but he was also a very popular figure in the parish. His expulsion from the vestry led to a bitter court case which was scheduled for a further hearing when the Morant Bay rebellion broke out.

This was not the only grievance of the people in St Thomas in the East. Their stipendiary magistrate, another brown man, T. Witter Jackson, was also a highly respected figure. As a neutral magistrate appointed by the Crown, Jackson was perceived as an impartial magistrate and very different from the planter-dominated magistracy. A month before the outbreak of the rebellion, parish officials therefore engineered Jackson's transfer out of the parish.

Although the tensions surrounding George William Gordon and T. Witter Jackson were specific to St Thomas in the East, the problems of a planter-dominated vestry and magistracy were symptomatic of island-wide difficulties in post-emancipation Jamaica. The common people were bitter about the continued political, social and economic domination of the whites. Among other things, this meant a lop-sided and partial judicial structure; for many blacks the only solution was an alternative legal system which they themselves controlled. Another problem centred around land: the people believed that their provision grounds belonged to them and that they should not have to pay rent for those lands. Access to land was a symbol of freedom, a freedom which some believed might even be denied to them. In addition, there were repeated complaints about the low level of wages paid on the plantations.

These grievances were not new. Protests over these issues were a recurring feature of the post-emancipation period. Even during the Morant Bay rebellion itself, there was much that was similar to earlier protests in Jamaica as well as to other social movements elsewhere. For example, one of the lasting images of the outbreak was Paul Bogle's insistence that he was not rebelling against the Queen. Eric Hobsbawm has described this sentiment as 'populist legitism'; in Hobsbawm's view the distant ruler 'represents justice' and symbolizes the aspirations of the people. This was true for peasant movements in Tsarist Russia as well as those in nineteenth-century Jamaica.[1]

Hobsbawm has also commented on the importance of social upheavals in revealing problems that 'cannot be studied at all except in and through such moments of eruption'.[2] Since the Morant Bay rebellion was one of those moments, this book seeks to give an accurate account of the rebellion. It provides a detailed narrative of the events on 11 October 1865 as well as of the days which followed the outbreak. As Jamaica has been characterized by a long history of protest, the book attempts to place the Morant Bay rebellion in the context of resistance during slavery as well as after emancipation. In addition, it tries to understand the conditions in 1865 which helped to spark the outbreak and the specific problems of St Thomas in the East. The religious and ideological orientation of those who marched into Morant Bay are also explored as is the response of the authorities to those events. The book examines the suppression of the rebellion and its political consequences. Because the Morant Bay rebellion became a *cause célèbre* in England, some attention is devoted to events there; however, the primary focus of this study is the rebellion in Jamaica.

Note on sources

Many historians have dealt with the Morant Bay rebellion, although in most cases they have done so as part of a larger work or as the culminating event in the post-emancipation period of Jamaican history. Two classic studies,

Philip D. Curtin, *Two Jamaicas: The Role of Ideas in a Tropical Colony, 1830–1865* (1955) and Douglas Hall, *Free Jamaica, 1838–1865: An Economic History* (1959) fall into this latter category. Curtin regards Morant Bay as 'another in the succession of riots since emancipation'; it was a demonstration which turned into a riot and then into a rebellion after the events at the court house on 11 October. For Hall, the rebellion was a local riot which was not markedly different from the riots in Falmouth six years previously. Hall believes that it was the reaction of the Governor and the nature of the suppression which distinguished Morant Bay.[3] Another study, Mavis Christine Campbell, *The Dynamics of Change in a Slave Society: A Sociopolitical History of the Free Coloreds of Jamaica, 1800–1865* (1976) adopts a similar perspective: she sees Morant Bay as 'nothing but a local riot' and in modern terms, as 'not unlike current "marches" or "sit-ins" '.[4] In my view, Curtin, Hall and Campbell underestimate the planning and organization of the rebellion; they also devote relatively little space to the outbreak itself.

Several other studies have discussed the rebellion but only as part of a larger work. Geoffrey Dutton, *The Hero as Murderer: The life of Edward John Eyre, Australian Explorer and Governor of Jamaica, 1815–1901* (1967) is a biography of Eyre and an attempt to rehabilitate the Governor. Although containing some useful information, it presents a biased and dated view of Paul Bogle and George William Gordon. In my earlier book, *Between Black and White: Race, Politics, and the Free Coloreds in Jamaica, 1792–1865* (1981), I consider Morant Bay principally in light of the response of the free coloureds to the outbreak. Bernard Semmel, *The Governor Eyre Controversy* (1962) is a very useful work but deals mainly with the aftermath of the rebellion in England. Two other books, Monica Schuler, *'Alas, Alas, Kongo': A Social History of Indentured African Immigration into Jamaica, 1841–1865* (1980) and Robert J. Stewart, *Religion and Society in Post-Emancipation Jamaica* (1992) are excellent studies of the period. However, Schuler concentrates on African participation in the rebellion and Stewart on the religious background to the outbreak.

Other works deal more fully with the rebellion itself. William A. Green, *British Slave Emancipation: The Sugar Colonies and the Great Experiment, 1830–1865* (1976) maintains that the uprising was a local action 'rooted in grievances which were common to blacks throughout the island'. For Green, Morant Bay might have led to other outbreaks elsewhere in the island had it been more sustained; moreover, he believes that the implications of the rebellion were 'broad and dangerous'.[5] Don Robotham, *'The Notorious Riot': The Socio-Economic and Political Bases of Paul Bogle's Revolt* (1981), is an important analysis of the rebellion. He rightly points to the premeditation and planning involved in the outbreak. Yet

Robotham concentrates on the background to the rebellion rather than on the outbreak itself.

Two recent studies examine Morant Bay as part of the history of protest in Jamaica beginning with the slave rebellion in 1831 and ending with the labour disturbances of the 1930s. Abigail Bakan, *Ideology and Class Conflict in Jamaica: The Politics of Rebellion* (1990) is a work of synthesis; she does not intend to provide a detailed historical account of the rebellion. Instead, her aim 'is to identify a general and recurrent pattern of ideological resistance among the direct producers over a broad historical period of development'. However, Bakan does emphasize the importance of land in understanding the rebellion. Thomas Holt, *The Problem of Freedom: Race, Labor, and Politics in Jamaica and Britain, 1832–1938* (1992) is the best treatment of the rebellion in the literature. He concludes that Morant Bay was a rebellion and sees areas of unity between sugar workers and peasants in the outbreak. For Holt, the Native Baptists were crucial in providing a vehicle for 'cultural resistance' and for bringing together a religious world view and a heightened political consciousness. But although impressive, Holt devotes only a chapter to Morant Bay in a larger study of Jamaica from 1832 to 1938.[6]

While I agree with Holt and also with Robotham's view of the rebellion, this study is different in that it focuses entirely on the uprising. *'The Killing Time'* seeks to provide more detail on the outbreak and spread of the rebellion as well as on the background to it, the reasons for its occurrence in St Thomas in the East, and the nature of the military and political suppression. In the process, it uses a variety of sources; however, it relies heavily on the evidence presented to the Jamaica Royal Commission, a commission of inquiry established to investigate the origins, outbreak and suppression of the rebellion.

This evidence is a crucial source for investigating the outbreak: it allows the observer to examine the society in ways which would otherwise not be possible. For example, in the wake of the rebellion there was a large number of anonymous, threatening letters which were found throughout the colony, many of which came to light in testimony before the Commission. Sometimes directed at specific individuals, the letters also reveal a widespread sense of injustice in the society at large. Moreover, the anonymous writers complained about some of the same problems which helped to set off the rebellion in St Thomas in the East. Paul Bogle was prompted to go further than the authors of these letters, but their existence suggests that his grievances were not unique.

Similarly, the inquiry into the disturbances revealed a highly politicized society, with a vocal dissident group developing in opposition to the government. Although George William Gordon was the most prominent of these figures, there were many others who were critical of the Governor and his policies. Consisting mostly of black men, these figures were rounded up after the rebellion and treated brutally. Several were hanged.

The evidence presented before the Jamaica Royal Commission is consequently a vital source for studying the rebellion and for a perspective on mid-nineteenth century Jamaica. However, there are problems with using the testimony of those appearing before the Commission. The Commission began its hearings more than three months after the outbreak of the rebellion. Following the repression of the rebellion the atmosphere in the colony was tense. No doubt some of the witnesses appearing before the commission were coached. The supporters of Governor Eyre sought to magnify the dangers of the rebellion, while his opponents were interested in minimizing the nature of the outbreak.

Yet there are ways to make use of this rich body of material. The Royal Commission not only interviewed over 700 people, it also published an appendix consisting of documents relating to the rebellion. The pre-rebellion correspondence between George William Gordon and Paul Bogle is an example of evidence which was not affected by the outbreak itself. The appendix to the report is therefore a crucial source. But the testimony before the Commission cannot be ignored. Although individual witnesses may have lied, this did not distort the general picture drawn from hundreds of witnesses. In looking at the repression of the rebellion, for example, it is possible that certain events detailed before the Commission never occurred. But there is no doubt about the savage and wanton nature of the suppression by various forces. This is equally true of the evidence revealing planning and organization of the rebellion.

Governor Eyre appeared before the Commission and also provided a considerable body of written evidence to it. Like the accounts of planters during slavery, this material has been discounted as biased and *parti pris*. In Eyre's case there is every reason to be careful about his submissions, especially about his belief in the widespread nature of the conspiracy. Yet some of the material which Eyre submitted was very valuable. It included evidence collected for the Attorney-General as well as transcripts of court cases held in the early part of 1866 involving men and women implicated in the rebellion. It would also be a mistake to discount Eyre's testimony totally and that of the leading whites and browns in the island. This is particularly the case when missionary accounts, newspaper reports, Colonial Office correspondence and contemporary records can supplement the analysis.

There are a number of additional considerations about the evidence given to the Royal Commission. There is a great deal of it, and the weight of the evidence is highly suggestive. In reviewing the testimony, it also becomes clear that this rebellion is comparable to other serious outbreaks; analogies to the 1831 slave rebellion in Jamaica, for example, are therefore possible. Despite the inevitable exaggerations and post-rebellion paranoia, the evidence on the events preceding the rebellion and, in particular, on the atmosphere during much of 1865, is important in understanding the basis of the rebellion. The Royal Commission performed a useful service in 1866; its labours are still valuable almost 130 years later.

One of the pleasures of research, especially about a topic like the Morant Bay rebellion, is the animated discussion which surrounds the topic. I have had the good fortune of being able to discuss my research, often at great length with a variety of very patient, although sometimes vociferous friends. Among those who have withstood the barrage are Bridget Brereton, David Barry Gaspar, Paul Gilje, Woodville Marshall and James Walvin. Some of the same people have gone further and critically read the manuscript. I am grateful to Bridget Brereton, David Barry Gaspar, Catherine Hall and Kusha Haraksingh for their comments on the manuscript as a whole. James Walvin has been especially helpful: he read the manuscript, looked at subsequent drafts of various chapters and responded unfailingly to numerous requests for advice. Veront Satchell provided very useful research assistance in Jamaica, and Barry and Merle Higman offered superb hospitality on several research trips. A year spent as a Rockefeller Fellow at the Atlantic Studies Program at Johns Hopkins University in 1987–88 proved invaluable, and I am grateful to the head of the program at that time, David William Cohen, for his assistance. While at Johns Hopkins, I was able to seek the advice of, among others, Franklin Knight and Sidney Mintz. The editor of the Warwick series, Alistair Hennessy, has gently prodded this book to completion.

I am grateful to those who provided funds for research on the topic: The British Academy, the University of Warwick, and the Rockefeller Residency Program at Johns Hopkins University. I have also benefited from giving papers on the subject to a variety of audiences. This includes seminars at the Institute of Commonwealth Studies and the Institute of Historical Research at the University of London, at Johns Hopkins University, at St Antony's College, Oxford and at the University of Warwick. I have also profited from discussing my work at several conferences: among them were the ASSERCA meetings in Marburg, the Society for Caribbean Studies meetings in England, and other conferences in Pittsburgh, Erlangen and London. Some of these papers have appeared in print and I am grateful to the following publishers for permission to incorporate material from them: to the KITLV Press for my essay, '1865: Prologue to the Morant Bay Rebellion in Jamaica', *Nieuwe West-Indische Gids/New West Indian Guide*, 65 (1991), to James Currey for material from 'Post-Emancipation Protest in Jamaica: The Morant Bay Rebellion', in Mary Turner, ed., *Chattel Slaves into Wage Slaves* (forthcoming) and to Königshausen & Neumann for material from 'From Slave Rebellions to Morant Bay: The Tradition of Protest in Jamaica', in Wolfgang Binder, ed., *Slavery in the Americas* (1993).

I have had considerable assistance at a variety of archives and libraries. In Jamaica, the staff at the National Archives, the National Library of Jamaica and the University of the West Indies Library have all gone out of their way to aid my research. This was also the case in England and, in particular, at the Public Record Office, the British Library, the library of the School of Oriental and African Studies (which houses the Methodist Missionary Society papers), the library of the Baptist Missionary Society, Rhodes House, Oxford (which contains the Anti-Slavery Society papers) and the Senate House Library and the library of the Institute of Commonwealth Studies, both at the University of London. I have also profited from the collections at the US National Archives in Washington.

As usual, Ruth Heuman commented on the manuscript as it progressed and, more importantly, encouraged the project all along the way. My children, Daniel and Adam, are too young to have been involved seriously in this project. But, in their own way, they made it all worthwhile; the book is dedicated to them.

Notes

1   E.J. Hobsbawm, *Primitive Rebels: Studies in Archaic Forms of Social Movement in the 19th and 20th Centuries* (New York: W.W Norton & Co., 1965), pp. 119–20.

2   E.J. Hobsbawm, 'From Social History to the History of Society', in *Essays in Social History*, ed. by M.W. Flinn and T.C. Smout (Oxford: Clarendon Press, 1974), p. 17.

3   Philip D. Curtin, *Two Jamaicas: The Role of Ideas in a Tropical Colony, 1830–1865* (Cambridge, Mass.: Harvard University Press, 1955), pp. 195, 178, 196, quote on p. 195; Douglas Hall, *Free Jamaica, 1838–1865: An Economic History* (New Haven: Yale University Press, 1959), pp. 249–50.

4   Mavis Christine Campbell, *The Dynamics of Change in a Slave Society: A Sociopolitical History of the Free Coloreds of Jamaica, 1800–1865* (Rutherford, N.J.: Fairleigh Dickinson University Press, 1976), p. 337.

5   William A. Green, *British Slave Emancipation: The Sugar Colonies and the Great Experiment, 1830–1865* (Oxford: Clarendon Press, 1976), p. 390.

6   Abigail Bakan, *Ideology and Class Conflict in Jamaica: The Politics of Rebellion* (Montreal and Kingston: McGill-Queen's University Press, 1990), pp. 11, 87, quote on p. 11; Thomas Holt, *The Problem of Freedom: Race, Labor, and Politics in Jamaica and Britain, 1832–1938* (Baltimore: The Johns Hopkins University Press, 1992), pp. 301, 300, 291, quote on p. 291.

Part I:

The outbreak

Another vestryman saw people in the crowd brandishing the police arms they had taken from the police station and heard them cry 'Colour for colour!' and 'War, war!' As the mob surged forward, Baron von Ketelhodt cried out, 'Peace!' and other officials called out 'Peace in Her Majesty's Name!' But the people responded 'No Peace! Hell today!'

The Court House, Morant Bay, 11 October 1865

CHAPTER 1 | The massacre at Morant Bay

On 11 October, 1865, several hundred blacks marched into the town of Morant Bay. As one observer put it, they went into the town 'like a mob, dancing and blowing horns'.[1] They carried a red flag, and they were in at least two (and perhaps three) groups emanating primarily from a village known as Stony Gut about four miles away in the hills above the town. Among the crowd and probably at its head was Paul Bogle, the leader of the Morant Bay rebellion and a small farmer from Stony Gut.[2] The 11th was the day when the vestry, the political body which administered the parish of St Thomas in the East, was holding one of its regular meetings.

The crowd that day was unlike any other which had ever made its way to Morant Bay. Vestrymen were familiar with crowds which 'used to come down there sometimes on vestry days and kick up a row – make a noise'. But this gathering was different: the people were armed and 'came in with some intention'.[3] Only a small number had guns but most of the others had either sharpened sticks or cutlasses. The crowd was also highly organized; the men marched four abreast, with the women on their flanks. As one observer noted, they 'came in rows . . . they were well packed together close behind each other, but not at all straggling; they advanced slowly and deliberately'. Though dressed in ordinary labourers' clothes, they looked more like troops than like an irregular mob.[4]

From the point of view of the authorities there were other worrying aspects about this crowd. Although the majority were coming from Stony Gut and neighbouring villages in the area, many were from elsewhere. A manager of the Jamaica Cotton Company's estate in St Thomas in the East, Arthur Warmington, who was also on his way to Morant Bay, found large numbers of people on the road from Manchioneal going to Bath and then toward Morant Bay, a total distance of over twenty miles. He was surprised to see a great number of people walking on the road with cutlasses, because 'it was not usual for them to walk up the public road . . . like that except when they are near the estates'. One group, from a more nearby settlement known as John's Town, had a good deal of encouragement from women along the road. About two or three miles from Morant Bay, Warmington heard women crying out, 'Flog them John's Town.' He also saw a large number of men and women assembling near a river about a mile from Morant Bay.[5]

Even more menacing was the statement of leading members of the crowd. As they passed by the druggist's shop on the way into town, they knelt down and tasted some dirt and swore that 'we will kill every white and Mulatto man in the Bay, and when we finish, we will return and go to the estates.'[6]

The crowd's first objective in Morant Bay was the police station. There were only two or three policemen inside or near the station, one of whom, Henry Good, hastened to block the crowd from entering. However, he was knocked down, stabbed and beaten. A second policeman, George Fuller Osborne, tried to escape but was caught by Paul Bogle. Bogle released Osborne only after ordering the policeman to remove his police jacket.[7] Inside the station the crowd also attacked another policeman, William Lake. According to Lake, one of the members of the crowd raised his cutlass to kill him, but another man prevented it, saying 'it is your colour; don't kill him. You are not to kill your colour.'[8] The crowd then removed all the swords, guns and pistols and demanded ammunition. But the police had none; moreover, none of the guns had any flints, rendering them useless. Having determined that there were no more weapons in the station, the crowd marched resolutely with their drum and fife playing toward the court house, where a meeting of the parish vestry was taking place.[9]

The head of the parish, Custos Baron von Ketelhodt, had already been warned of potential trouble. A German who had married an Englishwoman and settled in Jamaica, Ketelhodt was the principal magistrate of the parish and chaired meetings of the vestry. Concerned about the situation, he had called up the volunteer militia to guard the vestry that day and had written to the Governor requesting troops, expressing concern that the forces at his command would be insufficient to uphold the law. At the end of his letter the custos had added ominously that 'the shells are at this moment blowing to collect men all through the Blue Mountain Valley . . . .'[10]

The immediate cause of the troubles was a court case held four days previously, 7 October. According to Custos Ketelhodt, over 150 men had come into Morant Bay that Saturday 'armed with sticks and preceded by a band of music' and with the intention of rescuing a man who was to be tried in court, were he found guilty. During the proceedings a boy was convicted of assault and ordered to pay a fine of 4s. and costs of 12s.6d. However, another man, James Geoghegan, interrupted the court, arguing that the boy should not pay any costs. Geoghegan was ordered out of the court, but he continued to make a noise while he was leaving. When a justice on the bench ordered him to be arrested, the crowd prevented it. The police apparently grabbed Geoghegan in the square, but the mob pulled him away. According to the clerk of the parish, some '40 or 50 people with sticks

[were] licking at the police. The rioters were drawing away a man through the market, and the police trying to prevent them taking him away'. Fearing that the policemen would be injured by such a menacing crowd, the magistrates called the police back into the court house. In the process one of the policemen suffered a broken finger and at least one other member of the police was beaten. Paul Bogle was among the people involved in this scuffle.[11]

The next case was the one the crowd had come to witness. It concerned a trespass on Middleton, land bordering Bogle's village of Stony Gut. Middleton was owned by Wellwood Maxwell Anderson, a white planter who had become the Inspector-General of Immigration for Jamaica. He had leased the land to James Williams in April, 1865, who in turn rented it to small settlers. However, some of the settlers refused to pay rent on the grounds that 'the land was free' and maintained that Williams should reduce the rent. One settler claimed that he had 'been to the Record Office, and found that the land was given to them free, some years ago'. The settler warned Williams to reduce the rent; otherwise, he 'would not get any at all'.[12]

In this atmosphere it was likely that legal difficulties would arise between Williams and his tenants, although that Saturday's case concerned a trespass rather than non-payment of rent. One of the settlers, Lewis Miller, had apparently allowed his horse to stray on Williams' land. Miller was found guilty of the offence and fined 20s. Paul Bogle, Miller's cousin, advised him to appeal against the fine and acted as Miller's surety. While this case was being tried, the court house had filled with people involved in the skirmish with the police. One justice reported that the 'bearing of the people . . . was most threatening and insolent, and calculated to intimidate us'. The justices felt it was therefore impossible to make any arrests that day.[13]

The following Monday the justices issued warrants against twenty-eight people for the assault on the police at the court house. On Tuesday the police proceeded to Stony Gut, Bogle's village, to execute the warrants. They found Bogle in his yard, read him the warrant, and sought to arrest him. But Bogle refused to go and instead shouted for help. As one of the policemen reported it, as soon as Bogle appealed for help, 'the shell blew, and the drums rolled at the same time', and the police were surrounded. Immediately, upwards of 300 men armed with cutlasses and sticks appeared out of the nearby canefields and out of the chapel in the village. Although the police tried to escape, several were caught.[14] They were handcuffed, threatened with death, and eventually forced to swear an oath of loyalty. According to one of the policemen, he had to kiss the Bible and say, 'So help me God after this day I must cleave from the whites and cleave to the blacks.'[15] While at Stony Gut the policemen also witnessed other men taking the oath.

Paul Bogle spoke to the men in a language I did not understand. The men then took the oath, they kissed a large book, the Bible. Paul Bogle gave each of them a dram of rum and gunpowder which they drank.[16]

Bogle ordered three of his lieutenants, Colonel Bowie, his brother Moses, and James Davies to drill three gangs of men. The men carried sticks, cutlasses and lances and practised marching a short distance away from Bogle's house.[17] Before being freed, the police learned that Bogle would be coming to Morant Bay with his men the following day.

Bogle confirmed his intentions in a petition to the Governor, probably written while the police were still being held. In it, Bogle and his allies complained that 'an outrageous assault was committed upon us by the policemen of this parish, by order of the Justices, which occasion an outbreaking for which warrants have been issued against innocent person, of which we were compelled to resist'. The petition continued:

> We therefore, call upon your Excellency for protection, seeing we are Her Majesty's loyal subjects, which protection if refused to will be compelled to put our shoulders to the wheel, as we have been imposed upon for a period of 27 years with due obeisance to the laws of our Queen and country, and we can longer endure the same . . . .[18]

When the police were eventually released from Stony Gut later that day, they immediately reported what had happened and warned the parish officials of Bogle's plans.[19] The custos was thus enabled to call on the small group of volunteer militia to protect the meeting of the vestry.

The volunteer militia, made up mostly of whites and browns, was composed primarily of bookkeepers and overseers, that is, lower-level members of the plantation hierarchy. They were not professional soldiers. The largest group available for duty on Wednesday, the 11th, was the Number 1 Company of Volunteers from Bath. Twenty-two of them came into Morant Bay that morning, led by Captain Edward Hitchins.[20] The sergeant-major of the corps, E.N. Harrison, indicated how untrained many of them were for their duties. On the way into town a few rounds of ammunition were handed out to the men, and they were shown, apparently for the first time, how to load with ball cartridges.

When the volunteers marched into Morant Bay they found everything 'quiet, a few women only dancing before us to the music of our drum corps'. They were probably relieved to hear that the Stony Gut people were not planning to come into town. Instead, the volunteers believed that the people of Stony Gut were armed, but waiting in the village to resist any attempts to take Bogle and the others to town. While the meeting of the vestry was taking place in the court house, the militia had lunch and were resting or strolling around the parade.[21]

Suddenly, around 3 o'clock in the afternoon, a man galloped into the parade (the central part of the town facing the court house), shouting that 'the negroes are coming.' The volunteer bugle was sounded, and Hitchins ordered his men to their posts. The corps now also included eight volunteers from the Number 2 Company at Morant Bay, but it should have been a much larger contingent than that. Many members of the militia from the town had clearly not reported for duty. About ten minutes later they saw a crowd of about 400 people coming toward them.[22]

The crowd had come together from different roads leading in to the parade. They appear to have entered Morant Bay together but taken alternative routes which joined at the parade. These moves seemed well orchestrated. As the crowd began to march toward the court house, one of the volunteers observed an African with a pistol in front of the mob and reported that the crowd was advancing 'with a blowing of shells or horns, and a beating of drums'.[23]

By this time the members of the vestry had come onto the balcony of the court house. From his vantage point one of the vestrymen reported seeing the armed crowd marching in what he termed 'regular soldier style'. Another vestryman saw people in the crowd brandishing the police arms they had taken from the police station and heard them cry 'Colour for colour!' and 'War, war!' As the mob surged forward, Baron von Ketelhodt cried out, 'Peace!' and other officials called out 'Peace in Her Majesty's Name!' But the people responded 'No Peace! Hell today!'[24]

Ketelhodt then asked for a copy of the Riot Act and began reading it. But he was so alarmed by what was happening that he had difficulty getting through it. He had not progressed very far when the crowd began throwing stones at the militia. A volunteer observed a woman he knew named Geoghegan throw the first stone, followed by a hail of stones from other women in the crowd. The crowd hurled glass bottles as well as stones, and some proved effective. Several of the volunteers were injured, including the captain.[25]

The crowd was now close enough to attack the volunteers. Members of the mob managed to get between the volunteers and the court house and struck them from behind. Several volunteers were badly beaten and had their guns taken away from them.[26] In the face of this onslaught, either the custos or the captain gave the order to fire. Several members of the crowd were killed, possibly as many as seven, and others were wounded. The crowd briefly retreated, but then charged the volunteers before they could reload. Rev. Stephen Cooke, the Anglican curate from Morant Bay who formed part of the vestry, later suggested that a more effective militia or even a military commander could have dispersed the crowd. But the failure of the volunteers to fire in succession gave the crowd their opening. They rushed the militia, forcing them and the vestrymen to withdraw into the court house.[27]

Once inside the building the militia and vestrymen barricaded the doors. Shooting continued. The crowd scattered behind nearby buildings, but continued to throw stones and shoot at the court house, and the troops returned fire. At one point the custos sent out an old black man with a white handkerchief seeking peace; however, he disappeared and never returned. Later in the afternoon, probably around 5 o'clock, Ketelhodt tied a handkerchief to the end of an umbrella and hung it out of a window. When the mob was told that it meant peace, they replied that they had come for war, not peace. Ketelhodt even volunteered to give himself up to the crowd, if they would spare the others in the court house. But at least two or three voices cried out that they wanted him and every white and mulatto man there.[28]

The situation was quite desperate, yet some people managed to escape from the court house. After about an hour and a half inside the court house, for example, Baron Ketelhodt's son-in-law jumped out of one of the windows. He was shot at, but managed to get away. At least one person managed to get into and then out of the court house. Seeing the shooting and then the 'white flag' from the court house, Mrs Cooke, the wife of Rev. Cooke, sent a servant to 'see if Mr Cooke wanted anything'. Although the servant did not find Rev. Cooke, the Baron and the Inspector of Police gave him letters to carry directly to the Governor.[29]

After about two hours, members of the crowd decided that the best method of attack was to burn the court house down and force the volunteers and vestrymen to come out. It is likely that women were responsible for this plan. One witness claimed that a woman from the Stony Gut area, Rosanna Finlayson, 'said they must go and get a fire stick and trash, and set the schoolroom on fire. She said the white people were locked up in the court house, and if they set fire to the schoolroom the whole people would be burnt up alive'. Five minutes later the school house was on fire. It was adjacent to the court house and it was not long before that building began to burn as well.[30]

Women were also instrumental in encouraging the men in the crowd to continue their attack on the court house. After the volunteers had fired at the crowd some of the men had withdrawn. But women on one of the roads leading into the town reportedly told the men:

> Now, you men, this is not what you said in the mountain. You said you would come to the Bay and do so and so, and now you leave all this work to the women; go to the Parade and see what the Volunteers do to the men there.[31]

With the court house on fire, the volunteers and vestrymen could no longer remain there. They had a number of quick discussions about what to do; several decided to jump out of a back window while others removed the barricades and ran down the front stairs of the court house. Some made their way to the neighbouring home of Charles Price, a black builder who was also sitting on the vestry that day, escaping the collapse of the court house roof by a matter of a few minutes. In the process, several of the parish officials and militiamen were either wounded or killed. Price's home, which was known as the 'fort house', then also began to burn.[32]

The situation for the vestrymen and volunteers was hopeless. One of the members of the volunteer corps, Lieutenant Hall, was killed in Price's house and another was badly wounded. Several of the vestrymen were also hit. At one point the men inside the building thought they saw a steamer coming to the rescue, but that proved to be a mirage. As they were surrounded and the building was on fire they all seemed doomed. Rev. Victor Herschell, the Anglican minister in Bath, offered a prayer, and a vestryman, Arthur Warmington, shook hands with two others in the building and made them promise to send his wife and baby to England if they survived and he did not. They then all sought other hiding places.[33]

By this time it was dark. Some of the officials and militiamen were able to hide in the penguins, thick prickly bushes growing near the court house. Others were caught by the mob, badly beaten, and sometimes mistakenly left for dead. Many others were killed by the crowd, including John Walton, one of the magistrates who had presided at the court case on 7 October, Arthur and Alexander Cooke, both sons of Rev. Stephen Cooke, and Edward Hitchins, the captain of the militia.[34]

The custos was unable to escape. One volunteer heard Ketelhodt asking, 'What are you beating me for? What have I done to you?' as he was dragged along by the crowd and beaten to death.[35] Charles Price, the prominent black whose house had been a temporary refuge, was also attacked by the crowd, but there was a debate about what to do about him, largely because of his colour. A policeman reported the following exchange:

'Price, don't you know that you are a black nigger and married to a nigger?' They said, 'Don't you know, because you got into the Vestry, you don't count yourself a nigger.' He said, 'Yes, I am a nigger.' They said, 'Take a looking glass and look on your black face.' And Price said, 'Yes, I am a nigger.'[36]

A vestryman who was also hiding nearby heard a member of the crowd warn that they had 'orders to kill no black; only white and brown'. Another replied, 'But he has got a black skin and a white heart.'[37] Price's politics would not have helped his plight; he was a political supporter of Baron von Ketelhodt and also had close business connections with Rev. Herschell.[38]

The crowd decided to keep guard on Price, but then the women said:

'We work for him on the road and he not pay us, and we burn bricks for the church at Morant Bay, and he not pay us. You need not keep him till before day.'

Price was then beaten to death, despite offering £200 for his life.[39] Money did not necessarily save people. Rev. Herschell offered his attackers £300 to save his life, but to no avail. 'Damn the parsons: kill him,' was the crowd's response.[40]

Many of those killed had been specifically targeted by the crowd. For example, Lieutenant Hall, the volunteer shot in Price's house, was the collector of petty debts at Bath. In that capacity he had sought to collect money from an individual; the man learned that there was to be 'a row' at Morant Bay and that the volunteers would be there. He went to Morant Bay with the intention of killing two people, Hall and his deputy.[41]

The more prominent figures, such as Custos Ketelhodt and Rev. Herschell, had also angered much of the populace. Both men were political opponents of one of the parish's representatives to the House of Assembly, George William Gordon. Gordon was a radical coloured politician who was very popular in St Thomas in the East. Ketelhodt had sought to expel Gordon from the vestry, and the case had aroused considerable hostility toward Ketelhodt among the people in the parish. One of the areas of Gordon's electoral strength was Stony Gut, the village which was at the heart of the rebellion.

There was a further complication involving Ketelhodt and Herschell. According to George Price, a former member of the government and a planter, Ketelhodt had illegally given permission for Herschell to become the contractor for building repairs at Herschell's chapel at Bath. The repairs were extensive and, since Herschell had no knowledge of building, he had contracted Charles Price to do the work. The job was done improperly and Herschell found himself financially embarrassed over the whole business. As a result of an appeal by Ketelhodt, Herschell and Price, the government agreed to provide extra funds for the project. For George Price this was an example of the type of illegality practised by the local authorities in St Thomas in the East. It caused a great deal of hard feeling among the people in the parish.[42]

In addition, both Ketelhodt and Herschell had experienced problems with their labourers. At Oxford, Ketelhodt's estate in the parish, there were complaints about low pay for the workers. Many of the people who worked on the estate came from Stony Gut and the surrounding villages. Herschell also had an estate, an abandoned sugar plantation near Bath known as Potosi. There was a dispute between him and some of the settlers who had occupied the land before he purchased it, and a court case was pending. One historian has described Herschell as 'litigious' and a legal stickler, especially over the problem of boundaries.[43] On the morning of the rebellion,

Henry Lawrence, Gordon's overseer on his estate in the parish, predicted that 'the negroes know who fit for retribution' and that 'the Baron and Mr Herschell will be dead'. Lawrence added that Dr Major, another member of the vestry, would be safe.[44] Lawrence proved to be correct. Ketelhodt and Herschell were killed, but Major was rescued. Major's case is instructive about the crowd's view of doctors. As the crowd was about to kill him, Major called for Bogle, because he regarded Bogle 'as the most distinguished officer in that hellish scene . . . and was the only human being to be appealed to that night . . . .' Since Major was a doctor he was saved to care for the wounded among the crowd.[45] So was Arthur Warmington, who claimed he was a doctor. Warmington had taken refuge in an outhouse with some volunteers. The crowd soon discovered their hiding place and killed or wounded several of the occupants. As they pulled Warmington out of the privy the people cried, 'Kill him, kill him; down with the white man. Colour for colour; kill them all.' Warmington remembered that the crowd had spared a doctor and declared that he was one also. Bogle accepted Warmington's assertion but forced him to swear that he would not dress white people's wounds, otherwise Bogle would kill him. Warmington was taken to the home of a druggist, who promised to protect him.[46]

Several of the volunteers and vestrymen were badly beaten and left for dead. One volunteer, R.G. Harrison, and his brother were attacked, and his brother was killed. The crowd dragged R.G. Harrison down a hill and thought that he was dead as well, though members of the crowd returned to examine him two or three times. He remained still, despite losing his trousers and boots. Later, when things were quieter, he hid in a bush near the sea until daylight.[47]

Another volunteer, M.N. Wolfe, was severely wounded by men wielding cutlasses. When he pretended to be dead the crowd stripped him of his uniform and underwear and left him naked. Wolfe recounted what happened next:

> Two other rebels came to me when I was lying on the ground, and they said, 'This is one of the Volunteers; he is dead, the d—d son of a bitch.' As he said so, the other one said, 'Come let us see', and they came and turned me over on my back; then they came and searched if I was dead. They came and felt my chest to see if it was blowing, and they felt my nose. I stopped my breath as well as I could, and when they found no breath was coming, they believed I was dead, and they moved off about the distance of four or five yards. One of them returned with a cutlass, and said to the other, 'Come let us cut off his head', and he immediately came and placed his knees down upon my chest, with one hand extended, and he pointed the cutlass at my throat.

But his companion advised against it and suggested they search for others who were still alive.[48]

Some volunteers were caught trying to hide in the bush. One, W. Mitchell, heard men in the crowd expressing a desire to go home because they feared that the soldiers were coming. But the women said, 'No, search the bush, plenty more in the bush.' The men responded, 'No more', but the women insisted, 'Plenty more.' They rigged up a light on a long bamboo pole and found Mitchell in the bush. He was pulled out, beaten, and robbed but eventually taken to his employer, a shopkeeper in Morant Bay. Members of the crowd then demanded Mitchell's salary for saving his life.[49]

A planter and vestryman, William Payne Georges, lay undiscovered in the penguins. He had been wounded in the court house and when Price's home was under siege, but successfully avoided detection. At about 1 a.m. the next morning, Georges decided to head toward the rectory. He was surrounded by a dozen people, and one of them wanted to know: 'Who is that?' I said, ' A friend.' They immediately sung out, 'No friend – white man, chop him down.' A man lifted his cutlass, but Georges had a pistol and fired at him. The others ran away, and Georges proceeded to the rectory. He wrote a dispatch to the custos of Kingston, Lewis Q. Bowerbank at 6 a.m. that morning, informing him that he 'was about the last of the few whites who are left to tell the mournful tale'.[50]

Despite the bloodshed the crowd did not consist solely of people anxious to kill the vestrymen or the volunteers. Many actively aided some of the injured men. James Moore Ross was a volunteer who, although wounded, tried to escape to the wharf. A woman was helping him when Bogle appeared and threatened to kill Ross. The woman shouted to Bogle, 'Don't kill him; he is nearly dead already.' Ross managed to get to the wharf and onto a boat and to safety.[51] Francis Bowen, a magistrate and a planter who sat on the vestry, had a similar experience. He escaped from the court house just after the militia had fired its volley into the crowd. Bowen was followed and stoned but managed to get onto the road leading to the wharf. There he saw men beating the sub-collector of customs, Brooks Cooke. As he ran past this affray,

> a man with a gun and fixed bayonet stopped me, and putting the bayonet against my side said, 'Which side you belong to?' (he was a black man). I said, 'For God's sake don't put that into me.' Immediately then a black man called Thompson bawled out from the wharf, 'For God's sake don't do that, it's Mr Bowen from Coley, he is a good man.'

Bowen lunged toward Thompson and pleaded for a place to hide. Thompson told Bowen to run onto the wharf, where the boat, the *Eleanor* was in port. Bowen hid in an outhouse, while some other men hailed the boat for him.

Fortunately for Bowen, the captain was able to rescue him.[52] These were not isolated incidents. For instance, another volunteer, W.W. McGowan, had been badly hurt and left for dead. The crowd had removed his boots, shirt and money. He remained on the ground until the next morning when a member of the mob came across him, realized he was not dead, and threatened to behead him. A woman whom McGowan did not know offered him a glass of water, but the man threatening the volunteer knocked it out of her hand. She then offered 4s. for McGowan and another wounded volunteer, saying that McGowan was her brother. According to McGowan, her action and the timely arrival of British troops saved his life. *The Colonial Standard* also noted that several blacks sought to save the lives of some of the crowd's victims and hoped that they would be rewarded accordingly.[53]

Before leaving Morant Bay the crowd marched to the district prison located in the town. Again, they proceeded in a military fashion, headed by Paul Bogle. There were three companies of ten men each, led by Bowie, Craddock and Simmonds as well as nearly three hundred other people at the prison. One of the officers in charge of the prison reported that as the mob entered the gaol, Bogle ordered a sentry to be put at the gate. The crowd liberated the fifty-one prisoners in the gaol, but Bogle insisted that the prisoners 'must get their own clothes, for he would not like to rebel against the Queen, and he would not strike as a rebel against the Queen, and so they wanted their own clothing'. The prison officer had to break open the chest where the personal clothes of the prisoners were kept and hand them out. Bogle also had the prison officers swear on a Bible that they would no longer serve as public officers; in addition, the officers 'must go home and work for [themselves]'. Bogle then formed the prisoners into a line and marched them out of the prison.[54]

The events at the Morant Bay gaol illustrated the significant degree of organization of the crowd. It was clear that there were specific gangs, with captains in charge of each. One volunteer, Joseph Williams, had been beaten by several of these gangs as he sought to escape. He reported that the captains included McLaren, Ennis Napier and Scipio Cowell. A resident of Morant Bay, Cecilia Gordon, had heard captains ordering men to march and to stand guard in various locations in the town. She identified two of the captains as Grant and Stewart. Yet it was Bogle who was clearly in overall charge. Whenever a question of the treatment of a captive or of tactics arose, Bogle generally gave orders and was referred to as 'General Bogle'.[55]

The organized nature of the crowd may explain the lack of pillaging in the town. Apart from the burned-out buildings there was little other destruction in Morant Bay. The crowd demanded gunpowder from Mrs Lundie's shop, they took bread from the bakery, and a range of items, including tobacco, fish, candles and soap, from Marshalleck's store. But even there, they left the rum and other spirits.[56] The crowd had come to attack the vestry; they were not intent on destroying or looting the town. For them, the vestry was the symbol of oppression: its leading members were involved in disputes with the people over land, justice and wages. Moreover, Bogle and his allies were angry about the expulsion of their spiritual and political leader, George William Gordon, from the vestry. Their fury was reflected in the massacre at Morant Bay.

The events at the court house, at the prison, and in the town occurred before any troops could arrive. When they did land the next morning, the 12th, the troops found the dead and many of the wounded in the area around the court house. In all, eighteen of the officials and the militia were dead, and thirty-one others wounded.[57] Seven members of the crowd had been killed. But the rebellion was not yet over; it would spread throughout the parish of St Thomas in the East before being savagely repressed.

Notes

1   Papers, In the Special Commission, 6 March 1866: The Queen v. Bogle, Henry Theophilus and others for Felonious Riot, Evidence of John Dubruison, p. 355.

2   Papers, In the Court held under Special Commission, January 1866: The Queen v. Bogle and others, Copyevidence for Mr Attorney-General, Statement of Stephen Cooke, p. 389.

3   JRC, Evidence of Brookes Cooke, pp. 52–3.

4   JRC: Evidence of Edward House, p. 202; Evidence of Edward William Major, p. 28.

5   JRC, Evidence of Arthur Warmington, pp. 57–8.

6   JRC, Evidence of William Alvarenga, p. 136.

7   JRC: Evidence of Henry Good, p. 30; Evidence of George Fuller Osborne, p. 32.

8   JRC, Evidence of William Lake, p. 79.

9   Papers, In the Court held under Special Commission, January 1866; The Queen v. Bogle and Others, Copyevidence for Mr Attorney-General, Statement of Robert Evan Jones, p. 442.

10 JRC, Evidence of Edward Eyre, Custos of St Thomas in the East to the Governor's Secretary, 10 October 1865, p. 84. Shells were used as a method of communication in Jamaica. Generally, these were conch shells, whose ends were knocked off. It was then possible to produce a very large noise by blowing through them; the sound could be heard two or three miles away. The Maroons made use of cows' horns for the same purpose, although they also developed a type of Morse code with their horns. Generally, the shells were used for collecting people, as in the case of the Blue Mountain Valley just prior to the Morant Bay rebellion. See Geoffrey Dutton, *The Hero as Murderer: The life of Edward John Eyre* (Sydney and Melbourne: Collins & Cheshire, 1967), p. 264, n.6.

11 JRC, Evidence of Edward Eyre, Custos of St Thomas in the East to the Governor's Secretary, 10 October 1865, p. 83; Papers, In the Court held under Special Commission, January 1866: The Queen v. Bogle and others, Copyevidence for Mr Attorney-General, Statement of Stephen Cooke, p. 389. See also the description of the disturbance in PRO 30/48/44, Cardwell Papers, 'Jamaica', by Lewis Q. Bowerbank, p. 17.

12 JRC, Evidence of James Williams, p. 184; *The Colonial Standard and Jamaica Despatch*, 20 October 1865.

13 *Ibid.*; Papers, In the Court held under Special Commission, January 1866: The Queen v.

Bogle and others, Copyevidence for Mr Attorney-General, Statement of Francis Bowen, p. 396.
14 JRC, Evidence of William Fuller, p. 80.
15 CO 137/140, Storks to Cardwell, 19 February 1866, no. 28, Enclosure: Statement of William Fuller, Policeman, 5 January 1866.
16 *Ibid.*, Statement of James Foster, rural constable, 5 January 1866. The combination of rum and gunpowder was not an unusual mixture to confirm an oath; it was also administered by slave leaders to their adherents when organizing rebellions. See Robert J. Stewart, *Religion and Society in Post-Emancipation Jamaica* (Knoxville: University of Tennessee Press, 1992), p. 137.
17 JRC, Evidence of James Foster, p. 135.
18 Report, p. 14.
19 JRC, Evidence of John Burnett, p. 229.
20 JRC, Evidence of Edward Norman Harrison, p. 15; *The Morning Journal*, 13 November 1865.
21 Papers, Statement of Edward Norman Harrison, Serjeant-Major, St Thomas in the East Volunteers, 6 January 1866, p. 24.
22 JRC: Evidence of Wallace Wood McGowan, pp. 115–16; Evidence of H.J. Cowie, p. 473; Evidence of Edward Norman Harrison, p. 15; *The Morning Journal*, 13 November 1865.
23 Papers, In the Court held under Special Commission, January, 1866: The Queen v. Bogle and Others, Copyevidence for Mr Attorney-General, Statement of McGowan, p. 387. Although there is no further evidence on the identity of the African in front of the mob, it could have been one of the indentured labourers brought from Africa in the wake of emancipation. See Monica Schuler, *'Alas, Alas, Kongo': A Social History of Indentured African Immigration into Jamaica, 1841–1865* (Baltimore: The Johns Hopkins University Press, 1980).
24 Papers, In the Court held under Special Commission, January 1866: The Queen v. Bogle and others, Copyevidence for Mr Attorney-General, Statement of Francis Bowen, p. 396; JRC: Evidence of Arthur Warmington, p. 58; Evidence of James Britt, p. 178.
25 Papers: Deposition of Robert M. Whittle, Junr., p. 150; In the Special Commission, 5 March 1866: The Queen v. Bogle, Henry Theophilus and others for Felonious Riot, Evidence of Stephen Cooke, p. 352; JRC, Evidence of James Britt, p. 178. For a comparison with the prominence of women in the riots of eighteenth-century England, see E.P. Thompson, 'The Moral Economy of the English Crowd in the Eighteenth Century', *Past & Present* 51 (1971), pp. 115–16.
26 JRC, Evidence of Edward Norman Harrison, p. 17; Papers, R.G. Harrison, Volunteer, to J.S. Williams, p. 78.
27 Papers, Statement of Edward William Major, p. 28; JRC, Evidence of Rev. Stephen Cooke, p. 37.
28 Papers, In the Court held under Special Commission, January 1866: The Queen v. Bogle and others, Copyevidence for Mr Attorney-General, Statement of Stephen Cooke, p. 389.
29 JRC, Evidence of Baron Alfred Ketelhodt, p. 5; Papers, In the Court held under Special Commission, January, 1866: The Queen v. Bogle and others, Copyevidence for Mr Attorney-General, Statement of Robert Milne, p. 414.
30 Papers, In the Special Commission, 7 March 1866: The Queen v. Bogle, Henry Theophilus and others for Felonious Riot, Evidence of Charlotte Carter, p. 360.
31 JRC, Evidence of Cecilia Gordon, p. 180.
32 Papers, Statement of Edward William Major, pp. 28–9.
33 Papers, Statement of Arthur Warmington, p. 168.
34 Henry Bleby, *The Reign of Terror: A Narrative of Facts Concerning Ex-Governor Eyre, George William Gordon and the Jamaica Atrocities* (London: William Nichols, 1868), p. 33; Papers: Letter from Rev. Stephen Cooke, p. 129; Deposition of Robert M. Whittle,

Junr., p. 150; Statement of Edward William Major, p. 28.

35 Papers, Statement of Edward Norman Harrison, p. 26.
36 JRC, Evidence of Henry Good, p. 30.
37 JRC, Evidence of William Payne Georges, p. 4
38 George Price, *Jamaica and the Colonial Office: Who Caused the Crisis?* (London: Sampson, Low, Son, and Marston, 1866), p. 130. See also Price's letter to the editor of *The Morning Post*, reprinted in *The Colonial Standard and Jamaica Despatch*, 28 December 1865 and the comment on Price's politics in *The Morning Journal*, 11 January 1866.
39 JRC, Evidence of Henry Good, p. 30.
40 Papers, Statement of Arthur Warmington, p. 168.
41 Papers, Statement of Edward Norman Harrison, p. 25.
42 Price, *Jamaica and the Colonial Office*, p. 130.
43 JRC: Evidence of James Taylor, p. 450; Evidence of the Hon. A. Heslop, p. 331; William Law Mathieson, *The Sugar Colonies and Governor Eyre, 1849–1866* (London: Longmans, Green & Co., 1936), p. 199.
44 CO 137/400, Storks to Cardwell, 19 February 1866, no. 28, Enclosure: Eyre to Cardwell, January, 1866.
45 Papers: Statement of Edward William Major, p. 29; In the Court held under Special Commission, January 1866: The Queen v. Bogle and others, Copyevidence for Mr Attorney-General, Statement of James Bonner Barrett, p. 396.
46 Papers, Statement of Arthur Warmington, p. 169.
47 Papers, R.G. Harrison, Volunteer, to Mr J.S. Williams, 3 January 1866, pp. 78–9.
48 JRC, Evidence of M.N. Wolfe, p. 234.
49 JRC, Evidence of W. Mitchell, p. 142.
50 JRC, Evidence of William Payne Georges, p. 4; CO 884/2, Confidential Print, no. 2: Papers Relating to the Insurrection in Jamaica, October, 1865, Printed for the Use of the Cabinet, December, 1865, p. 15, The Hon. W.P. Georges to the Hon. L.Q. Bowerbank, 12 October 1865, 6 a.m. – Morant Bay.
51 Papers, In the Court held under Special Commission, January, 1866: The Queen v. Bogle and Others, Copyevidence for Mr Attorney-General, Statement of James Moore Ross, p. 444.
52 *Ibid.*, Statement of Francis Bowen, pp. 396–7.
53 JRC, Evidence of W.W. McGowan, p. 117; *The Colonial Standard and Jamaica Despatch*, 16 October 1865. John Gorrie confirmed that women saved or assisted several people at Morant Bay; see his *Illustrations of Martial Law in Jamaica. Compiled from the Report of the Royal Commissioners, and Other Blue Books Laid Before Parliament*, Jamaica Papers, no. 6 (London: Jamaica Committee, 1867), p. 3.
54 Papers, In the Special Commission, 7 March 1866: The Queen v. Bogle, Henry Theophilus and others by Felonious Riot, Evidence of Sligo Campbell, p. 359; JRC: Evidence of Sligo Campbell, p. 140; Evidence of W. Cuthbert, p. 139.
55 Papers, In the Special Commission, 7 March 1866: The Queen v. Bogle, Henry Theophilus and others by Felonious Riot, Evidence of Joseph Hardy Williams, p. 358; JRC: Evidence of Cecilia Gordon, p. 180; Evidence of Edward William Major, p. 28; Papers, Deposition of Robert M. Whittle, Junr., p. 150.
56 Papers, Statement of Robert Evans Jones, Sworn: 3 January 1866, p. 33; JRC: Evidence of Mary Ann Thomas, p. 191; Evidence of Daniel Marshalleck, pp. 42–3.
57 The dead included three old and feeble men; they were paupers who were at the meeting of the vestry and unable to escape the burning court house. See JRC, Evidence of Edward Major, p. 1066.

CHAPTER 2 | The spread of the rebellion

The attack on Morant Bay was only the beginning of the rebellion. It spread through the parish of St Thomas in the East, to the borders of St David to the west and to Portland to the north and east. Various groups of blacks attacked property, took prisoners, and, in two cases, killed whites associated with the plantations.

The Blue Mountain district

The events at Morant Bay had made it clear that whites and browns were targets of the crowd. This would continue in the days which followed. In the attack on the vestry certain individuals were marked out by the crowd, some of whom reportedly discussed future plans that evening. One group agreed to collect more men, apparently at Stony Gut, while another gang intended to travel in the direction of 'the River district, and that on the way down they were to get hold of that fellow Wallace, the overseer at Lyssons and to take his head off if they got him'.[1]

Lyssons, a sugar plantation, was a short distance to the east of Morant Bay. It was just possible to make out the burning court house from the estate, where a passing white man, Henry Mais, sought refuge. Travelling to Morant Bay on the afternoon of the 11th, he was advised by a former employee not to proceed to the town, as 'the war is commenced' and he and his buggy would 'be chopped up' if he went any further. Mais spent the night at Lyssons along with Wallace, two bookkeepers, and the captain of a ship who offered help. Late that night Mais heard gangs of people yelling and learned 'that they intended to come and take off the head of everybody on the estate'. A guard of eight or ten blacks from the estates was set up to protect the whites, and early the next morning Mais escaped to the safety of the ship in the bay. A labourer who accompanied Mais to the ship was stopped on his way home by a group of blacks and made to 'take an oath by swearing to God with Bible in hand that "I must join them to kill the whites." '[2]

In the other direction, toward the north-west of the parish and near Stony Gut, gangs of people attacked a shop in the village of Chigoe Foot Market, about four miles from Morant Bay. At about 1 a.m. on the morning of the 12th and again an hour later, Matthew Cresser, who ran the shop, was forced to give people food and drink. Most of them were armed with cutlasses and sticks, and at least one had a volunteer's rifle. Later that morning a mob entered the shop, took more food and drink as well as all the cutlasses, threatened to kill Cresser, and made him a prisoner. They forced him to accompany them to Stony Gut, where he found another shopkeeper who had also been taken prisoner. Both were unharmed and escaped that evening, although Cresser's shop was further sacked.[3]

During the next few days many of the estates in the north-west of the parish were pillaged. At several, the management of the estates or the headmen were able to escape or to deflect the attacks. Isaac Panton, a black headman on Hall Head estate, close to Chigoe Foot Market, was told by his labourers on Thursday morning that they would not work that day. They were afraid of the consequences: 'if we go to work, they will come in and kill all.' Most of the labourers joined the people who subsequently raided other estates in the Blue Mountain district. Panton himself escaped into the cane fields.[4]

The bookkeeper of neighbouring Blue Mountain estate was not so fortunate. About fifty people armed with guns, cutlasses and sticks approached the estate and one of them, an African named Henry Stewart, 'chopped' the white bookkeeper, Cochrane, with a cutlass. Cochrane subsequently died from his wounds. The crowd also threatened the brown overseer, James Cressy, and Beresford Fitzherbert, the son of the owner. According to Fitzherbert, members of the crowd claimed he was a volunteer and had 'shot the negroes at Morant Bay'. When the overseer, Cressy, intervened to protect Fitzherbert, the blacks responded, 'We don't know one buckra from another, we will kill them all.'[5] But Cressy managed to save Fitzherbert's life. The crowd took Fitzherbert's money and some rum but did no damage to the estate.[6]

At other estates in the north-west of the parish quick thinking by head people, who were in charge of the labouring gangs, saved whites. At Serge Island estate a headwoman of one of the gangs, Jane Messam, was able to protect the manager, William Miller. As a group of about twenty-five people, most of whom came from nearby Garbrand Hall estate, approached Serge Island estate armed with cutlasses, sticks and a gun, Messam hid Miller in a garret. Although the crowd had come 'to take Mr Miller's life', she convinced them to return later to deal with Miller. The crowd turned back, allowing Miller to escape to Kingston. Serge Island was subsequently sacked; when Miller came home three weeks later, his stores, clothing and household possessions were either missing or ruined.[7]

The armed crowd which attacked Coley estate, just to the north and east of Serge Island, was equally half-hearted about its stated intention to kill whites and coloureds. Two ill bookkeepers at Coley fled into the woods as the crowd advanced onto the estate, but were caught and returned to the barracks. The blacks insisted that the bookkeepers, brothers named M'Dowell, go with them to Stony Gut and 'join them skin for skin'; if not, they would 'take off our heads'. When it became clear that the M'Dowells were unable to travel to Stony Gut, one member of the crowd said to 'swear them and leave them'. The bookkeepers then swore to join the people and kissed the Bible. They escaped when the crowd left Coley.[8]

A visitor to Coley, a coloured man named George Armstrong, also sought to hide from the crowd but was taken prisoner and brought to Font Hill, a black settlement. There he found three other prisoners and encountered the leaders of the crowd, Dacres and Cowell. Again, as with the M'Dowells, the crowd was eager to have Armstrong join them. The man who captured Armstrong wanted him 'to taste each other's blood as a pledge' that Armstrong would join their party. Armstrong remained a prisoner until the following Tuesday but was unharmed. Indeed, one of the leaders of the blacks, Dacres, had wanted him made a prisoner as a form of protective custody. Dacres was concerned about an imminent Maroon attack in which it was likely that Armstrong would be killed since the Maroons 'spared nobody that was not of their party'. In addition, Paul Bogle had 'directed them to take no more lives, but to make prisoners of all they could.'[9]

The last plantation to be attacked in the area was Monklands, close to the borders of St David's. On the 12th about fifty armed people came to the estate, seeking the owner, Mr Paterson. He had already fled to Kingston, and his wife was hiding in the bush. The crowd took some food and some liquor out of the plantation store, although no rum in case it had been poisoned. They also made it clear that they would not harm Mrs Paterson. Early the next morning the crowd returned, again demanding Mr Paterson and then his gun and powder. They found a gun in the store and also 'took whatever they wanted out' of the store.[10] In addition to the gun, the crowd was after recruits, just as it had been on some of the other estates. In the case of Monklands one of the estate workers observed a young man with a paper and pencil who said, 'You must join the disciples, and if you join they put your name down.'[11] When the blacks left on Friday afternoon they put a guard on the shop to make sure that nothing further was taken. On the Saturday the crowd returned and totally plundered the shop.[12]

Paul Bogle also visited two of the plantations which had been attacked, Coley and Monklands. Bogle's experience at Coley suggests that he did not have control over the various groups involved in pillaging the estates. When Bogle arrived at Coley on Friday, the day after the first raid on the estate, he approached the plantation's shop and asked for something to drink. On learning that the people had already taken everything from the shop, Bogle made clear his opposition to plundering. He ordered two men to be flogged for their role in taking the goods and fired a volley over their heads as a warning to others.[13] As at Morant Bay, Bogle was not interested in the looting of property or in its destruction.

Bogle also had difficulty attracting recruits. He ordered the young men at Coley to accompany him to Monklands to confront the soldiers who had been sent to put down the rebellion. When many refused to join him, Bogle warned that 'if they would not go he would take away their lives.' One black estate worker was reluctant to join Bogle until he heard Bogle call for tamarind switches and guns. When Bogle arrived at Monklands the next day with his new recruits, he learned that Mr Paterson had left and that the estate shop was untended. Although Bogle took some drink from the shop for the people, he claimed he had come to protect Paterson.[14]

Bogle's vision of the nature of the rebellion was very different from that of the people who attacked the estates from Hall Head estate to Monklands. Most of them were from the surrounding area, either from neighbouring estates or settlements. They did not share Bogle's strictures against looting, although they did seek to gain supporters for the rebellion. To the east of Stony Gut, at Bath and in the Plantain Garden River district, similar events also unfolded.

Bath and the Plantain Garden River district

The people who marched into Bath on the morning of the 12th did so in larger numbers than those in the Blue Mountain district. Observers estimated that between 200 and 400 people entered the town that morning. One storekeeper, William Kirkland, whose shop was to be severely damaged by the crowd, described them 'marching in ranks with flags flying, drum beating, and a horn blowing'.[15] Their first stop was the home of Maria Hitchins, the wife of the captain of the volunteers.

Mrs Hitchins had already learned that the crowd was headed towards her. Although she knew that her husband had been killed at Morant Bay, she received a letter from him early on the Thursday morning. In the letter, which he had written while the court house was still under siege, Hitchins warned his wife that people would be coming for the volunteers' ammunition stored at their home. She was therefore able to hide the ammunition under the floorboards and flee with her young children to the woods.[16]

The crowd then attacked the shops in Bath. As they were still in search of ammunition, their first demand was for guns and powder. The clerk at Mr Ford's store reported that the people took all the guns and ammunition in the store. This was not all; during the day, more people entered Bath and plundered the other stores in town, including Mr Reid's, Mr Kirkland's, and Mr Mark's.[17]

But there was some concern in the crowd about the plundering. One of the leaders expostulated with the people to return the goods taken from Mr Ford's shop: 'we don't want cloths, we want a ton of powder; we do not come here to thieve, we come to kill.' The message was repeated later that day when another group sought to kill Kirkland, who was also the chief magistrate in Bath. Kirkland and many of the white and coloured residents of the town escaped to the bush.[18]

Although the leaders of the crowd did not succeed in convincing the people to return the goods to the shops, their presence indicates a significant degree of organization. Observers noted that men were carefully drilled and put through military manoeuvres on the evening of the 12th. Horatio Reid, who worked at Ford's store, heard the beat of a drum and orders such as 'Shoulder arms, head parry, and shorten arms.' He also reported that the blacks planned to burn down the court house. However, when they realized how close it was to the church, the crowd abandoned the idea: they were afraid the church might burn down, 'and they would not like that as they were getting a black parson, as the other planter one was killed.'[19]

The crowd did not generally consist of people from Bath. Instead, it was made up of men and women from black settlements such as Torrington and Sunning Hill to the west of Bath. As successive waves of people came into the town there were also blacks from villages closer to Bath. By the end of the day a large number of them were in the town, and they effectively controlled it. A coloured carpenter, John Hamilton, commented that the town was so crowded with people carrying cutlasses and sticks that, like many other residents, he had to hide in the bush. Hamilton also reported on the leader of the 400 men who marched into Bath, John Edwards. Edwards, who lived at Torrington, was master of a Wesleyan school and captain of the men who drilled in front of Ford's store.[20]

It was not only the town of Bath which was attacked. The next day, the 13th, Rev. Herschell's estate, Potosi, which was only a few miles from Bath, was looted. When Herschell's servant, Phillip Finlay, arrived at the estate on the 13th, he learned that Mrs Herschell had fled and found that most of the goods in the house had been taken or destroyed. Finlay recounted seeing two men sitting at a table serving Herschell's liquor. The daughter of the Potosi overseer reported that people had come to the estate in search of guns. They told her that 'they were just from the war and got authority to come and look for rifles.'[21]

Apart from Bath and the neighbourhood around it, the Plantain Garden River district was another major target. It was the most significant sugar-producing area in the parish and consisted of a cluster of plantations bordering the Plantain Garden River. One of the leading rebels in the district was Prince McLeod of Johns Town. *The Morning Journal* described him as the Paul Bogle of the Plantain Garden River district and claimed that McLeod 'incited the people in that district to rebellion and acts of violence and imposed unwilling men into his service'.[22] As in the case of Bath and the Blue Mountain district, local people made up the majority of those who plundered the plantations.

Golden Grove plantation was the first estate in the district to come under attack. It was a large plantation, employing over 500 people. The overseer and bookkeepers on the estate fled, but one bookkeeper who was unwell, John Mais, remained in the barracks. Mais reported that the crowd either demolished or took everything from the overseer's house and the book-keepers' barracks. When the crowd entered the great house, however, and threatened to destroy it, some of the people from Morant Bay 'called to them and made them desist as well as leave everything there untouched, saying that the house and contents was wanted for General Paul Bogle.'[23] Unlike the other great houses in the district, the one at Golden Grove was spared.

The crowd at Golden Grove was also searching for Alexander Chisholm, the overseer, whom they wanted to kill. One member of the crowd threatened to kill Mais unless he revealed where Chisholm was. According to Mais, the people wanted to 'chop' Chisholm 'because he was a bad overseer to them'.[24] Chisholm was not the only planter the crowd was after; their specific targets included three planting attorneys: Samuel Shortridge of Golden Grove, James Harrison of Hordley estate, and Augustus Hire of Amity Hall. As one woman living on Rhine estate near Bath observed, the blacks on the 12th not only named these planters but were also singing a song as they marched by:

> Buckras' [whites] blood we want,
> Buckras' blood we'll have.
> Buckras' blood we are going for,
> Till there's no more to have.[25]

The crowd was more successful in its objectives at Amity Hall, an estate not far from Golden Grove. There were several white and brown men at the estate on the evening of the 12th, including a coloured visitor and stipendiary magistrate, T. Witter Jackson, two men seeking refuge from the mob at Golden Grove, Chisholm and Dr Crowdy, a visitor from England, Mr Creighton, and the attorney of Amity Hall, Augustus Hire and his son, Henry. Henry Hire remembered hearing the crowd shout, 'Colour for Colour!' as they approached the estate at about 11 p.m.[26] Jackson, the stipendiary magistrate, believed that he could reason with the crowd but was badly beaten at the entrance to the house. In the rampage which followed, Augustus

Hire was mortally wounded, his son was attacked and left for dead, Creighton was badly hurt, and only the doctor, Crowdy, was spared. Chisholm managed to escape unharmed. Amity Hall great house was ransacked.[27] Many months later, two visitors to the island, Thomas Harvey and William Brewin, described the scene:

> We found the house in much the same state as the rioters left it –
> doors and windows smashed in; furniture broke to pieces; human
> blood still visible on the floor, and the whole a scene of wreck and
> ruin . . . .[28]

Augustus Hire was an obvious target of the rioters. Like Baron von Ketelhodt and Rev. Herschell, Hire had experienced serious problems with the people in his district. In Hire's case the difficulty was over land. Acting for the owners of Amity Hall over some nearby property, Hire had authorized a survey on the land known as Rowland's Field. Hire had been unable to collect rent from people he believed were squatting on the land. However, when the surveyor, along with Hire, began work in July 1865, they were surrounded by an armed crowd of over 100 blacks. The crowd seized the surveyor's chain, broke it, and became 'very violent'. Despite having the ringleaders arrested, Hire and his surveyor met considerable resistance when they tried again the following day. Hire recorded the precise words of one man, Henry Doyley, who grabbed the surveyor's chain; when Hire asked him what right he had to the land, Doyley responded, 'What God Almighty make land for? You have plenty; we have none.' The surveyor also reported that the crowd told him that 'if we wanted war, we should have war.'[29] Hire's recourse was to try the people involved in the scuffle in the Circuit Court; the case was scheduled to take place the week after Hire's murder.[30]

This was not an uncommon dispute. By the 1860s there were frequent disputes over land, especially as in Hire's case, where settlers had taken possession of land which the owners wished to reclaim. As Thomas Holt has suggested,

> the people had developed the idea . . . that they had rights to the
> land. Such convictions were rooted deep in the moral economy of
> the Afro-Jamaican peasants. They were convictions they were
> willing to fight for, sometimes in violent and angry confronta-
> tions.[31]

There was an additional grievance which some of the people working at Amity Hall had expressed. According to a schoolmaster who lived on the estate, John Anderson, the people complained bitterly about their wages. As Anderson put it, there were 'continual complaints' about the low pay at Amity Hall.[32]

The bitterness over the issue of land and the people's frustrations about pay help to explain their anger at Hire. But it was not just creole blacks who were involved in the attack on Amity Hall. Africans, who had been brought to Jamaica after the end of emancipation and who had worked initially under indenture, also participated in the disturbances. It is likely that it was Africans who killed Hire: an African man named Luce was executed for the murder and another was charged with it as well. Certainly, the presence of an obeah stick covered with blood and hair on the main door at Amity Hall suggests an African-inspired orientation among the blacks in the crowd.[33]

Amity Hall bordered two other plantations in the Plantain Garden River district, Hordley and Holland. Diana Blackwood, the headwoman of a gang at Hordley, could hear the noise of the crowd at Amity Hall and the sacking of the great house. She recalled the crowd shouting, 'Hip! hip, hurrah! We have taken Sebastopol!' when Hire was killed. For them it was akin to the famous siege of the Sebastopol fortress in the Crimean War ten years earlier. A little while later Blackwood could make out one group yelling, 'Hordley! Hordley!' and another, 'Holland! Holland!' It soon became apparent that the crowd had decided to attack Hordley.[34]

The Hordley estate workers at first sought to resist the crowd. When that proved impossible several rushed to the attorney, James Harrison, and advised him to escape: 'Massa, it no use, ladies and all of you must run; don't fire a shot, they will murder everyone; they have murdered everybody at Amity Hall.' The people then advised the ladies and children to hide in the bush. It was only a short time before the crowd entered the great house and began 'to smash and destroy everything'.[35]

The women and children who escaped made up a sizeable group. There were twenty-four of them, whom Joseph Wood, a coloured bookkeeper, and Diana Blackwood directed out of the house. Blackwood hid them in the cane until early in the morning, when she took them to her house close to Hordley. Protecting the whites posed significant dangers for Wood and Blackwood. Both were chased by members of the crowd, and Blackwood had to leave her house when the crowd learned what she had done. But Blackwood was able to take the women and children out of her house in time for them to escape detection.[36]

The steps taken by Diana Blackwood to protect the managerial personnel and their families highlight an important feature of the rebellion. As at Serge Island estate, where a headwoman deflected the mob from the attorney of the plantation, blacks were instrumental in saving the lives of many of those under threat. In the case of Serge Island as well as Hordley, it was elite blacks, headpeople, who remained loyal to the white and brown attorneys, overseers and bookkeepers. But at Hordley class allegiances alone could not explain the actions of the people. As James Harrison reported it, many of the people on his estate defended him again the next day when the mob came looking for him. Harrison recalled the crowd threatening that 'if you don't tell us [where Harrison is], we will cut your throat.' But the response was, 'I don't know where massa is, and I would not tell you if I did.'[37] The Methodist missionary stationed at Morant Bay, Rev. R.M. Parnther, reinforced these views about the loyalty of many blacks during the rebellion. In a letter home that could have described Blackwood, Parnther wrote that

> in the midst of the tragic scenes, there were those of the black people who not only had no connexion with the rebellion, but at the risk of their own lives, protected the properties; and saved, instrumentally the lives of their Employers and their families.[38]

As in the Blue Mountain district and at Bath, those who attacked the Plantain Garden River district were generally from the nearby settlements. One of the bookkeepers at Hordley calculated that there were between 500 and 600 people who besieged Hordley and Amity Hall. Among them were large numbers of women. James Harrison observed that many of the blacks came from the villages of Pera, Springfield and Arcadia, and Diana Blackwood identified several residents of Hayning, a village five or six miles from Hordley. Although they did not work at Hordley, many of them were labourers on the other estates in the area.[39]

The attacks on the plantations in the Plantain Garden River district continued on Friday, the 13th. Early that morning the watchman at Holland estate, a plantation bordering Amity Hall, warned the overseer, R.J. Stewart, that a large crowd was approaching. Stewart fled on horseback and was followed for nearly ten miles until he came to the sea. There he devised an ingenious escape: Stewart made a raft out of his shirt and some bamboos and thereby foiled his pursuers. He did not land until after dark because some of them returned to the beach in the afternoon after destroying his house.[40]

Holland estate was not the last one to be plundered. Along with Amity Hall and Hordley, Duckenfield, Plantain Garden River estate, Winchester and Wheelersfield were all extensively damaged.[41] According to one account, 'every respectable house in the district had been totally destroyed in the interior; all the contents, clothes, furniture, books, pictures, everything was destroyed or carried off'.[42] Nor was this the end of the rebellion; on the 13th it spread north to the town of Manchioneal.

The Manchioneal area

Manchioneal was a small town in the north-east part of St Thomas in the East. On Friday the 13th, in the early afternoon, a group of approximately fifty people marched into the town, armed with cutlasses and sticks and shouting, 'Colour! Colour!' They were from the Plantain Garden River district and were 'blowing shells and making a great noise'. One observer recalled the blacks saying that they would kill all the whites and browns they could catch. Since they were soon joined by many more people, the crowd in Manchioneal that day consisted of several hundred men and women.

Their leader was John Pringle Afflick, a black man who was married with grown children and had land as well as three horses and a donkey. According to one witness, Afflick went from house to house encouraging people to join the rebellion and threatening those who refused.[43]

As elsewhere in St Thomas in the East, the people had specific targets. Their first one was Mr Bunting's store. Bunting, a coloured lieutenant of the volunteers, was surprised when he saw 'a lot of men with cutlasses and sticks assemble in front of my store . . . .' Although he was aware that the blacks were approaching Manchioneal, Bunting doubted reports that they would kill all the whites and browns. His view was that the crowd would go after overseers on the plantations and would not attack the 'storekeepers who generally obliged them with credit'. Bunting managed to escape by boat, but he could see his house on fire and later learned that his store had been sacked as well.[44]

The looting in Manchioneal was not limited to Bunting's shop: the crowd broke into a shop owned by Charles Kirkland where 'they took out everything and broke the windows and doors'. The mob repeated the process at another store some distance away. They also plundered the police station but did not find any guns there as a policeman had hidden the one weapon before they arrived.[45] However, it was not only stores and the police station which the blacks were after; they were also seeking the volunteers. Since Bunting was the captain of the volunteers he was a prime target. The crowd also assembled at the home of private Fisher, where one man cried out, 'Where is the Manchioneal Volunteers; if you don't come out this night we will take their heads off one by one.'[46]

As in the Plantain Garden River district, there were individuals whom the crowd vowed to kill. One was the Wesleyan missionary, Rev. Foote. The people were not concerned about Foote's preaching; instead, it was his role in collecting rents from settlers at Grange Hill which angered them. A former policeman heard the threats against Foote and helped the missionary and his family escape to Port Antonio.[47]

Many other whites in the area also fled to Port Antonio. John Hinchelwood, the proprietor of Mulatto River, left his estate on the 13th. The man in charge of the stock, Charles Nelson, recalled the arrival of a large crowd at the estate later that evening. According to Nelson the crowd broke open the store where the rum was kept and accidentally started a fire. It burned down the great house, although Nelson sought to save as much of the contents as he could. The crowd returned the next morning to take what was left in the house along with the turkeys, geese and sheep which had survived.[48]

Many other houses in the Manchioneal area were looted over the next two or three days. One planter, Christopher Codrington, reported that, with only two exceptions, 'every house was either burnt or broken up, and everything taken out of it, all furniture and silver was lost'. Codrington estimated that Hinchelwood's loss at Mulatto River exceeded £1,000. In addition, a volunteer who worked as a gunsmith, F.J. Flemming, was made a prisoner and threatened with death. But Flemming's captor left him in a shop at Manchioneal, allowing Flemming to escape. The crowd took all the guns in the shop where Flemming worked.[49]

The crowd returned to Manchioneal on Saturday and Sunday. A goldsmith from Manchioneal, Alfred Eadie, reported that 'a vast quantity' of people gathered on Sunday, in preparation for advancing further on the following day. Eadie recalled that on the Monday the blacks 'commenced blowing the shell' to get recruits for the attack on the parish of Portland to the north.[50]

The people of Port Antonio, the largest town in Portland, were expecting just such an attack two days earlier, on the Saturday. So were the whites and browns who had fled to the town from St Thomas in the East. Among them was the former Inspector of Police, John Ashley Lord. Lord had been visiting friends in Manchioneal when he learned about the rebellion. He and his hosts escaped to Port Antonio 'after a night of untold anxiety and watching, as the Rebels were within 12 miles of us'. When Lord and his friends reached the town on Friday they learned that the blacks would arrive the next day. As Lord recounted it, 'messages came in on the 14th, sent by the Rebels to Port Antonio by the market negroes, that they, the Rebels would be down by 12 o'clock a.m. that day, and have Mr Hinchelwood's and Rev. Mr Foote's heads . . . .' The attack never materialized, and Lord concluded that the rebels were delayed by the 'pillaging and burning' of properties such as Mulatto River. On Monday, the 16th, the dispatch of troops toward Manchioneal scattered the blacks.[51]

By then it was clear that the rebellion had spread throughout St Thomas in the East. Whether it was Monklands on the borders of St David or Mulatto River in the north-east corner of the parish, there were significant similarities in the nature of the outbreak. In each area local people from each district made up the majority of the attacking crowds.[52] While small settlers who owned their own property formed a significant proportion of these groups, estate labourers were also an important element. This was especially the case in the Plantain Garden River district, where Africans were heavily involved in plundering the estates.

It is therefore possible to suggest a link between small settlers and estate labourers who acted together in the days following the initial attack on Morant Bay. The sugar workers were responding to the demands for higher wages and better working conditions on the estates while the peasants were in favour of more land. Moreover, given the nature of the Jamaican peasantry, most of them would have gained some experience on the estates, either working part-time during the year or for longer stretches at various points in their lives.[53] Protests and demonstrations were hardly new to either the workers or the peasants, as will be apparent from an examination of the culture and politics of protest in the post-emancipation period.

Notes

1   JRC, Evidence of Stephen Cooke, p. 36.
2   JRC, Evidence of Henry Mais, p. 377; CO 137/400, Storks to Cardwell, 19 February 1866, no. 28, Enclosure: Astwood to Eyre, 6 January 1866, no. 1, Statement of Joseph Estall, 18 January 1866.
3   JRC, Evidence of Matthew Cresser, pp. 143–4.
4   JRC, Evidence of Isaac Panton, p. 413.
5   *The Morning Journal*, 13 November 1865; JRC, Evidence of Beresford Fitzherbert, p. 13.
6   JRC, Evidence of James Cresser, p. 137. See also parts of a letter from Fitzherbert to his father recounting details of this incident in *The Colonial Standard and Jamaica Despatch*, 4 January 1866.
7   JRC: Evidence of Jane Messam, p. 972; Evidence of William C. Miller, pp. 62, 919.
8   JRC, Evidence of P. M'Dowell, p. 93.
9   JRC, Evidence of George Armstrong, p. 302.
10 JRC: Evidence of Evelina Williams, pp. 123–4; Evidence of Mrs A. Paterson, p. 98.
11 JRC, Evidence of Douglass Johnson, p. 232.
12 The anger of the crowd could also have arisen because of the exploitative practices of the estate shop. Such shops often made use of the truck and credit system which could be found elsewhere in the region. Howard Johnson has described it very well for the Bahamas: 'The credit system and the indebtedness which it induced became an effective technique for mobilizing and maintaining a stable labour force, and payment in truck served to perpetuate the indebtedness'. See his ' "A Modified Form of Slavery": The Credit and Truck Systems in the Bahamas in the Nineteenth and Early Twentieth Centuries', *Comparative Studies in Society and History*, 28 (October, 1986), pp. 729–53.
13 JRC, Evidence of W. Anderson, pp. 160–1.
14 *Ibid.*, p. 161.
15 JRC: Evidence of R.W. Kirkland, p. 114; Evidence of John March, p. 252; Evidence of William Pitt Kirkland, p. 265.
16 JRC, Evidence of Maria Hitchins, p. 17.
17 JRC: Evidence of Horatio Nelson Reid, p. 222; Evidence of Anna Susannah Carter, p. 598.
18 JRC: Evidence of Anna Susannah Carter, p. 598; Evidence of William Pitt Kirkland, p. 265; Evidence of E. Gentle, p. 65.
19 JRC, Evidence of Horatio Nelson Reid, p. 222.
20 JRC, Evidence of John Hamilton, pp. 481–2.
21 JRC: Evidence of Phillip Finlay, p. 484; Evidence of Frances Macrae, p. 170.
22 *The Morning Journal*, 13 November 1865.

23 Papers, Statement of John Mais, p. 39.

24 JRC, Evidence of John Mais, p. 458.

25 JRC, Evidence of Mrs Major, p. 34. Planting attorneys represented the interests of absentee owners; however, they were planters rather than lawyers. The overseer ran the estate and was responsible for its day-to-day management. The job of a bookkeeper consisted primarily in looking after the small stock on the plantation, supervising the transport of the sugar to the wharves, and generally tallying the production of sugar. See Edward Brathwaite, *The Development of Creole Society in Jamaica, 1770–1820* (Oxford: Clarendon Press, 1971), pp. 142–3.

26 JRC, Evidence of Henry F. Hire, p. 314.

27 CO 137/394, Eyre to Cardwell, 7 November 1865, no. 271; JRC: Evidence of Dr Crowdy, p. 10; Evidence of Alexander Chisholm, p. 1048.

28 Thomas Harvey and William Brewin, *Jamaica in 1866: A Narrative of a Tour Through the Island, with Remarks on its Social, Educational and Industrial Condition* (London: A.W. Bennett, 1867), p. 13.

29 JRC: Evidence of Edward Eyre, Hire to Myers, July, 1865, p. 988; Evidence of Roger Swire, p. 951.

30 JRC, Evidence of The Hon. Alexander Heslop, pp. 330–1. See also Harvey and Brewin, *Jamaica in 1866*, p. 19.

31 Thomas C. Holt, *The Problem of Freedom: Race, Labor, and Politics in Jamaica and Britain, 1832–1938* (Baltimore: The Johns Hopkins University Press, 1992), p. 267.

32 JRC, Evidence of John Anderson, p. 959.

33 BMS, 'Jamaica Affairs', vol. 2, p. 142: clipping from *The Morning Star*, 31 March 1866, p. 5; JRC, Evidence of Lt Herbert B. Adcock, p. 699. For a brief discussion of obeah, see p. 85.

34 JRC, Evidence of Diana Blackwood, p. 847; *The Colonial Standard and Jamaica Despatch*, 16 October 1865.

35 JRC: Evidence of James Harrison, p. 45; Evidence of Joseph Wood, p. 846.

36 JRC, Evidence of Joseph Wood, p. 846; Evidence of Diana Blackwood, p. 847.

37 JRC, Evidence of James Harrison, p. 46.

38 MMS 199, Parnther to the General Secretary, 20 December 1865, Highbury, Morant Bay.

39 JRC: Evidence of Joseph Wood, p. 846; Evidence of James Harrison, p. 46; Evidence of Diana Blackwood, p. 532; CO 137/499, Storks to Cardwell, 19 February 1866, no. 28, Enclosure: Eyre to Cardwell, January, 1866, Statement of E.N. Harrison.

40 JRC, Evidence of R.J. Stewart, pp. 337, 339.

41 JRC: Evidence of W.G. Astwood, p. 264; Evidence of Lt Herbert B. Adcock, p. 700.

42 JRC: Evidence of W.G. Astwood, p. 264. See also Arthur Warmington's account of the damage in the Plantain Garden River district in his letter to the editor, 26 October, in *The Jamaica Guardian*, 31 October 1865. Warmington was the manager of the Jamaica Cotton Company's estate in St Thomas in the East.

43 JRC: Evidence of Thomas Henry Bunting, p. 204; Evidence of F.J. Flemming, p. 420; Papers, Statement of James Rose, p. 38.

44 Papers, Statement of Thomas Henry Bunting of Manchioneal, 2 January 1866: Declared to before me this 2nd day of January 1866, Maurice Jones, JP, p. 75.

45 JRC: Evidence of W. M'Pherson, p. 380; Evidence of Edward Kelley, p. 184.

46 JRC, Evidence of W. M'Pherson, p. 380.

47 *Ibid.*, p. 381; JRC, Evidence of J. Field, p. 105.

48 JRC, Evidence of Charles Nelson, p. 151.

49 JRC: Evidence of Christopher Codrington, p. 582; Evidence of F.J. Flemming, p. 421.

50 JRC, Evidence of Alfred Eadie, p. 422.

51 Papers, John Ashley Lord, Late Inspector of Police, to Eyre, 6 January 1866, p. 144, Subenclosure 6, Part III; JRC, Evidence of Alfred Eadie, p. 422. The principal inhabitants

of Port Antonio took refuge on board an American ship, the *Reunion*, in order to escape the rebels: see JRC, Evidence of Edward Eyre, p. 86.

52   Hamilton Hume, *The Life of Edward John Eyre, late Governor of Jamaica* (London: Richard Bentley, 1867), p. 211.

53   Holt, *The Problem of Freedom*, p. 300.

Part II:

The politics and culture of protest

Every one of you must leave your house, takes your guns, who don't have guns take your cutlisses down at once. Come over to Stoney Gut that we might march over to meet the Maroons at once without delay. Blow your shells, roal your drums, house to house, take out every man, march them down to Stoney Gut, any that you find in the way takes them down with there arms; war is at us, my black skin, war is at hand from to-day to to-morrow.

Letter from Paul Bogle and others, Stony Gut, 17 October 1865

CHAPTER 3 | The tradition of protest in Jamaica

Jamaica has a long history of resistance, stretching from the early years of slavery through the post-emancipation period. During slavery the resistance took a variety of forms, from passive acts of protest such as malingering and sabotage to violent rebellion. The Maroons, run-away slaves who established communities in the interior of the island, also attacked plantations and, in the early eighteenth century, threatened the viability of the colony. It was the rebellions and the slave conspiracies, however, which left a more direct legacy for the rebels at Morant Bay.

Slave rebellions in Jamaica have been far more numerous than elsewhere in the British Caribbean and on a considerably larger scale than those in the United States. In Barbados, for example, there were no major rebellions for over a century from the late seventeenth century to the early nineteenth.[1] The largest outbreak in the United States, the Nat Turner Rebellion in 1831, consisted of only seventy slaves. Many rebellions in Jamaica, on the other hand, involved hundreds of slaves; in the most serious outbreaks, thousands of slaves took part.

There have been a number of explanations for the significant number of rebellions in Jamaica, including the high ratio of slaves to whites. Jamaica had a heavy concentration of slaves compared to the number of whites on the island: in the seventeenth and eighteenth centuries slaves outnumbered whites by more than ten to one and by more than thirteen to one in the nineteenth century. This was markedly different from Barbados, where a more stable white population meant that the comparable ratio there was four slaves for every white. In the United States only two states had slave populations which slightly outnumbered the whites; in every other state, whites were in the majority.

Some have also argued that the ratio of creole slaves (those born in the colony) to African slaves was important. In this view, creole slaves had more at stake in the system and were less likely to rebel than African slaves, especially those who had recently been imported to the colony. Again, there was a greater percentage of Africans in the Jamaican slave population than in Barbados or in the United States. While this ratio may be significant for Jamaica in the seventeenth and eighteenth centuries, it has less bearing in the nineteenth when creole slaves led a major rebellion.

Other factors might also be useful in explaining the slave rebellions in Jamaica. The marked degree of absentee ownership among whites in the island contrasts sharply with the patterns of white resident ownership in Barbados and in the United States. Also, Jamaica's geography, with a mountainous and often inaccessible interior, offered hiding places for rebels. A further element (which was not unique to Jamaica) was the impact of social, religious and political ideas, especially toward the end of the eighteenth and beginning of the nineteenth centuries. The campaigns of the abolitionists, first to abolish the slave trade and then slavery itself, influenced the slaves as did the example of the Haitian revolution.[2]

Recent refinements to these arguments suggest that slave rebellions were more likely to occur where the forces of control were weakened or distracted and also when slave expectations were frustrated.[3] This was particularly the case when slaves believed they were to be freed, but that the planters or local authorities were withholding their freedom. An examination of some of the major rebellions in Jamaica bears out many of these observations.

The first serious slave rebellion which the British encountered in Jamaica occurred in 1673, less than twenty years after they first arrived in the island. It involved 300 slaves, mostly from the Gold Coast (Ghana), who worked on a large plantation in the parish of St Ann. They murdered their master and fled to the interior of the island. There, the slaves resisted attacks against them and, according to a contemporary writer, were 'never dislodged'. Indeed, the slaves

> almost destroyed the first parties that pursued them which not
> only discouraged other parties from going against them but also
> Encouraged many other negroes to rise, committ barbarities, and
> then fly to them severall instances of which Soon followed.

These rebels formed the basis of one of the two major Maroon communities on the island.[4]

This was not an isolated outbreak. The last quarter of the seventeenth century witnessed several more rebellions, the largest of which occurred in 1690. In that year more than 500 slaves, almost all from the Gold Coast and belonging to an estate in the parish of Clarendon, broke out in rebellion. Although many of them were captured or killed, others appear to have joined the existing band of Maroons.[5]

The number of rebellions increased significantly in the eighteenth century. Mary Turner, an authority on the slave rebellion of 1831, regards riots and rebellions against slavery in eighteenth-century Jamaica as 'endemic'; moreover, she calculates that such outbreaks occurred on average once every five years. Since Maroons were involved in many of these rebellions, the whites waged a campaign against them between 1725 and 1740. But the attempt to suppress the Maroons proved to be costly and difficult. Between 1730 and 1734, for example, the whites spent £100,000 in a vain effort to destroy the Maroons. When peace was finally declared in 1739, part of the treaty stipulated that the Maroons should return runaway slaves to the whites. Yet slave rebellions and riots continued to plague the colony.[6]

The most serious rebellion of the eighteenth century broke out in 1760. Known as Tacky's rebellion, after the name of the African rebel chief, it occurred while the British were engaged in the Seven Years' War against Spain and France. This meant that imperial forces were more concerned about external attacks than internal rebellions. Moreover, the war played havoc with the economy: sugar exports were reduced by half and the cost of imported goods was doubled. In assessing the rebellion, Michael Craton concludes that slaves were encouraged to resist because of the weakening of the armed forces.[7]

The rebellion was one of the bloodiest in Jamaica's history. It lasted for six months and resulted in the death of sixty whites and the loss of over 1,000 slaves, 500 of whom were either killed or committed suicide and another 500 transported out of the colony. The Akan-speaking Coromantee slaves from the Gold Coast who were at the heart of the outbreak aimed at 'the entire extirpation of the white inhabitants; the enslaving of all such negroes as might refuse to join them; and the partition of the island into small principalities in the African mode . . . .'[8] The rebellion was an island-wide conspiracy which shocked the planters and was equal in its impact to the Christmas rebellion of 1831 as well as the Morant Bay rebellion over a century later.[9]

There were fewer outbreaks in the first few decades of the nineteenth century, although several conspiracies were discovered in 1823 and 1824. Yet the most serious slave rebellion in Jamaica's history was yet to come. It broke out two days after Christmas in 1831. Although the rebellion lasted less than two weeks, it did massive damage to property and involved thousands of slaves. One estimate suggests that 20,000 slaves may have been involved in the rebellion, more than 200 of whom were killed during the rebellion and a further 300 executed. Property valued at over £1,000,000 sterling was destroyed.[10] The Christmas rebellion or the 'Baptist war', as it came to be known, was a crucial event in the abolition of slavery. In a variety of ways it also foreshadowed the Morant Bay rebellion.

As with events at Morant Bay more than thirty years later, the Christmas rebellion came at a time of economic and political stress. A severe drought had affected Jamaica and curtailed the production of ground provisions. Food was scarce and expensive, and when heavy rains hit the island, hunger was followed by epidemics of smallpox and dysentery.[11]

It was not only material conditions which created disaffection. There was also a heightened degree of political consciousness among the slaves stimulated by the resistance of local whites to the British government. In 1831, and under pressure from the Anti-Slavery Society, the British government took steps to ameliorate the condition of the slaves. It sent out a revised Order in Council outlining improvements to be enacted locally on behalf of the slaves. The response in Jamaica was predictable: the whites organized a series of island-wide meetings to denounce the interference of the Home government in its internal affairs. Whites even began to reconsider their allegiance to the Crown; if Britain would not protect the institution of slavery, perhaps the United States could be encouraged to do so.[12]

The whites discussed these developments openly and apparently with little concern about the possible effects on the slaves. The slaves were consequently made aware of the growing anti-slavery agitation in England. As the whites became more vociferous in their denunciation of the British government, many slaves came to the conclusion that they had already been freed, but that the whites were withholding their freedom. Since they believed that they were free, the slaves surmised that they would not meet any resistance from the King's troops in the event of a rebellion; indeed, the soldiers might even come to their aid. Some slaves even asserted that gunpowder unloaded from a naval ship during the rebellion was for them.[13]

This naive belief in the Crown had echoes at Morant Bay in 1865. Many people in Jamaica believed that the Queen could never have written 'The Queen's Advice', a government document which was circulated throughout the island that year. They also maintained that the Queen had sent them clothes and money during the summer of 1865, only to have the goods diverted by the planters to the Indian indentured labourers. At various stages of the rebellion, Paul Bogle made it clear that he was not rebelling against the Queen. There was even a hope that the Queen would replace the current set of white authorities and send others with whom the rebels could negotiate.[14]

The leadership of the Christmas rebellion was also comparable to that at Morant Bay. Sam Sharpe, the rebel leader, was an urban slave, educated and well thought of by his master. He was highly articulate and became a leader in the Baptist church as well as a 'Daddy' or 'Ruler' in the Native Baptist church. Much like Bogle, then, who was a deacon in the Native Baptist church, Sharpe used the organization of the church to organize the rebellion. As Mary Turner has suggested, 'the Baptist war . . . was essentially the Native Baptist war; its leaders shaped mission teaching to their own ends'.[15]

Sharpe planned a campaign of passive resistance for the period just after Christmas, 1831: the slaves would simply cease work until their owners paid their wages and thereby conceded that the slaves were free. However, Sharpe also developed an alternative strategy of armed rebellion in case passive resistance failed.[16]

Some of Sharpe's methods were quite similar to those employed by Paul Bogle. For example, like Bogle, he made use of oaths to exact loyalty from his confederates. At a meeting before the 1831 rebellion, Sharpe asserted that 'if "Buckra" would pay them, they would work as before; but if any attempt was made to force them to work as slaves, then they would fight for their freedom.'[17] The oath was taken on a Bible:

> Sharpe said we must sit down. We are free. Must not work again unless we got half pay. He took a Bible out of his pocket. Made me swear that I would not work again until we got half pay.

One version of the oath included promising 'not [to] trouble anybody or raise any rebellion'.[18] However, another oath taken just before the outbreak of the rebellion was more threatening: those accepting it vowed 'not to flinch till they had succeeded in getting their freedom'.[19]

The oaths taken by the slaves in 1831 and by the ex-slaves in 1865 represent a fusion of religion and politics, but one in which political goals were dominant. Both the Baptist war and the Morant Bay rebellion were political movements, but they were based around religious meetings and partly inspired by Baptist and Native Baptist traditions. As Mary Turner has commented on the 1831 rebellion, it demonstrated 'some degree of political maturity among the slaves. They had created a protest movement . . . in which religion had been subordinated to political aims'.[20] The same analysis applies to Morant Bay.

There were, of course, significant differences between the two rebellions. The Christmas rebellion was far more widespread than Morant Bay. It engulfed all of the western parishes of the island rather than being restricted to one parish, and it resulted in the destruction of far more property. Perhaps as many as ten times more participants took part in the slave rebellion than at Morant Bay. It is also possible to contrast the aims of those involved in the rebellions. In the Baptist war slaves were seeking their freedom, a freedom they defined as the right to work for wages on the plantations. At Morant Bay the rebels were intent on making their freedom more meaningful; they were therefore concerned about more specific grievances such as the lack of justice, access to land, and low and irregular pay.

Yet the course of each rebellion revealed some striking similarities. In each case, slaves and ex-slaves could be found who were opposed to the rebels or, at the very least, sought to protect the plantations on which they worked. These divisions sometimes reflected class differences within the plantation community. On one cattle pen in St James, for example, the head driver in 1831 sought to safeguard the buildings from being destroyed, only to find the slaves following the lead of a recently-released prisoner who set them on fire. Some slaves mounted guards to defend their estates, others worked normally during the rebellion to harvest the sugar without white supervision, and still others hid in the woods. Most of these responses were repeated during the Morant Bay rebellion.[21] The suppression of both rebellions was savage. Soldiers and militiamen seem to have regarded all blacks in the affected areas as enemies and subject to immediate retribution. Running away from the soldiers was regarded as sufficient proof of guilt and alleged ringleaders were often executed without trial. The courts martial were shams; in the Christmas rebellion, out of ninety-nine slaves tried at Montego Bay, eighty-one were executed. Prisoners were sometimes executed for minor offences, such as killing estate stock, and whole slave villages on some of the rebel estates were destroyed.[22]

The extent of the 1831 rebellion as well as the brutal manner in which it was put down had widespread reverberations in England. Most importantly, it had the effect of speeding up emancipation: the Act freeing the slaves was passed less than two years after the rebellion had begun. For the ex-slaves, too, the rebellion was not forgotten; it surfaced later during the riots and rebellions of the post-emancipation period.

Post-emancipation riots and rebellions

Recent research suggests that the Morant Bay rebellion was not an isolated phenomenon in the years following emancipation. During the period after 1838 there were numerous riots and conspiracies, several of which had the potential of becoming island-wide revolts. The rebellion at Morant Bay has overshadowed these earlier events, but it is important to place Morant Bay both in the context of slave rebellions and of resistance in the post-emancipation period.[23]

As with slave rebellions, the post-emancipation outbreaks had certain elements in common. Rumours of re-enslavement helped to spark the conspiracies and disturbances of 1839 and 1848 as well as Morant Bay itself. The threat of re-enslavement was often associated with the possibility of Jamaica joining the United States as a slave state. Other issues, including disputes over rents and wages as well as problems about land, were also conducive to riots and conspiracies in this period.[24]

Several of these elements were prominent in a conspiracy which came to light in July, 1839. It arose from a rumour that 'the white and brown people were going to surround the chapel on the 1st of August [the first anniversary of full freedom], and kill the black men, and make the women slaves again'.[25] Labourers in several western parishes including Westmoreland, St Elizabeth, St James and Trelawny consequently purchased guns and machetes to protect themselves. They also carried out target practice and drilling exercises and, quite significantly, adopted the names of the leaders of the 1831 slave rebellion in these drills.

The fear of re-enslavement was one of the driving forces of this conspiracy. Another was the problem of land. As Lorna Simmonds suggests, for the labourers 'acquiring land was the true indicator that freedom had been properly achieved'.[26] Ex-slaves were therefore prepared to 'fight' for access to land. As one labourer, Edward Campbell, put it:

> the black people were going to fight in August, if the white and brown people did not deliver up the land to them . . . .That there must be a fight to get their lands; that if the last fight [the 1831 slave rebellion] did not happen, they would not get their freedom so soon; and that everybody did not join in the last war, but now all were free, and must help in the fight that was coming.[27]

The Christmas rebellion was the model for these ex-slaves. Moreover, just as in that rebellion and at Morant Bay as well, there were reports that the Queen and her forces would be on their side. There was also a suggestion that the Maroons would come to the aid of the labourers. Although no outbreak occurred, whites reportedly left the affected areas in anticipation of a rebellion.

Nine years later, in 1848, another conspiracy was discovered among the ex-slaves in western Jamaica. This time the conspiracy was accompanied by a series of protests and riots. Again, the ex-slaves regarded 1 August as the day the whites would choose to re-enslave the blacks. The date was particularly significant, as it was the tenth anniversary of full freedom. In addition, the labourers and peasants were concerned about the threat of increased taxation as well as a lowering of wages on the estates.[28]

The late 1840s was a particularly difficult time for Jamaica. The British government had announced the equalization of sugar duties in 1846, resulting ultimately in the loss of protection for sugar produced in the British colonies. In Jamaica this created an economic crisis for the planters. They therefore sought to depress wages on the estates, often by as much as 25 per cent. However, many ex-slaves regarded this development as a first step toward the reintroduction of slavery.

The peasants and labourers were also disturbed by the planters' public outbursts. As in 1831, the planters held meetings to denounce the actions of the Home government. Again, annexation to the United States was raised as a possibility. This idea was given added credibility by reports in the American press which linked the distressed state of the island with the benefits of annexation. Moreover, the planters were complaining that freedom had been granted too quickly and were speculating on the chances of reimposing slavery.[29]

Just as the planters came together in their denunciation of the British government, blacks involved in the conspiracy sought to create unity by using colour to appeal for support. A headman on an estate in Hanover reported being approached by several men who said, 'Mr Brown, now you see we are all black, we must stand to our colour.'[30] There were also condemnations of brown people for helping the whites to suppress the 1831 rebellion. The 1831 rebellion as well as the Haitian revolution continued to serve as models of protest.

One of the complaints of the blacks was directed at 'White Man's' or 'Buckra Law'. The labourers were particularly incensed at their treatment by overseers and bookkeepers on the sugar estates. In addition, as in the 1831 slave rebellion, there were reports that black Baptist leaders were leading the resistance, although the Baptist missionaries denied any involvement in any such plans.[31]

The whites took the threat of revolt seriously. Some moved out of the threatened districts. Although the Governor, Charles Grey, was sceptical about an outbreak, he none the less transferred members of the West India Regiment to strategic points in the affected areas. Grey also sent a warship to Montego Bay and to Savanna-la-Mar to calm the western part of the island. In addition, Grey issued a proclamation designed to dispel rumours of re-enslavement. The proclamation made it clear that there was no intention to revoke emancipation.[32]

While there was no general outbreak, there were localised protests in various parts of the island. In July disturbances took place in Black River, St Elizabeth and also in Clarendon. Some of the people involved in these protests were aware of the conspiracy. Later in the year a riot occurred in Brown's Town, St Ann, in which two people were killed and several people seriously wounded. It was followed by a riot on an estate in St Thomas in the Vale that involved over 150 estate workers who resisted police seeking to execute warrants. However, the most serious outbreak during the year broke out in August on Goshen estate in St Mary.[33]

The main issue in the Goshen riots was taxation. The people on the estate objected to the high tax assessments made by the collecting constable, Richard Rigg, and to his appropriation of personal property because of unpaid taxes. Since Rigg was told that he would be killed if he came to Goshen, he brought along two policemen when he travelled to the estate. In the course of carrying out his duties, Rigg as well as the policemen were attacked and seriously wounded by a crowd of at least 200 people armed with sticks. When the police returned a week later to issue warrants against twenty-four people involved in the assault, they were confronted by 500 men and women armed with sticks and some weapons. This skirmish appears to have been carefully planned: the mob consisted of people from several other parishes as well as a few Maroons. In the mêlée some of the policemen were seriously wounded and all fled. Another detachment of police met the same fate the following week, and it took the 2nd West India Regiment to restore order.[34]

The Goshen riots were directed against the tax system, which the people on the estate considered unjust. Governor Grey also regarded the assessments as unfair and was worried about the possibility of a serious escalation in the level of violence. He had good reason to be alarmed: one of the policemen who went with Riggs to Goshen reported hearing the people say they would 'murder Mr Rigg, and the police in particular; and that the St James's's war would be nothing to what they would commence.'[35] Although seventeen years had passed since the 1831 slave rebellion, it clearly remained an important symbol.

Two other riots – both of which occurred in 1859 – were also significant precursors of Morant Bay. The first, which took place in February, was directed against the toll-gates in several parts of Westmoreland. Residents tore down the toll-gates in at least four different places in the parish, suggesting a concerted campaign against them. Public feeling against the tolls had been vented in a petition sent to the Governor six months earlier, but he had ignored it. When some of the offenders were tried for their part in the assault on the toll-gates, people attacked the police station. Peace was ultimately restored when troops arrived from Port Royal.[36]

The second major riot in 1859 developed over a property dispute involving Florence Hall estate near the town of Falmouth. The controversy was between a coloured man, Theodore Buie, and his Scottish aunt who sought to evict him from the property. Buie and about sixty others were arrested, but before they could be brought to trial a large crowd attacked the police station and freed them. As the assailants continued to stone the police station, the police fired on them, killing two women and severely wounding eight or nine others, one of whom died a few days later. During the riot, the crowd set fire to the police station and prevented anyone from extinguishing it. They also tried to burn down other parts of the town, and succeeded in destroying the Falmouth wharf. Together, the events at Falmouth and Florence Hall have usually been described as a riot, but there were commentators at the time who believed that the situation was far more serious and that it bordered on rebellion. Moreover, much of it occurred on 1 August, the twenty-first anniversary of full freedom. Although it may have been coincidental that the trial of Buie and his associates was set for that date, Simmonds maintains that 'it was the perfect time to protest the absence of fair justice for black Jamaicans . . . .'[37]

The riots in 1859 highlighted some of the issues which profoundly affected post-emancipation Jamaica and would prove crucial six years later at Morant Bay. High taxes, whether in the form of assessments or of toll-gates, were a serious problem for the mass of the people, especially as the

Legislature had shifted a heavy proportion of the taxes onto the ex-slaves and away from the plantocracy. The lack of justice, which was an important element in the Buie case, was one of the leading factors in the outbreak at Morant Bay. In both the Florence Hall riots and the Morant Bay rebellion, women were major actors and also major victims of the authorities.

The Morant Bay rebellion, then, was preceded by a long history of slave rebellions as well as a series of riots in the post-emancipation period. Many of the people involved in these riots continued to look to the rebellions as models of resistance, especially the 1831 Christmas rebellion. However, the agenda of the rioters was different in the period after emancipation. It included resisting any attempt at re-enslavement and regarded access to land as a measure of full freedom. Above all, this meant creating the conditions for a meaningful freedom. This would also be the agenda at Morant Bay.

Notes

1 Hilary Beckles and Karl Watson, 'Social Protest and Labour Bargaining: The Changing Nature of Slaves' Responses to Plantation Life in Eighteenth-Century Barbados', *Slavery and Abolition*, 8 (December, 1987), pp. 272–93.

2 Orlando Patterson, *The Sociology of Slavery: An Analysis of the Origins, Development and Structure of Negro Slave Society in Jamaica* (London: McGibbon & Kee, 1967), pp. 274–9.

3 Michael Craton, *Testing the Chains: Resistance to Slavery in the British West Indies* (Ithaca: Cornell University Press, 1982), p. 13.

4 Richard Hart, *Slaves Who Abolished Slavery*, 2 vols., (Kingston: Institute of Social and Economic Research, 1985) 2, p. 14; Patterson, *Sociology of Slavery*, p. 267.

5 Hart, *Slaves*, 2, pp. 17–18; Patterson, *Sociology of Slavery*, p. 268.

6 Mary Reckord (née Turner), 'The Jamaica Slave Rebellion of 1831', *Past and Present*, 40 (July, 1968), p. 108; Patterson, *Sociology of Slavery*, pp. 269–70. On the Maroons, see also Barbara K. Kopytoff, 'The Maroons of Jamaica: An Ethnohistorical Study of Incomplete Polities, 1655–1905', Ph.D. thesis, U. of Pennsylvania, 1973; Richard Price, ed., *Maroon Societies: Rebel Slave Communities in the Americas* (Garden City, N.Y.: Anchor Books, 1973); Hart, *Slaves*; Gad Heuman, ed., *Out of the House of Bondage: Runaways, Resistance and Marronage in Africa and the New World* (London: Frank Cass, 1986) and Mavis C. Campbell, *The Maroons of Jamaica, 1655–1796: A History of Resistance, Collaboration and Betrayal* (Granby, Mass.: Bergin & Garvey, 1988).

7 Craton, *Testing the Chains*, pp. 125–7.

8 Edward Long, *The History of Jamaica*, 3 vol. (London: T. Lowndes, 1774), 2, p. 447.

9 Craton, *Testing the Chains*, p. 138. See also the discussion in Hart, *Slaves*, 2, ch. 6.

10 Patterson, *Sociology of Slavery*, p. 273; Thomas C. Holt, *The Problem of Freedom: Race, Labor, and Politics in Jamaica and Britain, 1832–1938* (Baltimore: The Johns Hopkins University Press, 1992), p. 14; Edward Kamau Brathwaite, 'Rebellion: Anatomy of the Slave Revolt of 1831/32 in Jamaica', *The Jamaican Historical Society Bulletin*, 8 (December, 1981), pp. 80–1. See also Edward Kamau Brathwaite, 'The Slave Rebellion in the Great River Valley of St James – 1831/32', *The Jamaican Historical Review*, 13 (1982), pp. 11–30.

11 Mary Turner, *Slaves and Missionaries: The Disintegration of Jamaican Slave Society, 1787–1834* (Urbana: University of Illinois Press, 1982), p. 149.

12 Gad J. Heuman, *Between Black and White: Race, Politics and the Free Coloreds in Jamaica, 1792–1865* (Westport, Conn.: Greenwood Press, 1981), p. 84. British plans for ameliorating slavery began in 1823 when the first proposals to improve the condition of the slaves were dispatched to the colonies. However, whites in Jamaica resisted these directives, as they would again in 1831.

13 Turner, *Slaves and Missionaries*, p. 154.

14 JRC: Evidence of Sligo Campbell 140; Evidence of W. Cutherbert 139; Evidence of Raynes Waite Smith 744; Evidence of William Rennie, p. 418. For more information on 'The Queen's Advice', see ch. 4.

15 Turner, *Slaves and Missionaries*, p. 153.

16 *Ibid.*, pp. 153–4.

17 Henry Bleby, *Death Struggles of Slavery: Being a Narrative of Facts and Incidents which Occurred in a British Colony during the Two Years Immediately Preceding Negro Emancipation* (London: Hamilton, Adams and Co., 1853), p. 112.

18 CO 137/185, Trial of Samuel Sharpe, 19 April 1832, pp. 308, 309.

19 *PP*, 1831/32, (561) XLVII, 35.

20 Reckord, 'Jamaica Slave Rebellion of 1831', p. 123.

21 Turner, *Slaves and Missionaries*, pp. 158–9.

22 *Ibid.*, pp. 160–1.

23 Lorna Elaine Simmonds, ' "The Spirit of Disaffection": Civil Disturbances in Jamaica, 1838–1865' (M.A. thesis, University of Waterloo, 1982), p. 147.

24 *Ibid.*, p. 15; Michael Craton, 'Continuity Not Change: The Incidence of Unrest Among Ex-Slaves in the British West Indies, 1838–1876', *Slavery and Abolition: A Journal of Comparative Studies*, 9 (September, 1988), p. 145.

25 *PP*, 1840, (212) XXXV, McNeel to Smith, 23 July 1839, Evidence of Robert Murray, 40. The discussion of the 1839 conspiracy which follows is based on Lorna Simmonds' treatment of it: see Simmonds, ' "The Spirit of Disaffection" ', pp. 37–39.

26 Simmonds, ' "The Spirit of Disaffection" ', p. 38.

27 *PP*, 1840, (212) XXXV, 43.

28 Simmonds, ' "The Spirit of Disaffection" ', p. 77.

29 *Ibid.*, pp. 77, 80–1.

30 *PP*, 1847/48, (685) XLIV, 11.

31 Robert J. Stewart, *Religion and Society in Post-Emancipation Jamaica* (Knoxville: University of Tennessee Press, 1992), p. 152.

32 Simmonds, 'The Spirit of Disaffection', pp. 83–4.

33 *Ibid.*, pp. 84, 88.

34 *Ibid.*, pp. 85–6. See also Holt, *The Problem of Freedom*, p. 205.

35 *PP*, 1849, (280) XXXVII, 53.

36 Douglas Hall, *Free Jamaica, 1838–1865: An Economic History* (New Haven: Yale University Press, 1959), p. 248; Simmonds, ' "The Spirit of Disaffection" ', p. 123.

37 Anon., *The Florence Hall Controversy and the Falmouth Riots* (Falmouth, Jamaica, n.d.[1859]), pp. 10–13; Holt, *The Problem of Freedom*, pp. 267–8; Simmonds, ' "The Spirit of Disaffection" ', p. 128.

CHAPTER 4

Prologue to the Morant Bay rebellion: The Underhill meetings

The year 1865 opened to a spate of gloomy reports about the economic condition of the island. Indeed, even before 1864 had ended, *The Falmouth Post*, a leading paper in the northern part of the colony, commented on the 'signs of growing poverty in the midst of us. There is hardly a counting-house in the country whether on Estates or in our Stores from which evidence of the magnitude of the fact may not be drawn. The lamentation over the material decadence of the country is almost universal.'[1]

The main cause of this distress was the state of the sugar market. The price of sugar had dropped, in some cases below the cost of production. A planter paper, *The Colonial Standard*, reported on 'the cry of alarm and distress that has burst forth from all classes in the country'.[2] The American Civil War added to Jamaica's economic problems; it resulted in a dramatic increase in the cost of food and clothing. At a time when estates were reducing the amount of sugar under cultivation as well as their wage bill, prices for imports were increasing dramatically. Work on the estates was harder to find, and when it was available, wage rates had frequently declined.[3]

To add to these difficulties, Jamaica was also suffering from a severe drought. In some parishes it was the worst drought anyone could remember. A prediction from one of the major sugar-producing parishes, Trelawny, forecast the loss of several sugar estates, if conditions persisted. The report concluded 'that if there be not a speedy change for the better, the manufacture of Sugar and Rum in Jamaica will, ere long, be numbered amongst the things that were'.[4] Neighbouring Hanover faced a similar fate: a correspondent there noted that 'our prospects are very bad: not a drop of rain: crops are short, and plants for next year are suffering materially. Poor Jamaica! What is to be done with bad seasons, bad returns, and bad prices?'[5]

Even for a press given to hyperbole, these remarks were evidence of the seriousness of the situation. But the drought was not just hurting the large estates; the peasants who depended on ground provisions were badly affected as well. There was a universal dearth of ground provisions, which forced up the price of food. Some commentators blamed the peasantry for becoming involved in the religious revival of the early 1860s and ignoring their agricultural plots. Whatever the cause, there was little doubt about the dramatic consequences for the mass of the population.[6] For the people, one solution was to steal food. It was certainly clear that the theft of ground provisions had become commonplace. In his opening speech to the Legislature in 1864, Governor Eyre observed that 'the great increase and almost universal prevalence throughout the country of larceny of provisions or of domestic animals, calls for the most prompt and stringent measures to repress an evil which frustrates the toil of the industrious, and paralyses all efforts at improvement or comfort.'[7] In some ways Eyre's strictures were unnecessary. The number of prisoners in the island's penitentiaries had jumped from 283 inmates in 1861 to 629 by 1864. A year later the figure was 710 prisoners; more significantly, 617 of them were committed for larceny.[8]

These developments in Jamaica were not unknown to officials in Britain. But they were highlighted by a letter in January 1865, from Edward Underhill, the secretary of the Baptist Missionary Society, to the Secretary of State for the Colonies. An English Baptist minister, Underhill had visited Jamaica in 1859 as part of a tour of the West Indies and published a book about it in 1862. In his letter Underhill described the increasing distress of the black population in Jamaica. For Underhill there was no doubt about 'the extreme poverty of the people' which was evidenced 'by the ragged and even naked condition of vast numbers of them'.[9] He noted the increase in crime, and especially of larceny. The immediate cause of these problems was the drought, but there were longer-term explanations as well. Underhill believed that there was a lack of employment in Jamaica. Since there was less work on the estates and since the drought had caused a general failure of the provision grounds, the people either had to 'steal or starve. And this is their present condition'.

For Underhill the Jamaican Legislature was partly responsible for the perilous state of the colony. Although he did not elaborate on the island's legislation, Underhill criticized the high levels of taxation (especially on the mass of the population), the abortive immigration schemes, and the Assembly's denial of political rights to the ex-slaves. Worst of all, British capitalists had ceased investing in Jamaica; unless this changed and 'employment can be given to its starving people, I see no other result than the entire failure of the island'.

To avoid this catastrophe, Underhill made several suggestions. He called for an inquiry into the island's legislation, its taxation, and its general economic condition to find out where things had gone wrong. In addition, Underhill advised that the peasantry produce more exportable commodities and especially minor products such as coffee and tobacco rather than sugar. But it was not his recommendations for saving Jamaica which aroused so much interest; rather it was Underhill's description of the state of the island and its people which generated such feeling.

The Colonial Office forwarded Underhill's letter to Governor Eyre, who circulated it to the custodes and heads of religious denominations all over the colony. Eyre asked his informants for their views about the general accuracy of Underhill's allegations and about the causes of the current crisis, although he believed that Underhill had exaggerated the case. The letter was first published in the *Jamaica Guardian* on 21 March.[10]

Much of the response to Underhill's letter reinforced the picture of a colony in decline. One of the most thoughtful replies came from Richard Hill, a stipendiary magistrate appointed during the apprenticeship period and the senior resident magistrate in St Catherine. In thirty years as a stipendiary magistrate, Hill had never seen Jamaica 'sunk so low, in the wretchedness of "difficulty of living" as at present'. There was little doubt that the American civil war had significantly worsened the economic plight of the colony. In addition, the severe drought of the past two years as well as a series of epidemic diseases, including small pox and typhoid fever, had made matters much worse.

For Hill, a further problem was the increasing population in the post-emancipation period. When coupled with a 50 per cent decline in the number of plantations in Jamaica after 1834, this meant a serious shortage of work for the ex-slave population. Hill calculated that 'a great proportion of the community . . . now have no profitable occupation . . . . They are from necessity idle, because they cannot get employment, and they are drifting into the vicious condition of people living how they can.' The result was an increasing prison population, often committed to gaol for stealing food.[11]

The report of the Baptist Union reinforced many of Hill's conclusions and supported some of Underhill's claims. Based on the findings of Baptist missionaries all over the island, the Union pointed to the severe lack of employment, despite the desperate means often adopted by people to find work:

> It appears that in some districts numbers of people are known to walk from 6 to 30 miles in search of work, that numbers even in crop time, applying to the Estates for employment, are turned back without obtaining it: that at the present time in consequence of drought, and in some cases from partial cultivation, some Estates are working short time; and that in many districts creole labour has been displaced either wholly or in part by that of Coolies, Chinese, and Africans.

This was the case during the high season; after the sugar had been harvested, there was even less work available.

The consequence of an excess supply of labour was a sharp drop in wages. While task work had usually taken the place of day labour, the amount of labour involved in a task had sometimes been significantly increased. At the same time, wages had been reduced, often by as much as 25 per cent. The Baptists did not blame the planters for lowering their labour costs, but they wanted the Governor to understand 'the actual condition of the labouring population of the country, that your Excellency may see the general truthfulness of the representations contained in Dr Underhill's letter . . . .'[12]

An Anglican minister in the parish of Westmoreland, Henry Clarke, agreed that, at least in his part of Jamaica, the people were 'in a distressing state of poverty'. Low wages were partly to blame for this situation: the top rate of one shilling per day was insufficient to feed and clothe a man, even without taking into account the additional costs of his family. To add to this problem, the high import duties on many necessities as well as taxes on such working items as horses, mules and wheels were 'calculated to starve the people . . . and must result in reducing all classes of the community to poverty'.[13] Clarke's analysis of Jamaica's plight, like that of Richard Hill and the Baptist Union, echoed many of Underhill's sentiments. Yet there were many who disagreed with Underhill's letter and with his description of Jamaica.

A planter with estates in Metcalfe and St Mary and a member of the government, Henry Westmorland, found that Underhill had painted a far too gloomy picture of the black population and of the colony generally. Unlike some districts in the island which were suffering from drought or other problems, his parish and his plantations were flourishing. Westmorland's labourers worked only half-days, and his properties were often short of labour. Another member of the government, Dr Hamilton, reinforced Westmorland's claim that in most cases, the difficulty on plantations was to attract a sufficient number of workers. Hamilton also pointed to the success of many small settlers, especially in their production of crops such as ginger, honey and pimento. For Hamilton, the small settlers were 'a thriving race, their number is rapidly increasing, the cultivation of minor products is augmenting and if in some districts distress does exist, it does not prevail as a general rule among the agricultural population'.[14]

Others who replied to Eyre's request for information admitted that Jamaica's situation was very serious. However, they blamed the problem on the people themselves. Samuel Oughton, a Baptist missionary in Kingston, was aware of the widespread poverty in the island and the increase in crime. But Oughton did not believe that

> these accumulated evils are to be wholly or principally attributed
> to excessive droughts, inability to obtain employment or dear salt
> fish and calico; . . . the real cause in the great majority of cases is,

in my opinion, only to be found in the inveterate habits of idle-
ness, and the low state of moral and religious principles which
prevail to so fearful a degree in our community.[15]

Eyre agreed. He believed that the poverty and crime in the colony was due
to the apathy and indolence of the community. In responding to Underhill,
the Colonial Office adopted this line. After carefully looking into Underhill's
allegations, officials decided that the peasantry were 'not suffering from
any general or continuous distress from which they would not be at once
relieved by settled industry'.[16]

Much of the Jamaican press also adopted this approach to Underhill's
letter. *The Colonial Standard* denounced Underhill's suggestions as 'social-
ist doctrines of prevention' and declared that the letter was full of
misrepresentations. It maintained that the real problem was that 'sugar does
not pay as it ought, because the gentlemen of Mr Underhill's stamp preach
against slavery, and prefer to sweeten their tea with slave sugar to paying
him one penny extra per pound for that which is produced by a man and a
brother . . . .'[17] *The Guardian*, also a pro-planter newspaper, disputed
Underhill's claim that the people were starving and argued that the drought
was hardly a new phenomenon for Jamaica. On the other hand *The County
Union*, a paper published in Montego Bay, agreed with Underhill's description of the distress in the country. Another independent newspaper, *The
Sentinel*, maintained that there was a great deal of truth in Underhill's
allegations, although it had reservations about some of the statements in the
letter.[18] Ultimately, however, the meetings which arose in the wake of
Underhill's letter, rather than the views of the island's press or Eyre's
correspondents, provided a better test of the people's assessment of the
crisis facing Jamaica.

Petitions and public meetings

The first significant petition in 1865 was a memorial from the poor people
of St Ann to the Queen. Although Eyre maintained that it was the first
public response to Underhill's letter, the petition was prepared before that
letter appeared in the island press.[19] Nor was it the outcome of a large public
meeting, like most of the subsequent petitions. The St Ann petition was
none the less important: in it, the people of St Ann complained about their
inability to find work on the estates and about the low price of their
alternative crop, pimento, which was not worth harvesting. Since their own
provision grounds were exhausted from overuse, the petitioners were forced
to rent land. But the cost was exorbitant and there were other problems as
well:

In many instances our provisions is destroyed by cattles, and if the proprietors find the most Simple fault, three months notice is given and we have to destroy our provisions, at the same time numbers of us having a large family of 11 or 12 children depending on the provisions for subsistence.

They appealed to the Queen to rent them Crown land at low rates; they would then

> put our hands and heart to work, and cultivate coffee, corn, canes, cotton and tobacco and other produce [;] we will form a company for that purpose if our Gracious Lady Victoria our Queen will also appoint an agent to receive such produce as we may cultivate. . . .[20]

The petition was sent to the Governor, who forwarded it to the Colonial Office. In his accompanying despatch Eyre made his own views about the memorial very clear. He regarded it as the 'first fruit' of Underhill's letter and expected others in a similar vein. For Eyre, these petitions would have the effect of making the peasantry 'discontented with their lot and disinclined to conform to the laws which regulate their taxation, their civil tribunals or their political status, all of which they have been informed are unjust, partial or oppressive'.[21]

Other petitions followed the one from St Ann, although they were the result of very different gatherings. As Abigail Bakan has suggested, these subsequent meetings provided a means of political expression which had been denied to the majority of the population.[22] The usual pattern was for a group of freeholders to ask the custos of a particular parish to choose a time and a place for a meeting. The request from a group in the parish of St David was typical:

> We the undersigned Freeholders and other inhabitants of this Parish, respectfully request your honor will be pleased to grant us a place, and appoint a time, where we might meet for the purpose of expressing our sentiments in reference to the distressed condition of the inhabitants occasioned by the drought and other causes, that we might adopt a memorial for presentation to Her Majesty's Government.[23]

The freeholders generally signed their names, and several of these requests were published. In some cases the custos organized the meeting, advertised it in the press, and chaired it.

Several of these public meetings adopted broadly similar petitions. The memorials complained about the state of the island and some of its institutions, but were not highly critical of the plantocracy. At a large gathering representing the parishes of Clarendon and Manchester, the petitioners approved of Underhill's letter; at the same time, they sympathized with the plight of the planters. Their second resolution, for example, viewed 'with alarm the continual decline of the proprietary body'. Like those attending the Underhill meetings in St James and Hanover, they complained about the 'crushing weight of taxation' and called on the British government to establish an inquiry into the causes of Jamaica's decline. Similarly, the memorialists were concerned about the 'unrighteous competition they have to maintain with the slave grown produce of Cuba'; accordingly, they wanted Spain to observe her treaties with Britain regarding the slave trade.[24]

The Underhill meeting in St James was also held in May. A newspaper reporter described it as 'so mixed and weighty a gathering – so solid a demonstration – never in our memory has been got together in this town'. Prominent planters, merchants, and ministers were present as well as labourers, and the custos chaired the meeting. As in Clarendon and Hanover, speakers voiced their concern about the high level of taxes, but here the attack was directed specifically against the House of Assembly. Wellesley Bourke, a brown member of the House from St James, maintained that many assemblymen met 'for one purpose – the perpetuation of taxes and an upholding of the corruption that involved the people, the planters, and the whole island, in one general poverty'.[25]

Like the attacks on the slave trade, these diatribes against the House won considerable support. For instance, two planters who could not attend the St James meeting wrote to Bourke on the subject. In their view, 'the evils we have most to fear . . . are the House of the Assembly and the present Executive Committee, in whom we may briefly say nine-tenths of the country . . . have no confidence'.[26] Such statements expressed a concern for the state of the colony, but they clearly did not envision any significant changes in the social or political hierarchies in the island. The resolutions at the meeting in St James did not threaten the status quo. But even at this meeting, and more importantly at other types of gatherings, there was a very different response to Underhill.

One of the speakers who followed Wellesley Bourke at St James was the Baptist missionary, Rev. Edward Hewitt. But he claimed to be speaking as 'a British subject and citizen of Jamaica' rather than as a Baptist. Hewitt had observed the growing poverty in the island, especially evident in the poorer clothing worn by his parishioners. However, he directed his main attack against the high taxes which helped to support the Established church, adding that 'we are taxed enormously for Immigration purposes. All of you have to pay.' This statement was immediately denied by a leading planter on the platform who, along with several others, then walked out of the hall. Although this temporarily disrupted the meeting, Hewitt carried on. He argued that '13,500 Immigrants have been brought to Jamaica and what good has this done for the country. It is you the labourers who ought to work and then you will prosper.'[27]

Hewitt's views were reinforced by another Baptist missionary, Rev. J.E. Henderson. He was concerned about the huge debt the colony owed, part of which had been created to import immigrant labour from India. Henderson asked:

> Have they done any good? (Voices, 'No, no, no.') Do they pay taxes? (Voices, 'No, no, no.') The natives who are the labouring population are driven away from the estates, and coolies taken in their stead.[28]

This anti-planter, anti-immigration line was not only taken up by Baptists. During the public meeting in Hanover, a planter was discussing the need to abolish the export duty on sugar and rum which had been imposed to help meet the costs of importing labour, when, 'as by a preconcerted signal, stentorian lungs gave forth, with a vigour and a power which were irresistible. "*No, no, they would have no immigration.*"'[29] The uproar continued when the next speaker, the clerk of the peace, suggested that the picture of distress in the island should not be exaggerated. According to one report:

> The demonstration which followed this simple observation beggars description, and such as is never witnessed save at the closing scene of a strongly-contested and exciting election . . . Clenched fists were lifted above the crowd, and seemed to threaten the annihilation of any one who would dare to assert that the picture of poverty was capable of being overdrawn![30]

There were obviously strong sentiments at some of these meetings opposing the planters' views on immigration and any attempts to counter the picture of distress in the island. Elsewhere, the criticisms were not limited to just these issues.

There were other Underhill meetings which differed from the quasi-official ones in St James and Hanover. Also held in May and June, several of these were organized by the Underhill Convention, a group of blacks who strongly supported Underhill's letter. The Convention appears to have been behind the meetings which took place in Kingston, Spanish Town and St David.[31]

The Underhill meeting in Kingston was chaired by George William Gordon, the most prominent opponent of Governor Eyre in the House of Assembly. Those who submitted resolutions included local preachers, some attached to the 'Tabernacle', a Native Baptist chapel Gordon had helped to establish in Kingston. There were also black politicians and other independent clergymen involved in the gathering, whom a member of the administration later described as 'political agitators'.[32]

The speakers at the Kingston meeting were generally hostile to the government. Rev. Edwin Palmer, a black Baptist pastor, complained that the

> people were poor and destitute, the planters robbed them of their wages, that they were trampled under foot, the government was oppressive, that the merchants in Kingston would employ none but white or coloured men in their stores which was a disgrace and a shame, that the time would soon come when they would be compelled to do it.

Palmer described a new law authorizing whipping as directed only at blacks and aimed at re-introducing slavery. He was not alone in such attacks. A vestryman from St David, Samuel Clarke, reportedly warned the audience that whites could no longer 'keep down negroes, and although you won't give us education we will show them that we shall yet have a position in the country'.[33]

While other speakers carried on in a similar vein, the resolutions adopted at the Kingston meeting provided strong support for Underhill as well as a radical critique of the government and the ruling class of Jamaica. One resolution complained about the 'class legislation' of the island and suggested that 'the time has arrived when the masses of this country must speak out their woes, labouring as they do under many wrongs and disabilities . . . .' The memorialists were also opposed to the enormous expenditure to import labour and pointed to 'the systematic abnegation of every principle involving the Education of the Masses and other measures of a preventive and ameliorating character'. The partial nature of the law, lack of jobs, low wages and general distress in the colony: all came under their scrutiny. But what may have worried the authorities most was their call

> upon all the descendants of Africa in every Parish throughout the Island, to form themselves into Societies and hold Public Meetings, and co-operate for the purpose of setting forth their grievances, especially now, when our philanthropic friends in England are leading the way.[34]

The resolutions of the Kingston meeting were couched in much stronger language than those from St James, Hanover and Clarendon. There was more open defiance of the authorities and more demands for change. The petitions of the meetings in Spanish Town and St David were less pointed but even more specific than those of their Kingston counterparts.

At the Spanish Town Underhill meeting, the resolutions centred on the desperate situation of the artisans and tradespeople of the town. Since so little work was available, many of them 'have been compelled to leave their homes to seek employment in foreign climes, and many others are only deterred from doing so, because they do not know what is to become of their families in their absence'. As in Kingston, the petitioners complained about the high import duties on raw materials and finished products; the duties made it almost impossible for local artisans to compete with imported mass manufactured goods. The memorial concluded by corroborating Underhill's statements about the state of the colony and by thanking the British philanthropists for their concern about Jamaica.[35]

For Eyre, the Spanish Town meeting was a counterpart of the one held at Kingston. Some of the same black politicians who opposed the government, such as William Kelly Smith and Joseph Goldson, were prominent at both meetings. A vestryman for St Catherine, A.C. Sinclair, was also very concerned about the Spanish Town meeting and regarded it as a 'revolutionary gathering'.[36] Yet the chairman of the meeting, A.H. Lewis, who was one of the representatives of the parish in the assembly, described it as orderly, without 'the least attempt at any expression which could lead to disaffection'.[37] None the less, the meeting clearly sympathized with Underhill's letter.

The St David's meeting also applauded Underhill's efforts on behalf of the island. But the petition was specifically concerned about the plight of the small settlers. One of the resolutions maintained that labourers on the estates were

> not honestly and adequately paid for their labour; that great wrong and injury attends the small settlers in the destruction of their provision grounds by the unlawful and unrestricted freedom of large herds of cattle belonging to proprietors of estates and pens.
> . . .

The memorial also complained about the lack of justice in the Jamaican courts: the petitioners believed that there was 'a law for the rich and a law for the poor'. To improve the situation generally for the small settlers as well as for the traders, the St David's meeting suggested the establishment of an Island Agricultural Loan Bank or Joint Stock Company. The gathering also called for the establishment of a committee known as the Central Communicating Committee 'to correspond with the yeomen throughout the island on subjects of agriculture and other branches of native industry'.[38]

This meeting was marked by acrimony, especially toward the custos of St David, W.P. Georges. One of the resolutions described the custos as 'one of our bitterest enemies' and complained that Eyre had sought information on the Underhill letter from Georges. St David, like St Thomas in the East, was a politically divided parish. According to Georges, the Underhill meeting in St David had been organized by his leading political opponent, Samuel Clarke, and 'others who delight in Political Excitement'.[39]

Whatever the differences within the parish, however, these resolutions made it clear that there were serious problems between the planters and the small settlers. This was especially the case in the courts but also involved damage done to the provision grounds of the labouring population. The treatment of estate workers was also taken up at an Underhill meeting in St Mary in late June. In addition to airing some of the same issues as at the Kingston and Spanish Town meetings, the St Mary petitioners pointed to the 'present low prices paid as wages to labourers . . . and that so tardily'. This reinforced reports of estate workers being paid in arrears and some-times kept waiting for months for their pay.[40]

The series of Underhill meetings from April to late June clearly high-lighted the crisis affecting Jamaica. No one doubted the impact of the drought or the result of the depressed sugar market. The repeated pleas about the lack of jobs, the plight of the small settlers, the low pay for estate work, and the state of the law, should have alerted colonial officials to a different range of problems. But the reaction of the Governor as well as of the Colonial Office was to stigmatize the supporters of Underhill and to ignore some of the critical difficulties facing the island.

Many of the Underhill meetings appointed deputations to present their petitions to the Governor. Like several other groups, the representatives of the Kingston meeting were received by Governor Eyre, informed that he would forward their resolutions to the Colonial Office, and left in no doubt that the Governor could not support them.[41] Writing to the Colonial Office just ahead of this meeting, Eyre made clear how much he differed from Underhill's supporters:

> My own conviction is that the pressure which now undoubtedly exists amongst a portion of the population, and which from the long continuance of the drought has become intensified during the last few weeks, owes its origin in a great measure to the habits and character of the people, induced by the genial nature of the climate, the facility of supplying their wants in ordinary seasons at comparatively little exertion and their natural disposition to indolence and inactivity, and to remain satisfied with what barely supplies absolute wants.[42]

The Colonial Office shared these views. Its response to the original petition of the poor people of St Ann was drafted by the head of the West India Department, Henry Taylor. The government's view was that

> . . . the prosperity of the Labouring Classes as well as of all other classes depends in Jamaica, and in other Countries, upon their working for Wages, not uncertainly or capriciously, but steadily and continuously, at the times when their labour is wanted, and for so long as it is wanted, and that if they would use this industry,

and thereby render the Plantations productive, they would enable the Planters to pay them higher Wages for the same hours of work than are received by the best Field Labourers in this Country . . . and they may be assured that it is from their own industry and prudence, in availing themselves of the means of prospering that are before them, and not from any such schemes as have been suggested to them, that they must look for an improvement in their condition.[43]

Known as 'The Queen's Advice', this document was widely circulated in Jamaica: 50,000 copies were disseminated in July to all parts of the colony.

Most copies of 'The Queen's Advice' were distributed around the island without any apparent protest. However some people refused to circulate it. Henry Clarke, an Anglican minister in Westmoreland, wrote in his journal that the document 'only tells [the peasantry] that they are very well off, and that if they would work on the estates when they are required to work they would soon be rich. I shall destroy every copy of it as it is really provoking the people to rebellion.' A group of Baptist missionaries in St James also found that it was inapplicable to their parish; they observed that the copies which had already been circulated had caused 'an amount of irritation most painful to observe'. Like many other people in the island, the missionaries did not believe that the Queen could have written the document. They maintained that she 'could never have addressed the suffering poor without one kind word of sympathy for them in their distress brought upon them by circumstances over which they had no control'. Eyre dismissed these comments by portraying the Baptists as troublemakers who had participated in the Underhill meeting held at Montego Bay.[44]

Conspiracies, further public meetings and George William Gordon

Conditions in Jamaica during the summer of 1865 did not improve. The drought continued in most parts of the island, and further gloomy predictions appeared in the press. In Vere, there was no work for the people and 'stealing and starving in all directions'. There was a serious question about maintaining control in the parish: *The County Union* reported that 'a state of anarchy is gaining ground that will soon bid defiance to the civil power under its most energetic exercise'.[45] The situation was no better in St Elizabeth. A letter writer to *The Morning Journal* warned that if things did not change there, 'a dire fate awaits Jamaica and her people'.[46]

As if to fulfil this prophecy, rumours of a conspiracy in western Jamaica began circulating in late July. At first the targets were some of the leading planters in St Elizabeth. One of them, Raynes Waite Smith, represented the parish in the Assembly and was a former member of the government. A storekeeper near Smith's plantation had found an anonymous letter which attacked Smith. The letter claimed that the Queen had sent Smith a large quantity of rice, but he had either kept it for himself or used it to feed his Indian indentured labourers. Smith had also heard that some people planned to take over his large house; according to one rumour, the house 'would do very well for them by-and-by'.[47]

This was only one of the elements of the reported conspiracy. The custos of St Elizabeth and president of the Legislative Council, John Salmon, wrote to Governor Eyre alerting him to rumours of an outbreak expected on 1 August, the anniversary of emancipation. Salmon believed that some of the people would resist paying taxes on that day or would seek to appropriate land.[48] There were also other rumours about the forthcoming rebellion. Some small settlers in St Elizabeth had informed a magistrate that a large group of blacks planned to proceed to Black River, the most important city in the parish. Once there the women would take whatever they required from the shops.[49] A doctor living in the parish reported a similar story:

> The storekeepers, for instance, said remarks were constantly dropped in their stores, such as when people came to buy a bit of cloth they would say, 'You stop, August will soon come, and cloth will be cheap.'[50]

One of the causes of the threatened disturbance was a report that the Queen had sent a large amount of money for the people of St Elizabeth to purchase land. However, the custos had kept it for himself. Another was a continuing concern among ex-slaves about the possibility of being re-enslaved. According to a Catholic priest who was familiar with western Jamaica, the fear of re-enslavement was not limited to the people of St Elizabeth but had spread through St James and Westmoreland as well.[51]

The prospect of a rebellion prompted many families to flee to Black River for protection. By the end of July they had come to believe that the blacks were intent on killing whites and browns.[52] A doctor who worked among blacks in the parish, Alexander M'Gatty, reported that by that time 'the parish was in a wild state of excitement'.[53] The custos was clearly very frightened; he was particularly worried about leaving his family on his plantation while he dealt with the situation at Black River. Salmon blamed the Underhill meetings for the threatened outbreak:

> The general opinion among proprietors white, Colored and Black is that all this disturbance and ill feeling is to be attributed to the late assertions which have been made that the negroes are ill treated and cheated and unfairly dealt with and oppressed and that

if permitted to be reiterated there will be no peace or security for property or life.[54]

St Elizabeth was not the only parish where trouble was expected at the beginning of August. The custos of St James, G.L. Phillips, informed Eyre that he had received anonymous letters 'conveying threats of Fire and Robbery' because of the prevailing high prices in the shops and the low wages paid on the plantations. One rumour predicted that the outbreak would begin in St James, and another was that the leaders of the plot came from there as well.[55]

Under these circumstances Eyre requested that two men-of-war be sent to the affected areas, the first to Black River and the second to Montego Bay and Lucea. Although the Governor did not believe that an outbreak was likely, he thought it wise to take these precautions. In his correspondence with the commodore in charge of the fleet, Eyre suggested that 'if the ships were to have a little gun practice in each of the Ports it might be useful in letting the Peasantry know of their presence'.[56] Whether or not the threat was a real one, Salmon reported that the ship sent to Black River, the *Bulldog*, had achieved the desired result. All was quiet in the parish. At the very least, the visit of the *Bulldog* pleased many of the people in the parish who were allowed to inspect the vessel.[57]

After a lull in early July the Underhill meetings continued. The gatherings in August and September were similar to those organized by the Underhill Convention. Moreover, George William Gordon was heavily involved in these later meetings. In his newspaper, *The Watchman and People's Free Press*, and in a placard which appeared in St Ann and in St Thomas in the East, Gordon actively encouraged the people in the two parishes to attend the meetings. To attract support in St Ann, he made use of Underhill's letter, the poor people's petition of St Ann, and the government response to it:

People of St Ann's,
Poor people of St Ann's
Starving people of St Ann's
Naked people of St Ann's.

You who have no sugar estates to work on, nor can find other employment, we call on you to come forth, even if you be naked, come forth and protest against the unjust representations made against you by Mr Governor Eyre and his band of Custodes.[58]

At the meeting itself in St Ann, a native pastor who had also been involved in the Kingston meeting, Rev. James Crole, expressed great concern about the 'oppressed, distressed, wretched and deplorable condition' of the mass of the population. In his view, the 'oppressive system of government' was the cause of their plight.[59]

Gordon used similar tactics to drum up support for the meeting in St Thomas in the East. In the placard he was particularly abusive toward the custos, Baron von Ketelhodt:

> People of St Thomas ye East, you have been ground down too long already. Shake off your sloth, and speak like *honourable* and free men at your meeting . . . But can you and the inhabitants of St Thomas ye East longer bear to be afflicted by this enemy to your peace – a custos whose feelings are foreign to yours?[60]

As in many other parishes in the island, Ketelhodt, as custos of St Thomas in the East, had been asked to hold a public meeting on the state of the island. Although he had agreed to have the meeting at the court house on 12 August, Ketelhodt postponed it at the last minute. None the less, the meeting was held in the market place opposite the court house.[61]

Gordon chaired the meeting, which was attended by many men who were later implicated in the rebellion. For example, Paul Bogle, James McLaren and Samuel Clarke were present and were among those who either proposed or seconded resolutions. A schoolmaster from Amity Hall in St Thomas in the East, John Anderson, reported that this was not the only Underhill meeting in the parish. Anderson had been at an earlier such meeting at Stoakes Hall, and he had brought resolutions from that meeting to the larger gathering at Morant Bay. There is a possibility that this pattern of holding local gatherings which fed resolutions to the larger parish meeting was replicated elsewhere in the island.[62]

Some of the resolutions adopted at the Morant Bay meeting reiterated complaints which had been aired at other Underhill meetings. There was concern about the increasing level of taxes, the difficulties of finding employment, and the problem of low wages. As in the Kingston meeting, which Gordon also chaired, those present attacked 'the oppressive nature of many of the Acts which have recently passed the Legislature of this island [and] are such as to create feelings of apprehension for the future well-being of society . . . .' There was also considerable bitterness directed at the custos for his 'illegal and oppressive conduct towards the rights of the constituency of this parish and the island generally . . . .' Ketelhodt's attempt to postpone the meeting was seen as 'unconstitutional'; furthermore, the meeting concluded that 'the generally arbitrary, illegal and inconsistent conduct of the custos is destruction to the peace and prosperity of the affairs of the parish'.[63] The final Underhill meeting in Vere in early September would repeat some of these sentiments.

Gordon presided over the meeting at Vere, just as he had at several other Underhill meetings. Again, as in St Thomas in the East, the custos, Lewis

MacKinnon, refused to allow the meeting to take place in the court house. MacKinnon justified this stance by pointing out that 'these meetings do an infinite deal of mischief' and allow men he considered agitators to gain notoriety. But the meeting, held in the town of Alley, went ahead in the open air under a large tree.[64]

There are various versions of Gordon's speech at the meeting, which lasted upwards of an hour. But there is little doubt that Gordon strongly attacked the Governor using highly emotive language. In one report, Gordon called Eyre 'a bad man' who 'sanctions everything done by the higher class to the oppression of the poor negroes'. Similarly, Gordon derided 'The Queen's Letter': she would never have written such a document which was 'all trash'. He also complained about the lack of justice in the parish, the low level of wages, and the general poverty of the people. Indeed, Gordon had hoped to collect money for the Anti-Slavery Society but found that the people were too poor.[65]

Similar statements had been made at other Underhill meetings, although it is possible that Gordon's language was stronger than usual on this occasion. What differentiated this speech from many others was Gordon's alleged statement encouraging revolution and invoking the dreaded image of Haiti. According to two bookkeepers working in Vere, Gordon concluded his speech by telling the audience that they should not be afraid of the consequences of attending the meeting:

> I was told by some of you that your overseer said, that if any of you attended this meeting they would tear down your houses. Tell them that I, George William Gordon, say they dare not do it – it is tyranny, you must do what Hayti does; you have a bad name now, but you will have a worse then.[66]

Gordon's reported remarks about Haiti were published in the island press and also used as evidence in his court martial at Morant Bay. In subsequent conversations on the subject, Gordon denied ever having brought up the example of Haiti. The report which appeared in *The County Union* was written by William March, a coloured reporter who also worked for Gordon; it did not contain any such reference. Moreover, this version had been carefully scrutinised by Dr Robert Bruce, the coroner for Vere, and one of the organizers of the Vere Underhill meeting. On the other hand the account containing Gordon's alleged remark was prepared by men who were probably strongly opposed to Gordon's politics.[67]

Whatever the truth of the allegation, it was widely believed that Gordon had raised the spectre of Haiti. Even Gordon's ally in Vere, Robert Bruce, claimed that he wrote to Gordon after the meeting making it clear that he did not like 'the way [Gordon] spoke' and that he would not attend any more such meetings. Furthermore, Sidney Levien, the editor of *The County*

Union, was also concerned about the possible consequences of the meeting. He wrote to Bruce that he wished 'to shield you and them [the people of Vere] from the charge of anarchy and tumult, which in a short time must follow these fearful demonstrations'.[68] Levien was not alone in expecting trouble. Col Alexander Fyfe, the stipendiary magistrate for St David and a member of the Legislative Council, wrote an urgent letter in September to William Hosack, a member of the Executive Committee, warning the government that it was 'slumbering on a mine' but 'did not seem to realize the danger [it] was in'.[69]

Yet the local government as well as Whitehall remained unmoved either by the meetings or by the deteriorating conditions in the island. The Colonial Office response to the Underhill petition from Hanover arrived in Jamaica in September. In the dispatch the Colonial Office repeated its earlier homilies: it again counselled steady and continuous work.[70] In the face of an unyielding government it was becoming clear that the Underhill meetings could have little practical effect. If petitioning and peaceful meetings had failed, some people were preparing for war.

Notes

1   *The Falmouth Post*, 30 December 1864.
2   *The Colonial Standard and Jamaica Despatch*, 20 March 1865.
3   Gad J. Heuman, *Between Black and White: Race, Politics, and the Free Coloreds in Jamaica, 1792–1865* (Westport, Conn.: Greenwood Press, 1981), p. 171; *The Falmouth Post*, 6 January 1865. See also resolution number 1 of the Underhill meeting held in Savanna-la-Mar in April: *The Sentinel*, 1 May 1865.
4   *The Falmouth Post*, 25 April 1865.
5   *Ibid.*, 31 March 1865.
6   *The Colonial Standard and Jamaica Despatch*, 24 May 1865.
7   *The Falmouth Post*, 18 August 1865.
8   *Ibid.*; *The Morning Journal*, 4 September 1865.
9   *The Morning Journal*, 20 March 1865; Thomas C. Holt, *The Problem of Freedom: Race, Labor, and Politics in Jamaica and Britain, 1832–1938* (Baltimore: The Johns Hopkins University Press, 1992), p. 270. Underhill's letter was reprinted in his *A Letter Addressed to the Rt. Honourable E. Cardwell* (London, 1865). The quotations which follow are taken from Underhill's letter.
10 CO 137/388, Eyre to Cardwell, 2 March 1865, no. 40; Edward Bean Underhill, *The Tragedy of Morant Bay* (London: Alexander and Shepheard, 1895), p. 13. Unlike Eyre, Lord Olivier, a later governor of Jamaica, supported Underhill's letter: see Lord Olivier [Sydney Haldane], *The Myth of Governor Eyre* (London: Faber & Faber, 1936), p. 119.
11 CO 137/390, Eyre to Cardwell, 19 April 1865, no. 90: Hill to Austin, 15 March 1865.
12 CO 137/391, Eyre to Cardwell, 6 May 1865, no. 128: Report of the Baptist Union, 1 May 1865.
13 CO 137/390, Eyre to Cardwell, 19 April 1865, no. 90: Henry Clarke to the Bishop, 6 March 1865.

14 *Ibid.*: Westmorland's remarks on Underhill's letter; CO 137/391, Eyre to Cardwell, 23 May 1865, no. 135: Dr Hamilton's remarks on Underhill's letter.

15 CO 137/388, Eyre to Cardwell, 2 March 1865, no. 40: *Jamaica Guardian*, 25 February 1865.

16 CO 137/390, Eyre to Cardwell, 19 April 1865, no. 90; CO 137/391, Rogers to Underhill, 5 August 1865, attached to Eyre to Cardwell, 6 May 1865, no. 128.

17 *The Colonial Standard and Jamaica Despatch*, 2 May 1865; *Ibid.*, n.d., reprinted in *The Morning Journal*, 27 March 1865.

18 *Jamaica Guardian*, n.d., reprinted in *The Morning Journal, 27 March 1865; The County Union and Anglo-Jamaican Advertiser*, 24 March 1865; *The Sentinel*, 11 April 1865.

19 JRC, Evidence of Rev. Benjamin Millard, p. 782.

20 CO137/390, Eyre to Cardwell, 19 April 1865, no. 90: The Humble Petition of the Poor People of Jamaica and parish of St Ann.

21 *Ibid.*, 25 April 1865, no. 115.

22 Abigail B. Bakan, *Ideology and Class Conflict in Jamaica: The Politics of Rebellion* (Montreal and Kingston: McGill-Queen's University Press, 1990), p. 76.

23 *The Colonial Standard and Jamaica Despatch*, 12 June 1865.

24 *The Morning Journal*, 26 May 1865.

25 *Ibid.*

26 *Ibid.*

27 *Ibid.*, 27 May 1865.

28 *Ibid.*

29 *The Falmouth Post*, 23 May 1865.

30 *The County Union*, 23 May 1865.

31 *The Morning Journal*, 16 June 1865.

32 JRC, Evidence of Henry Westmorland, p. 859.

33 Papers, Statement on oath of George Fouché, 26 October 1865, p. 216.

34 *The Colonial Standard and Jamaica Despatch*, 6 May 1865.

35 *The Morning Journal*, 23 May 1865.

36 CO 137/391, Eyre to Cardwell, 7 June 1865, no. 143; *The Morning Journal*, 10 July 1865.

37 JRC, Evidence of A.H. Lewis, p. 839.

38 *The Colonial Standard and Jamaica Despatch*, 14 July 1865.

39 CO 137/392, Eyre to Cardwell, 12 July 1865, no. 174: The St David Resolutions, 26 June 1865; Georges to Austin, 10 July 1865.

40 *The Morning Journal*: 6 July 1865; 29 June 1865.

41 *Ibid.*, 18 May 1865.

42 CO137/391, Eyre to Cardwell, 6 May 1865, no. 128.

43 CO137/390, Cardwell to Eyre, 14 June 1865, no. 222.

44 Henry Clarke, 'The Journal of Henry Clarke', vol. 2, 31 July 1865; CO 137/392, Eyre to Cardwell, 22 August 1865, no. 210: Henderson, Dendy and Reid to Myers, 4 August 1865; CO 137/393, Eyre to Cardwell, 20 September 1865, no. 237: Henderson, Dendy and Reid to Jordon, 19 August 1865.

45 *The County Union*, n.d., reprinted in *The Morning Journal*, 17 July 1865.

46 *The Morning Journal*, 17 July 1865.

47 JRC, Evidence of Raynes Waite Smith, p. 744.

48 JRC, Evidence of Henry Westmorland, p. 857: Salmon to Eyre, 22 July 1865.

49 CO 137/392, Eyre to Cardwell, 7 August 1865, no. 198: Salmon to Eyre, 25 July 1865.

50 JRC, Evidence of Dr Alexander M'Gatty, p. 666.

51 JRC: Evidence of Henry Westmorland, p. 857: Salmon to Eyre, 25 July 1865; Evidence of Rev. Joseph Woollett, p. 548.

52 JRC, Evidence of Thomas Wheatle, p. 599.

53 JRC, Evidence of Alexander M'Gatty, p. 667.

54 CO 137/392, Eyre to Cardwell, 7 August 1865, no. 198: Salmon to Eyre, 28 July 1865.

55 *Ibid.*: Phillips to Austin, 26 July 1865; Smith to Salmon, 24 July 1865, private and confidential; JRC, Evidence of Henry Westmorland, p. 857: Salmon to Eyre, 22 July 1865.

56 *Ibid.*, Eyre to Commodore Cracroft, n.d. See also Don Robotham, *'The Notorious Riot':* *The Socio-Economic and Political Bases of Paul Bogle's Revolt* (Kingston, Jamaica: Institute of Social and Economic Research, 1981), p. 88.

57 CO 137/392, Eyre to Cardwell, 7 August 1865, no. 198: Salmon to Austin, 4 August 1865; Salmon to Capt. Wake, R.N., 4 August 1865.

58 JRC, Proceedings and Despatches on the trial of George William Gordon, p. 619; *The Jamaica Watchman and People's Free Press*, 21 August 1865.

59 Robert J. Stewart, *Religion and Society in Post-Emancipation Jamaica* (Knoxville: University of Tennessee Press, 1992), p. 165.

60 JRC, Proceedings and Despatches on the trial of George William Gordon, p. 619; *The Jamaica Watchman and People's Free Press*, 21 August 1865.

61 *The Colonial Standard and Jamaica Despatch*, 21 July 1865; *The Jamaica Watchman and People's Free Press*, 21 August 1865.

62 JRC: Evidence of Henry Clyne, p. 735; Evidence of John Anderson, pp. 958–9. For example, there were two meetings in the parish of St Elizabeth; see JRC, Evidence of Thomas Wheatle, p. 599.

63 JRC, Appendix, pp. 1156–7. According to Olivier, when the delegation from the meeting in St Thomas in the East sought to present their resolutions to Governor Eyre, he refused to receive them. Paul Bogle and James McLaren were part of the delegation. See Olivier, *Governor Eyre*, p. 165.

64 Papers, MacKinnon to Jordon, 27 September 1865, p. 230; JRC, Evidence of Joseph Williams, p. 852.

65 JRC: Evidence of James Humber, p. 444; Evidence of William March, pp. 888–9; Evidence of Dr Robert Bruce, p. 730.

66 JRC, Evidence of James Humber, p. 444.

67 JRC: Evidence of James Ford, p. 388; Evidence of William March, pp. 888–90.

68 JRC, Evidence of Dr Robert Bruce, p. 729.

69 JRC, Evidence of William Hosack, p. 925.

70 *The Falmouth Post*, 22 September 1865.

CHAPTER 5

Prologue to the Morant Bay rebellion: St Thomas in the East

St Thomas in the East, the scene of the Morant Bay rebellion, was predominantly a sugar parish. It had some of the richest properties in Jamaica, especially in the Plantain Garden River district, and many of its largest estates were owned by absentees. It was also one of the most politically divided parishes in the colony. In the 1860s these divisions deepened and help to explain why the rebellion broke out in Morant Bay.

George William Gordon and St Thomas in the East

Some of the bitterest disputes in the parish during the early 1860s involved George William Gordon. A coloured politician who first sat in the Assembly in the 1840s, Gordon was born around 1820 to a wealthy planting attorney, Joseph Gordon, and a slave woman. Joseph Gordon freed his son, George William, and paid for his early education. At about the age of ten the younger Gordon was employed by his godfather, James Daly, at Black River in the parish of St Elizabeth. Gordon subsequently commenced business as a produce merchant in Kingston and later became an extensive landowner in many parts of the island. By 1843 Gordon claimed to be worth £10,000. In the mid-1840s he married a white woman, Mary Jane Perkins; she was a widow whose mother had established a school for young ladies in Kingston. Gordon was one of the founders of the Jamaica Mutual Life Assurance Society and was appointed a justice of the peace in seven parishes across the island. He also became proprietor of the revived *Watchman* newspaper in the late 1850s.

However, Gordon's business affairs ran into serious difficulties, especially in the 1860s; he lost heavily in coffee dealings and, by 1865, he had accumulated liabilities of over £35,000. His father, who thought of Gordon as kind and affectionate as well as highly talented, maintained that his son had squandered the money away foolishly.[1]

Even before 1865 Gordon's politics were radically different from most other Jamaican politicians. By the late 1850s, Gordon was supporting the interests of the ex-slave population and saw himself increasingly as their spokesman. Lord Olivier described Gordon as 'a man of deep sensibility and of real benevolence of disposition' who was deeply affected by the injustices suffered by the common people. Gordon was 'irrepressibly voluble' and often indiscreet; his politics and his religious outlook dismayed the established authorities in the island.[2]

Originally a member of the Established church, Gordon later joined the Presbyterians, and also frequented the Congregational church. On Christmas Day 1861, he was publicly baptized by Rev. James Phillippo, Jamaica's leading Baptist missionary. Gordon had close links to the Native Baptists, especially to the group led by Paul Bogle in St Thomas in the East, and had his own Native Baptist chapel in Kingston known as the 'Tabernacle'. Bogle, a small landowner living in Stony Gut, a mountainous village about four miles inland from Morant Bay, served as Gordon's political agent in St Thomas in the East. Highly regarded in the district, Bogle grew some sugar and had just begun cultivating cotton when the rebellion broke out. For Thomas Harvey and William Brewin, he 'was a man of very limited education, but of considerable intelligence and energy, and besides possessing much influence over his own class and colour, was not without importance in the general affairs of the parish'. In 1865 Bogle was made a deacon of the Native Baptists in Gordon's 'Tabernacle'.[3]

Gordon's shift toward the Baptists alienated him from the man who took over the government of Jamaica in 1862, Edward John Eyre, himself a devout Anglican. The third son of a Yorkshire vicar, Eyre emigrated to Australia at the age of seventeen in 1832. He prospered as a sheep farmer and an overlander, taking sheep and cattle to the new settlements in South Australia. He also became famous as an explorer, having made the difficult journey across Australia from Adelaide to Albany. Eyre was subsequently given the job of protector of the aborigines at Moorundie in South Australia, where he was described as an 'exceptionally humane' official with an affinity for the aborigines. Before he was thirty, then, Eyre had found the means to earn a comfortable living and had been lauded for his feats of exploration as well as his work with the aborigines.

His later career was less successful. He served as Lieutenant-Governor in New Zealand and St Vincent and temporarily as Governor of the Leeward Islands, but encountered difficulties in each of his postings. In part, this may have been due to his personality; his most recent biographer, Geoffrey Dutton, described Eyre as 'shy, poor and solitary'. James Morris accurately characterized him as having 'matured into an inflexible man, prone to self-pity'. Perhaps because of his origins and background, Eyre lacked the self-confidence which colonists expected of men in high office. He certainly did not have the established wealth which was presumed of colonial officials of his stature. At the same time, his correspondence with the Colonial Office reveals a man who was self-seeking and anxious to further his own career.

These characteristics did not make it likely that Eyre would have an easy time in Jamaica when he was appointed Lieutenant-Governor in 1862.[4]

Eyre soon ran into difficulties with George William Gordon, who was to haunt Eyre's tenure in Jamaica and long after as well. As one of the magistrates in St Thomas in the East, Gordon had complained to Eyre's predecessor in office, Governor Darling, about the state of the gaol in Morant Bay. Soon after Eyre was in office, Gordon reported that the parish rector, Rev. Stephen Cooke, had sent an ill and poor man to the gaol where he had died. Gordon complained about the rector's illegal imprisonment of the man and also about the filthy conditions of the prison. In response, Eyre removed Gordon from the magistracy and criticized his behaviour over the matter. When the issue was raised at the Colonial Office, officials backed Eyre but also praised Gordon's attempt to improve conditions in the gaol.[5]

Gordon's demotion from the magistracy was not the only political blow he suffered in 1862. Earlier in the year he was defeated in an attempt to gain a seat to the House of Assembly for St Thomas in the East. His supporters in the parish, and especially Paul Bogle, were concerned about these setbacks but also determined to reverse them. In the first of two letters he sent to Gordon on 25 July, Bogle sympathized with Gordon:

> All hearts burnt to hear the way you are treated for our cause. But in suffering there are concilation for their is a rest is provide for those who toil and bear persecution for truth sake in heaven.

In his subsequent letter, Bogle requested a loan to pay the tax which would enfranchise Gordon's supporters at the next election. Bogle's role as political agent as well as his religious sympathies with Gordon are apparent in the letter:

> At a meeting held at the Liberal School Society meetings at the above named place [Stony Gut] to take into *consideration* what plans we might adopt for to recover your place that is lost in the *political* world, but in the *religious* one we are asurd your progress is great; may God Grant it so. Among other plans we resolve to have an hundred tax payers put on, *independent* of *freeholders*, and those who will or can pay without borrowing from us. So we sent to ask you as *responsible persons* to lend us 150l. [£150] to lend to those that will form the tax payers, to be paid back to us the *responsible parties* . . . by which way we will returnit to you (without *intress*).[6]

Bogle wanted to register the potential voters as taxpayers, who could qualify for the franchise if they were assessed at £3 per year. The problem was that recent legislation meant that a duty of ten shillings per voter had to be paid as well as any outstanding taxes before polling day.[7] It is clear that Bogle had carefully considered the electoral balance, because he also had sympathetic voters who would qualify on the basis of their freeholds.

There is no evidence to suggest whether George William Gordon provided the loan which Bogle requested. Yet it is clear that Bogle's work on behalf of Gordon paid off. In March 1863 Gordon won a seat to represent St Thomas in the East in the Assembly. Research on the voting records suggests that Gordon defeated his opponent, a planter, with the aid of the small settler vote. In July Gordon was also elected to the parish vestry as churchwarden.[8]

Bogle continued to act as Gordon's political agent after these electoral successes. Two years later, during the summer of 1865, Bogle wrote to Gordon pointing out that Gordon 'must provide something for me to vote upon for the year coming'. He also enclosed a list of election expenses for 1865, which included payments to several individuals as well as an indication of the nature of electioneering in Jamaica. Nearly £2 had been spent on refreshments; under this heading Bogle listed expenses for cheese, music, bread, ale, porter and rum. Stephen Cooke, the clerk of the peace for St Thomas in the East and a bitter enemy of Gordon's, confirmed the close political relationship between Gordon and Bogle. He also claimed to have heard the custos of the parish, Baron von Ketelhodt, warn Bogle about his association with Gordon but to no avail.[9]

Despite Gordon's election to the vestry in 1863, his position as churchwarden was soon under threat. Gordon's politics and his association with the small settlers and labourers in the parish were clearly at odds with that of the custos and the leading members of the vestry. Moreover, Gordon opposed much that went on in the vestry. Rev. Stephen Cooke, who was a close ally of Ketelhodt's and father of the clerk of the peace in the parish, was very active in seeking to get rid of Gordon. Cooke claimed that Gordon 'was the greatest nuisance any parish ever had. I never knew such a man in my life, he was attacking everyone.' Yet there was probably another motive for Cooke's actions. Cooke's attempts to remove Gordon from the vestry may well have been inspired by Gordon's earlier attacks on him over the condition of the gaol at Morant Bay.[10]

Gordon was aware that Cooke wanted him off the vestry. In a letter to Bogle in early 1864, Gordon indicated that he had headed off previous challenges to his position and believed he could do so again:

> I have again to contend with Rector Cooke's annoyance, he is trying to get me out of the churchwarden's office, but I have no doubt he will fail also this time.[11]

Two months later, however, Ketelhodt had Gordon bodily ejected from a meeting of the vestry. Cooke had successfully rounded up a majority of the magistrates, all of whom wanted Gordon expelled from the vestry. They outnumbered the elected vestrymen who opposed the Baron's proceedings. On the order of the custos, the police removed Gordon from the meeting and prevented him from returning to it.[12]

Gordon's expulsion from his elected position on the vestry caused dismay among the small settlers and labourers who supported him. Furthermore, many people in the parish had not forgotten Eyre's dismissal of Gordon from the magistracy two years previously. Rev. Cooke and Baron von Ketelhodt were implicated in both of these actions, and the two men were highly unpopular in the parish. It did not help matters that Ketelhodt's home was in the parish of St Andrew, thirty-five miles away. Although Ketelhodt owned a sugar estate in St Thomas in the East, a judge described the custos as 'a comparative stranger to the parish'.[13]

By contrast, the extent of Gordon's popularity became clear when he was returned as a vestryman in the parish elections of 1864. This was in spite of strenuous efforts by the ruling group in the parish to keep Gordon out of the vestry and to return nominees approved by the custos. The issue of George William Gordon and his treatment by the custos and by the Governor thus inflamed the parish for much of 1864. Nor was there an opportunity for feelings to subside the following year. Gordon was re-elected to the vestry in 1865 and also brought a legal action against Ketelhodt which lasted throughout much of the year.[14]

The case between Gordon and Ketelhodt was first heard before Chief Justice Sir Bryan Edwards in April, 1865. It hinged on the question of what constituted membership in the Church of England and whether Gordon's election as churchwarden was nullified because of his identification with the Native Baptists. According to *The Morning Journal*, Ketelhodt won the case to the surprise of nearly everyone present in the court and contrary to the judge's charge to the jury. The paper expected that a new trial would set aside this verdict, but it also pointed to the difficulties which confronted Gordon. While Gordon had to pay the legal expenses for the case out of his own pocket, the Executive Committee had sanctioned the expenditure of £250 for Ketelhodt's legal costs. This followed a decision by the vestry in St Thomas in the East to make that sum available to its custos.[15]

A new trial was held in August, 1865, but it upheld the earlier decision in favour of Ketelhodt. Gordon made it clear that he would pursue the matter further, and the Supreme Court decided on 10 October to grant yet another trial. At the time of the rebellion, then, a further trial between Gordon and Ketelhodt was expected. It seemed likely that the case would ultimately be tried before the Privy Council in England.[16]

During the trials and even before them, Gordon did nothing to hide his bitter feelings toward Ketelhodt, Cooke, and others on the vestry, including the Anglican curate in Bath, Rev. Victor Herschell. Making use of the apocalyptic language of the Baptists, Gordon described the custos and Herschell as 'a very wicked *band*, and the Lord will reward *them all*'. In the placard designed to round up support for the Underhill meeting in Morant Bay, Gordon went even further: he portrayed Ketelhodt as 'an unscrupulous and oppressive foreigner'. Recalling events at vestry meetings and the handling of funds to deal with an outbreak of smallpox in the parish, Gordon accused Ketelhodt of corruption:

> Do you see how, at every Vestry, he [Ketelhodt] puts off the cause of the poor until the board breaks up, and nothing is done for them? Do you remember how he has kept the small-pox money, and otherwise mis-distributed it, so that many of the people died in want and misery, while he withheld the relief, how that he gave the money to his own friends, and kept it himself, instead of distributing it to the doctors and ministers of religion for the poor?

As for Governor Eyre, he was 'an evil-doer' and 'the Lord will plenteously reward him'. Elsewhere, Gordon wrote that the Governor 'was a plague-spot on poor Jamaica'. This language was revealing. As Thomas Holt has concluded, it provided evidence that for Gordon as well as for Paul Bogle, 'religion shaped their world-view and gave a strong millennial undercurrent to their vision of political entitlement and social justice'.[17]

Political developments in St Thomas in the East could therefore become extremely significant. One issue of this kind which worried Gordon was a report that T. Witter Jackson, the coloured and very popular stipendiary magistrate in the parish, was to be transferred elsewhere. Stipendiary magistrates, who were paid a salary and therefore meant to be independent of the plantocracy, had originally been appointed during the apprenticeship period to deal with disputes between apprentices and their masters. They had equal jurisdiction with the unpaid justices, most of whom were planters and were regarded as biased against the ex-slave population. In the aftermath of full freedom, stipendiary magistrates continued to function as a paid body, working with the unpaid magistrates. But the stipendiary magistrates were heavily outnumbered by the other justices; their number declined in the post-emancipation period from a peak of sixty to six by 1865, compared to a total of 784 justices of the peace. Moreover, the stipendiary magistrates were limited in their role as impartial justices, as they had no paramount or exclusive jurisdiction over the other magistrates.[18]

According to Gordon, Cooke and Herschell had reported that T. Witter Jackson was drunk at a meeting of the vestry and that nine magistrates had falsely supported this allegation. The Governor, in deference to the wishes of Ketelhodt, had therefore decided to remove Jackson from St Thomas in the East. For Gordon, this proved that 'St Thomas ye East is about the *very worst* parish in the island, and now the Governor has given *another* cheer to magisterial oppression . . . .'[19] Like Gordon's expulsion from the vestry, Jackson's treatment at the hands of the magistrates in the parish further embittered the people.

Maladministration of justice and tension on the estates

Jackson's experience as a stipendiary magistrate in St Thomas in the East was further evidence of the divisions within the parish and of the maladministration of justice there as well. This was particularly the case in the lower courts of the parish, the courts of petty sessions. Petty sessions were held in the three principal towns of the parish: Morant Bay, Bath and Manchioneal. They dealt with criminal and civil cases, usually of a relatively minor nature. In criminal cases, for example, petty sessions were limited to misdemeanours such as petty theft, disorderly conduct and assault. For civil cases, the jurisdiction of these courts extended to cases of debt up to £10 and civil actions up to 40s. Punishments were determined by the magistrates or their clerks and were limited to terms of imprisonment up to six months and fines not exceeding £10. The clerk of the peace has been described as a local attorney-general; it was his duty to prosecute in criminal cases. Since the petty sessions dealt with minor cases, it was here that the peasantry usually appeared. More serious crimes were referred to the circuit courts, which also served as courts of appeal for the petty sessions.[20]

Even before T. Witter Jackson arrived in the parish in 1860, some of the justices were already opposed to his appointment. This hostility grew significantly worse when Jackson, who was also agent for immigration and therefore responsible for immigrants in the parish, denied one of the magistrates, John Walton, his allotment of immigrants. According to Jackson, Walton had been personally offensive to him. Jackson's action met with the subsequent approval of the Governor, Charles Darling.[21]

However, problems with Walton continued. In December 1862 Walton was involved in a row with a woman from Stony Gut, Gracey Tobin. Tobin was walking to work on Retreat estate one morning when she met the proprietor, Walton, riding on the path. Walton apparently did not give way for her to pass, and her hoe accidentally struck the horse. She turned round and said, 'Ask your pardon, my good horse.' But in response, Walton beat her severely, shouting 'You bitch! You wretch! You damned wretch!' Tobin took out a summons against Walton for assault, and the case came to court repeatedly for at least three months. Yet each time the case came up, the magistrate sitting with Jackson would step down, leaving Jackson alone on the bench and making it impossible to hear the case. This was a clear example of the magistrates in St Thomas in the East protecting each other, and it was only when Lieutenant-Governor Eyre intervened that a court could be formed. In the event, Walton was found guilty, although he was fined only a pittance and costs.[22]

This was not the only occasion when the magistrates in St Thomas in the East were unwilling to sit with Jackson on the bench. After an exchange of words between Walton and Jackson over another case, Walton and three other justices refused to conduct business with Jackson. They were aided in their efforts to exclude Jackson from the bench by Stephen Cooke. Cooke also sought to deny Jackson access to important legal documents and to form courts without informing him.[23]

The difficulties between Jackson and the other magistrates were not just personal. Jackson was known as 'the Nigger Magistrate', and he himself maintained that the 'negroes have a peculiar confidence in the stipendiary magistrates generally'.[24] For the mass of the population in the parish the problem was to obtain justice before a planter-dominated magistracy: of the twenty-eight magistrates in St Thomas in the East, twenty-four were members of the planter class. As stipendiary magistrate, Jackson represented the sole independent judicial authority in the parish. The planter magistrates were therefore eager to minimize Jackson's authority and preferably to get rid of him. In 1865 the magistrates finally succeeded in having Jackson transferred out of the parish.[25] As in the case of George William Gordon, a popular figure seen to be representing the interests of the small settlers and labourers lost his position in the parish. Jackson later recalled the reaction of a black politician from neighbouring St David, Sam Clarke, to his transfer. Clarke said 'in the most emphatic way, that the people would not submit to it'.[26]

Clarke's outburst may have been inspired partly by the harsh punishments meted out by the courts in St Thomas in the East. In his diary, T. Witter Jackson recorded some of these cases. One example concerned Thomas Bower, who was described as 'a very bad character' and who was accused of having stolen a piece of rope from the wharf at Morant Bay. For this crime his sentence was ninety days hard labour in the house of correction. In another case, H. Bryan pleaded guilty to stealing 'growing canes' at Coley estate and was sentenced to hard labour for two calendar months in the district prison. Jackson provided more detail in the case against an African immigrant, Robert Donaldson. A planter, William C. Miller, swore that he saw Donaldson come out of a cane field with a cane he had taken out of the ground which was valued at 3d. Donaldson did not return to the estate for a week thereafter and claimed in court that his child was sick and that he could not get any money; moreover, he offered to pay for the cane out of his wages. Instead, he was found guilty and sentenced to sixty days hard labour in the house of correction.[27]

Apart from the problem of heavy sentences, Jackson also provided evidence of the sheer difficulty of obtaining a hearing in some cases. A rural constable, Obediah Stewart, had arrested Thomas Fyffe, who was charged by his 'sweetheart', Eliza Spencer, of assaulting her with a cutlass. Stewart took the parties to Morant Bay, but was directed by a policeman to take them to Belvidere estate where T. Witter Jackson lived. Since Jackson was not at home, Stewart took Fyffe and Spencer to Morant estate, where another magistrate, Mr Paterson, asked that they be taken to the court house at Morant Bay. Paterson told them that he would join them shortly. Paterson eventually went to the wharf at Morant Bay, but in spite of his promises to try the case and Eliza Spencer pleading with him to do so, he refused to deal with it. They went to another estate seeking a magistrate, but he was also absent. Fyffe was then put in gaol for two nights, although it was not clear under whose authority this had been done. As Eliza Spencer then wished to withdraw the charge, Jackson agreed to Fyffe's release. Yet Jackson complained that there was no documentation on the case, even though Fyffe had spent time in gaol.[28]

Jackson protested bitterly about the way justice was handled in the parish. He was particularly upset by a case in which William Bogle charged James Geoghan, William Geoghan and James McFarlane for using threatening language against him. The three men were arrested and put in the 'lock-up' overnight. On the following day they were brought before Mr Justice Walton to be bailed, but Walton signed the bail bond without inserting the amount of the bond and leaving out McFarlane's name altogether. Although the men were to appear at the court house as part of their bail bond, the specific court house was not mentioned in the document. Moreover, Jackson had been assured six months previously that the 'lock-up' would no longer be used as a prison. He concluded that 'the Tyranny nourished by, and the Interests involved in this abominable place, are too . . . designing to be easily suppressed'. Moreover,

> the insufficiency of the offence to authorize the apprehension of the party accused, their illegal incarceration, and their subsequent liberation, on an informal and absolutely worthless Bail-Bond, disclose pernicious practices in the administration of the law, in this parish, that cannot be too speedily corrected.[29]

In a letter to Stephen Cooke, Jackson made it clear that he intended to show the custos 'how very slovenly the business in Your office is conducted and upon what insufficient grounds men may be apprehended and incarcerated in this parish . . . .' Yet when Jackson brought this problem to the attention of the custos, Ketelhodt replied that without a complaint from the parties involved, neither he nor any of the magistrates could interfere.[30]

However, this was not the most serious example of illegal detention which Jackson recorded in his diary. Even more worrying for Jackson was the case of Thomas Wainwright. In early September, 1862, two policemen had come to Wainwright's home to arrest him. Since he was ill, they left but returned the next day with six other policemen 'saying that Mr Paterson had desired them to bring him whether he could walk or not'. Although Wainwright wanted to know why he was being arrested, the sergeant in charge, a man named Gillespie, was unable to tell him, except that he believed it was connected with a robbery at a store in Morant Bay. Despite Wainwright's illness, he was brought to the 'lock-up' at Morant Bay and kept there seven weeks and two days. During that period he received no medical attention of any kind. Even more remarkably for Jackson, Wainwright 'was never taken before a magistrate for examination or confronted with anyone supposed to be his accuser, or afforded an opportunity of speaking in defence'. He never saw a warrant for his arrest or was directly charged with any crime.[31]

At the end of October, without any warning, Gillespie took Wainwright out of the 'lock-up' to appear before a magistrate, Mr McKenzie, to be bailed. McKenzie refused to deal with the case. The next day Wainwright was brought before another magistrate, Mr Walton, at Retreat estate, but he also declined to have anything to do with the case. Finally, on 30 October, Wainwright was released on the order of Mr Paterson. Clearly appalled at this treatment, Jackson brought it to the attention of Lieutenant-Governor Eyre. Yet although Eyre expressed sympathy over Wainwright's illegal detention, the Lieutenant-Governor concluded that it was up to Wainwright to bring an action against Paterson and against the policeman who had incarcerated him.[32]

Jackson was not alone in his concern about the lack of justice in St Thomas in the East. One of the judges on the Supreme Court of Jamaica, Justice Allan Ker, confirmed that the labourers in the parish could not rely on the administration of justice there. According to Ker the people lacked confidence in the decisions of the magistrates. While Ker maintained that this was not the cause of the Morant Bay rebellion, it none the less created a great deal of disaffection in the parish. Ker also pointed to the anomaly of magistrates sitting in judgement on cases in which they themselves were concerned. While the magistrates may have acted properly in most instances, the people of St Thomas in the East perceived that justice was not being done. It did not help that nearly all the magistrates were planters or men connected with the management of estates. As a black labourer in the parish, C. Walker, put it, there was no use summoning an employer before a court in the case of a disagreement over wages. When asked why this was the case, Walker replied that 'there is no justice at all; nobody would hear me.'[33]

The high cost of going to court, even in petty sessions, made it very difficult for most people to consider the possibility. For the plaintiff in a court case the costs were prohibitive. Even before a case was heard, fees included 2s. for an information, a further 2s. for a warrant or summons, 1s. for a copy summons, and 3s. for taking the minutes of evidence. There was an additional charge of 3s. for the hearing itself and extra costs for each witness who was to receive a subpoena. Noelle Chutkan has argued that a labourer would therefore have to pay at least a week's wages to get a case to court. The prospect of being a defendant in a case was equally frightening, because of the possibility of losing and being forced to pay costs.[34]

A planter in St Elizabeth, William Coke, complained about these excessive costs. He pointed out that a labourer might be involved in a dispute and be fined 2 or 3s., but then have to pay an additional 11s. in fees. For Coke this was a cause of serious grievances. T. Witter Jackson maintained that there was an additional problem in St Thomas in the East. He found that the clerk of the peace was charging illegally high fees which made matters even worse. Faced with exorbitant charges for going to court and with partial justice once they got there, the people in St Thomas in the East developed their own solution to the problem.[35]

There is evidence that the people in the parish established alternative courts. Much of this activity was centred around Stony Gut but also covered the area from Serge Island estate in the Blue Mountains to Manchioneal in the north-east of the parish. Paul Bogle and his associates were heavily involved in the organization of these courts. In practice, these courts issued summons, tried cases and exacted punishments. They also appointed or elected their own barristers, lawyers, judges, justices of the peace, police and clerks. For example, in a meeting held in 1863 at Stony Gut, the timing and dates of two petty sessions were agreed. Moreover, one of the resolutions at the meeting made it clear that standards of decorum were to be strictly maintained:

> Resolved, that all Person or Persons who shall wilfully Missbehave themselves in the Vecinity of the Court the same shall be committed for, trial if wont Submit be disbands as Unsivilise.

At the same meeting, Paul Bogle was appointed a justice of the peace; a month later, his son, William, was made clerk of the peace.[36]

Summonses were clearly carefully drafted. The manager of Serge Island estate, William Miller, discovered one which had been signed by one of the African indentured labourers working on his estate, John Lamont. In the summons, which was 'endorsed The Queen against James Millin', Millin was accused of 'abusive and Columnious Languages, tending to Provoke a Breach of the peace . . . .' Millin was therefore ordered

> In her magisties name to be and appear on Saturday the 4 day of
> March at the Court House Huntley Village Before such Justices
> of the peace, as shall then be there, to answer to the said Charge,
> and to be further dealt with according to Law.[37]

According to Miller, Lamont held court at Huntley, a village in the Blue
Mountains. Punishments usually consisted of cash fines or of specified
amounts of work. Although most of the surviving evidence about these
courts is restricted to St Thomas in the East, such courts seem to have
existed elsewhere in the island as well.[38]

There were obvious limits to the peasant courts. As Noelle Chutkan has
observed, justice in them could only be administered between co-operating
parties. The courts were not recognized by the plantocracy and would have
no effect on cases between planters and peasants or labourers. Moreover, it
is likely that these courts were a continuation of the people's courts developed during slavery in the Baptist and Native Baptist churches. In the words
of one of the black founders of the Baptist church in Jamaica, Moses Baker,

> we appoint judges and other such officers among us, to settle any
> matters according to the Word of God. We think ourselves forbid-
> den to shed blood, or to go to law one with the other before the
> unjust, but settle any matters we have before the saints.

As with these alternative courts during slavery, the courts at Stony Gut in
1865 were based on the religious community headed by Paul Bogle. Yet, as
Robert Stewart has pointed out, they also served as mock courts to prepare
its members for any appearance before the official judicial system.[39]

But the peasant courts may have had an additional function. Thomas Holt
suggests that the fees and fines associated with the courts were suspiciously
high and indicate the possibility that they were similar to the mutual aid
societies found among other black communities in the Americas. While the
courts may well have had this role, they also indicate a strong desire on the
part of blacks in St Thomas in the East to take charge of their own legal
affairs. In the face of a largely corrupt and highly inefficient judicial system
in the parish, it was one solution to the problem.[40]

Yet not everyone in St Thomas in the East had recourse to the law,
however it was defined. Some people in the parish were prepared to break
the law and to attack the plantations. Twice in 1864 and again in 1865,
estates in the parish were the subject of incendiarism. Golden Grove estate
in the Plantain Garden River district lost its trash house in July, 1864 as did
nearby Hordley estate in September. In early January, 1865, Duckenfield
estate, also in the same district, reported the loss of two large trash houses.
Again, it was strongly suspected that the fire had been set deliberately. The
attorney of Duckenfield, W.P. Georges, reported that 'it was only with the

greatest difficulty that the works [on the estate] were preserved'.[41] Finally in May, *The Falmouth Post* carried an account of a fire at the great house of Lyssons estate, a plantation fairly close to Morant Bay. As in the other cases, the authorities regarded it as the work of an incendiary. This time, despite efforts to control the blaze, the great house was destroyed. For *The Falmouth Post* these fires were to be regretted, but they were also an indication 'that there is something radically wrong . . . .'[42]

There were also other indications along the same lines. During the summer of 1865, *The Falmouth Post* reported several instances of extreme cruelty to animals in the parish. A mule was found burnt at Brown's Gut behind Morant Bay, two steers were stabbed at Lyssons estate, and a steer on Stanton estate suffered the same fate in a particularly brutal way.[43] As with the accounts of the fires on the plantations, these were highly unusual reports. They suggest that there was a marked degree of antagonism directed primarily toward the estates during this period, probably by their own workers. It is therefore possible that the dissatisfaction among estate workers with the level as well as the irregularity of their wages may have led to this type of destruction.

Many workers in St Thomas in the East complained about wages. One problem was the plantations' practice of always retaining a week's wages to ensure that workers returned to the estate. Labourers reported that they never received that pay if they were ill or chose to work elsewhere. There were also disputes about the size of tasks, which workers claimed was greater than the average labourer could perform in a day. In addition, labourers felt that their pay of 1s. per day was often unjustly cut on payday.[44]

This was also the case elsewhere on the island. In the parish of St Dorothy, workers were paid irregularly; one observer reported that 'often at the time of payment the manager refused to pay according to agreement, and forces the labourers to take less than their due'. Workers were also worried about the decline in wages. Don Robotham maintained that this reduction of wages had intensified after 1861. In the western part of Jamaica there were reports of wages being reduced by 25 per cent; elsewhere, this figure was as high as 50 per cent.[45]

To make matters worse, many estates in St Thomas in the East were short of cash and unable to pay their workers for long periods of time. The manager of the Manchioneal cotton estate testified that pay had to be suspended for eight weeks about three months before the outbreak of the rebellion. Reports after the rebellion was over indicated that labour relations had become worse. According to *The Morning Journal*, estates refused payment for work done the week before the rebellion 'and in some quarters the whip was freely used to coerce people to do more than the regular standard of work and in others the rate of wages was reduced to 6d.

per day'. These problems over wages, and especially the attacks on property, suggest a history of labour militancy in the parish.[46]

Research on two estates in St Thomas in the East during slavery provides early examples of this militancy. Mary Turner has demonstrated that the slaves on two estates in the parish, Blue Mountain and Grange Hill, used a variety of measures against the planters more commonly associated with contract and wage workers. These included the collective withdrawal of labour and the articulation of grievances to managers or masters. Often led by skilled slaves and by headmen, slaves on these estates were able to engineer the dismissal of white staff as well as secure terms of service well in advance of existing slave codes. This meant that slaves had two days off, Thursdays as well as Sundays, to work their provision grounds.[47]

The advent of full freedom in 1838 did not lessen conflicts between ex-slaves and their former owners in St Thomas in the East. Swithin Wilmot has documented the resistance of labourers on Golden Grove estate in the Plantain Garden River district to wage levels far below what they had earned in their free time during the apprenticeship period. To achieve higher wages and also access to their lands and homes, the workers went on strike. These ended successfully in September, 1838. Moreover, whenever the employers arbitrarily altered agreed wages or rent charges, the workers again struck, until their demands were met.[48]

Although the reports are not conclusive, it seems likely that this pattern continued in the 1860s. In the voluminous material collected after the rebellion at Morant Bay there are accounts of lengthy work stoppages after the traditional August holidays in 1865. This was particularly the case in the parish of Metcalfe, in the north-east of Jamaica. It was usual for workers to take a three-week break in August, but James Stewart, a manager of estates in the parish, recalled that the workers did not return to work until the middle of September. When Stewart inquired why they were staying away from work, his labourers said that they were waiting for the new law which would compel employers to pay them 4s. per day. The law was to come from St Thomas in the East.[49]

The clerk of the peace for Metcalfe, Gilbert Shaw, confirmed these accounts, although his inquiries suggested that the new law would increase wages to 2s. or 3s. per day. When these reports began to circulate in Metcalfe, Shaw found that labour was increasingly difficult to find. A report in *The Falmouth Post* adds some credibility to these accounts. In September the newspaper carried the news that the workers on several estates in St Thomas in the East had gone on strike for higher wages. While the strike was not confirmed, the paper's informant, a proprietor and magistrate, blamed the action on the agitation surrounding the Underhill meeting in the parish.[50]

Whether or not the strike occurred, there is little doubt that, by Septem-

ber, 1865, St Thomas in the East was in a turbulent state. In the middle of
the month its stipendiary magistrate, T. Witter Jackson, was transferred
from the parish. George William Gordon, one of the two representatives
from St Thomas in the East in the Assembly and the most popular figure
among the small settlers and workers, was involved in a highly publicized
trial with the custos, Baron von Ketelhodt. Although the Underhill meeting
in the parish had taken place in August, Ketelhodt had sought to postpone
it and denied the people access to the court house. Yet a month later, on
9 September, he gave permission to a black American Baptist, Rev. Samuel
Ringold Ward, to hold a counter-meeting in the court house. According to
Ward, his intention was to teach the people 'loyalty and good order'.[51] The
events in October at Morant Bay suggest that it was too late.

Notes

1 Rev. David King, *A Sketch of the Late Mr G.W. Gordon, Jamaica* (Edinburgh: William
   Oliphant and Co., 1866), p. 4; Gad J. Heuman, *Between Black and White: Race, Politics,
   and the Free Coloreds in Jamaica, 1792–1865* (Westport, Conn.: Greenwood Press,
   1981), p. 61; Rev. Duncan Fletcher, *The Life of the Honourable George W. Gordon, The
   Martyr of Jamaica.* 2nd ed. (London: Elliot Stock, 1867), p. 9; Ansell Hart, *The Life of
   George William Gordon* (Kingston: Institute of Jamaica, 1972), p. 24; W. Adolphe
   Roberts, *Six Great Jamaicans: Biographical Sketches* (Kingston: The Pioneer Press,
   1952), pp. 28, 30; JRC: Evidence of Mrs Maria Gordon, p. 726; Evidence of George
   Airey, p. 733; PRO 30/48/42, Cardwell Papers, Joseph Gordon to his wife, 23 October
   1865.
2 Lord Olivier [Sydney Haldane], *The Myth of Governor Eyre* (London: The Hogarth Press,
   1933), pp. 115, 97.
3 Hart, *George William Gordon*, pp. 20–21; JRC, Appendix, p. 1150; BMS, 'Jamaica
   Affairs', vol. 2, p. 142: Clipping from *The Morning Star*, 31 March 1866, p. 5; Thomas
   Harvey and William Brewin, *Jamaica in 1866: A Narrative of a Tour Through the Island,
   with Remarks on its Social, Educational and Industrial Condition* (London: A.W. Bennett,
   1867), p. 22.
4 Hamilton Hume, *The Life of Edward John Eyre, late Governor of Jamaica*, (London:
   Richard Bentley, 1867), p. 12; Heuman, *Between Black and White*, pp. 175–6; Geoffrey
   Dutton, *The Hero as Murderer: The life of Edward John Eyre* (Sydney and Melbourne:
   Collins & Cheshire, 1967), pp. 175–6; James Morris, *Heaven's Command: An Imperial
   Progress* (London: Faber & Faber, 1973), pp. 302, 306; Catherine Hall, 'Imperial Man:
   Edward Eyre in Australasia and the West Indies, 1833–66', in *The Expansion of England:
   Essays in the Cultural History of Race and Ethnicity*, edited by Bill Schwartz (forth-
   coming); Douglas A. Lorrimer, *Colour, Class and the Victorians: English attitudes to the
   Negro in the mid-nineteenth century* (Leicester: Leicester University Press, 1978), p. 198;
   C.V. Gocking, 'Constitutional Problems in Jamaica, 1850–1866', (D. Phil. thesis, Oxford
   University, 1955), pp. 442, 436.
5 Heuman, *Between Black and White*, p. 176; CO 137/367, Eyre to Newcastle, 24 July 1862,
   no. 52, Taylor's minute.
6 JRC, Appendix: Paul Bogle and others to George William Gordon, 25 July 1862; Paul
   Bogle to George William Gordon, 25 July 1862, p. 1150.

7   Heuman, *Between Black and White*, p. 130.

8   *Ibid.*, p. 128; Don Robotham, *'The Notorious Riot': The Socio-Economic and Political Bases of Paul Bogle's Revolt* (Kingston: Institute of Social and Economic Research, 1981), p. 84.

9   JRC, Appendix: Bogle to Gordon, 12 July 1865; St Thos. y East. Election Expenses and Paul Bogle. Memo. 12 July; Papers, Espeut to Myers, 6 January 1866, enclosure: Stephen Cooke, 5 January 1866, p. 124, subenclosure 6, part III.

10 JRC, Evidence of Rev. Stephen Cooke, p. 781.

11 JRC, Appendix, Gordon to Bogle, 22 February 1864, p. 1150.

12 JRC: Evidence of Rev. Stephen Cooke, p. 781; Evidence of Alexander Heslop, p. 333; *The Morning Journal*, 26 April 65: Report of the Home Circuit Court, Precinct of Kingston, 25 April.

13 JRC: Evidence of Dr Alexander Fiddes, p. 375; Evidence of Jasper Cargill, p. 946.

14 Jamaica Archives, 'Private Diary of Thomas Witter Jackson, Stipendiary Magistrate in St Thomas-in-the-East: April, 1863–January, 1865', 21 Oct 1864, p. 146.

15 *The Morning Journal*, 26 April 65: Report of the Home Circuit Court, Precinct of Kingston, 25 April; JRC, Evidence of Henry Westmorland, p. 869.

16 *The Falmouth Post*, 29 August 1865; *The Morning Journal*, 10 October 1865.

17 JRC: Appendix, Gordon to Lawrence, 30 January 1865, p. 1152; Placard: State of the Island, p. 619; Appendix, Gordon to Lawrence, 11 Sept 1865, p. 1154; Appendix, Gordon to Price, 16 September 1865, p. 1155; Thomas C. Holt, *The Problem of Freedom: Race, Labor, and Politics in Jamaica and Britain, 1832–1938* (Baltimore: The Johns Hopkins University Press, 1992), p. 293.

18 Noelle Chutkan, 'The Administration of Justice in Jamaica as a Contributing Factor in the Morant Bay Rebellion of 1865', *Savacou* 11/12 (September, 1975), pp. 79–80.

19 JRC: Appendix, Gordon to Lawrence, 21 September 1865, p. 1155; *Ibid.*, Gordon to Lawrence, 11 September 1865, p. 1154; Harvey and Brewin, *Jamaica in 1866*, p. 22.

20 Chutkan, 'The Administration of Justice', pp. 78–9.

21 CO 137/393, Eyre to Cardwell, 4 September 1865, no. 220, enclosure: Jackson to Jordon, 18 August 1865; Jackson, 'Diary', 15 August 1863, p. 103.

22 JRC, Evidence of T. Witter Jackson, p. 360; Jackson, 'Diary', 25 April 1863: Gracey Tobin v. John Walton, p. 5.

23 Jackson, 'Diary': 15 August 1863, p. 104; 24 January 1864, p. 42; 10 October 1863, p. 38.

24 JRC: Evidence of George Judah, p. 802; Evidence of T. Witter Jackson, p. 362.

25 Robotham, *'The Notorious Riot'*, p. 59; CO 137/393, Eyre to Cardwell, 4 September 1865, no. 220, enclosures: Ketelhodt to Austin, 20 July 1865; Hinshelwood to Ketelhodt, 11 July 1865; Rev. Mr Cooke to Ketelhodt, 14 July 1865; Jackson to Jordon, 18 August 1865; Governor's minute.

26 JRC, Evidence of T. Witter Jackson, p. 362.

27 Jackson, 'Diary': 11 April 1863, p. 2; 25 April 1863, p. 8; 12 March 1864, p. 46.

28 *Ibid.*, Memo, Belvidere, 27 June 1863, p. 17.

29 *Ibid.*, 2 January 1864, p. 40.

30 *Ibid.*: Jackson to Cooke, 5 February 1864, p. 122; Ketelhodt to Jackson, 5 March 1864, p. 135.

31 *Ibid.*, Jackson to Austin, 29 June 1863: Statement of Thomas Wainwright, pp. 100–1.

32 *Ibid.*: p. 101; Austin to Jackson, 30 September 1863, p. 108.

33 JRC: Evidence of The Hon. Mr Justice Allan Ker, pp. 285, 288; Evidence of T. Witter Jackson, p. 359; Evidence of C. Walker, p. 308.

34 Chutkan, 'The Administration of Justice', p. 79. See also Harvey and Brewin, *Jamaica in 1866*, p. 21.

35 JRC: Evidence of William Coke, p. 642; Evidence of T. Witter Jackson, p. 361.

36 JRC, Appendix: To the Honourable Geo. B. Clarke, 14 July 1863, pp. 1160–61; Memory of Meeting, 4 August 1863, p. 1161. See also Robotham, *'The Notorious Riot'*, p. 85.

37 JRC, Appendix, Miller to Espeut, 4 January 1866, p. 1161.

38 JRC: Evidence of William Miller, p. 919; Evidence of Edward Eyre, p. 1010. Eyre testified that the government had received information on mock courts being held in the parishes of St Andrew and St David as well as St Thomas in the East.

39 Chutkan, 'The Administration of Justice', p. 85; Robert J. Stewart, *Religion and Society in Post-Emancipation Jamaica* (Knoxville: University of Tennessee Press, 1992), pp. 131–2, quote on p. 131.

40 Holt, *The Problem of Freedom*, p. 289.

41 *The Falmouth Post*: 12 July 1864, 17 January 1865, 5 January 1865.

42 *Ibid.*: 12 May 1865; 17 January 1865.

43 *Ibid.*, 4 July 1865.

44 Harvey and Brewin, *Jamaica in 1866*, p. 18.

45 Edward Bean Underhill, *The West Indies: Their Social and Religious Condition* (London: Jackson, Walford, and Hodder, 1862), p. 232; Robotham, *'The Notorious Riot'*, p. 50.

46 JRC, Evidence of Arthur Warmington, p. 61; *The Morning Journal*, 28 February 1866.

47 Mary Turner, 'Chattel slaves into wage slaves: A Jamaican case study', in *Labour in the Caribbean: From emancipation to independence*, edited by Malcolm Cross and Gad Heuman (London: Macmillan Caribbean, 1988), pp. 16–17, 26–7.

48 Swithin Wilmot, 'Emancipation in Action: Workers and Wage Conflict in Jamaica, 1838–40', *Jamaica Journal* 19 (August–October, 1986), p. 57.

49 JRC, Evidence of James Stewart, pp. 543, 545.

50 Papers, Shaw to Westmorland, 2 January 1866, p. 50l, subenclosure 4; *The Falmouth Post*, 1 September 1865.

51 JRC, Evidence of Samuel Ringold Ward, p. 555.

CHAPTER 6 | Ideology, religion and rebellion

The events in St Thomas in the East immediately preceding the Morant Bay rebellion make it clear that the outbreak was not a riot or a spontaneous demonstration. In the month leading up to the rebellion and possibly even before then, there was a series of meetings in the parish which suggest deliberate planning and organization. The gatherings themselves were often similar and were usually chaired by one of the leaders of the rebellion. Since these meetings were frequently held in Native Baptist chapels, it is essential to examine the place of religion in the rebellion. Although the evidence is fragmentary, it is also important to investigate the aims of the rebels at Morant Bay.

Meetings, oaths and black volunteers

One meeting occurred on 15 August, only a few days after the Underhill meeting which George William Gordon had organized in Morant Bay. Two local accountants, one of whom was coloured and the other possibly white, reported that it took place in a house thought to be owned by Gordon in the town. Several of the rebellion's leaders were present, including Paul Bogle or his brother, Moses, James McLaren, and Scipio Cowell. When the accountants asked about the purpose of the meeting, those present refused to tell them, but made it clear that they would find out in the future. One of the people at the meeting, George McIntosh, was clearly upset that the accountants had not been at the Underhill meeting; as a result, he believed that they should be excluded from this one. Moreover, McIntosh accused them of being spies and, along with the others at the meeting, refused to let the accountants in.[1]

About a month later, and three weeks before the outbreak of the rebellion, there was a meeting which was more typical of the gatherings which were to follow. It occurred at a chapel at Church Corner in Morant Bay. A labourer, Francis Gordon, reported that he had heard about the meeting from Moses Bogle and James McLaren. McLaren, who could read and write, was later described as the secretary of the rebels. A labourer in his early twenties, McLaren sometimes took charge of services at the Native

Baptist chapel at Morant Bay. At the meeting at Church Corner he had a Bible on which people swore an oath; in addition, McLaren warned them that, 'You must not let your father or your mother know anything about it.' A black man living about a mile from Morant Bay, John Spence, was also present and noted that it was a large meeting with people from outside the town. Spence watched people kiss the Bible, presumably part of the procedure of taking the oath. He also heard that the people at the meeting 'wanted the *backlands* and were going to kill buckra'.[2]

The following week Alexander Bothwell, a carpenter and subsequently a special constable during the rebellion, attended a meeting at Spring Garden, about three miles north of Morant Bay and a mile south of Stony Gut. The meeting was held at a Native Baptist chapel run by William Bailey. One of the people later killed in the rebellion, Joseph Kelly, had asked Bothwell to attend the meeting, which took place on a Tuesday night about 8 o'clock. As in the meeting at Church Corner, participants were asked to take an oath, but Bothwell wanted to know what it meant. Kelly, who was chairing the meeting, responded that Bothwell would not be told unless he took the oath; otherwise, he would have to leave. Bothwell left.[3]

Less than a week before the outbreak another meeting was held at Church Corner. A black labourer who joined Bogle's march to Morant Bay on 11 October, George Thomas, was present and recalled that it was held in the house next to the Baptist chapel. According to Thomas, Paul Bogle had earlier sent a man to encourage the young people working on Nutts River estate to attend, and Thomas had joined them. Bogle and McLaren were there and announced that the meeting was private, but 'would be for the benefit of all the blacks'. As in the earlier meeting at Church Corner, McLaren gave them a Bible to kiss and also wrote their names on a list.

At this meeting, however, there was a more specific message from Bogle. Bogle emphasized the theme of the backlands, which he claimed belonged to the people but the whites had kept that information secret. In addition, there was the problem of wages, and Bogle recalled George William Gordon complaining about the low level of pay. Finally, Bogle raised the issue of justice and the court case involving Lewis Miller which was to come before the magistrates on 7 October. Thomas reported Bogle saying that 'we were to see him trial, and see him get justice, for the white man was taking too much advantage of them.' Bogle therefore wanted black volunteers in groups of fifty men, with a captain heading each such group.[4]

On 6 October, the day before the proceedings at the Morant Bay court house, a black man, George Lake, was present at another meeting. This time the meeting was held at Torrington, a village about a mile north-east of Stony Gut, and presided over by Bogle alone. Again, it was at a meeting-house or chapel and, on this occasion, Bogle himself gave each person a Bible and swore them. Bogle warned Lake that he was to tell the whole truth and nothing but the truth, so help him God, and then told him 'that a war was expected to take place in St Thomas in the East'. According to Lake, Bogle claimed that George William Gordon was behind them and would 'suffice with gun and powder' and that 'he would send people from foreign to come to Jamaica to have a war – to mix with Jamaica people and fight the war'. Bogle also provided details about the trial on Saturday and made it clear that whether Lewis Miller was found guilty or not, he wanted him rescued from the magistrates.[5]

The meetings before the rebellion were not held just in the vicinity of Stony Gut or in Morant Bay. There is evidence of a meeting between 7 and 11 October at Font Hill, a village four or five miles to the west of Stony Gut. One of those present at the meeting, William Anderson, was a young black estate labourer. While Anderson's testimony is more detailed than some of the other accounts, it also needs to be carefully examined. Anderson was sentenced to death during the rebellion, but was spared on the condition that he bring the troops to Stony Gut. Moreover, Anderson pointed out many of the people involved in the rebellion and subsequently served as the servant of Colonel Hobbs, who was in charge of the British troops from Newcastle. He was also confused about the date of the meeting. On the other hand, Anderson's evidence reinforces some of the existing testimony and was itself supported by others. In addition, he provided a reliable account of the Underhill meeting in St Thomas in the East.[6]

Anderson recalled that James McLaren was present at the Font Hill meeting. As at the other meetings, McLaren sought to have those present take an oath and would not divulge the purpose of the meeting without the oath-taking. McLaren was seeking volunteers, but when asked what the volunteers were to do, he replied that white volunteers were not told what to do and that they should get volunteers in the same way. More ominously, McLaren warned that 'when the people meet at Morant Bay, without a civil war there was no use in the island'. He believed that the white people should see that there were 'plenty black in the island . . . and cry out that they don't mean to pay any more ground rent again'. Anderson was also clear about the nature of the oath administered at these meetings. While it differed from place to place, he maintained that it was 'to pay no taxes and to kill every buckra in Jamaica'.[7]

Rev. Samuel Ringold Ward, a black American Independent Baptist minister who had a congregation in neighouring St David's, also provided evidence of McLaren's intentions and views about land. In a discussion with McLaren at the beginning of September, Ward recalled agreeing that McLaren had obtained his land at Font Hill for a nominal price. However, McLaren responded 'that the people wanted lands, and if the owners did not allow them to have lands there would be blood'.[8]

There was further confirmation of meetings in the vicinity of Font Hill just before the outbreak at Morant Bay. A black labourer living in the area, Alexander Cameron, remembered attending a meeting at which he was given a Bible to kiss and told to go to the vestry meeting on Wednesday. There the purpose of the meeting would become clear. Another black, John Moody, reported that after kissing the Bible, there was singing and praying.[9]

These meetings leading up to the rebellion had certain elements in common. At most of them an oath was taken, and the names of those present were written down. The meetings took place in chapels or meeting houses and often in those of the Native Baptists. The oath was meant to be secret, and the leaders sought black volunteers. There is evidence that both Paul Bogle and James McLaren expected a violent confrontation in the parish. When coupled with the events which followed, they provide evidence of planning of the rebellion. Since many of the leaders of the rebellion were Native Baptists and some of the meetings took place in their chapels, it is also important to assess the revolutionary implications of native religion.

Native religion and revolution

Toward the end of 1860 Jamaica experienced a religious revival which was to have a significant impact on developments in the island over the next several years. The Great Revival, as it was known, began in October among the Moravian congregations of western Jamaica and spread quickly among the Methodists and Baptists in the area. Originating in the United States in 1858, the revival had moved across the Atlantic to Ireland and Britain. Missionaries in Jamaica, faced with declining congregations after the 1840s, had sought to bring the movement to the island from the middle of 1859 onwards. Although at first unsuccessful, the missionaries found the revival suddenly taking hold in 1860. It spread to the rest of Jamaica during 1861 and lasted until the following year.[10]

While the missionaries clearly welcomed the revival, they were surprised by the intense excitement it generated. W. Claydon, a Baptist missionary who had congregations in Clarendon and Manchester, recounted some of the effects on his parishioners.

> The work is characterised by most agonising convictions, accompanied often by physical prostration; piercing cries for mercy, and heartrending groans, continuing, in some instances, for nine or ten hours . . . . I should observe, while under conviction they confess to all the sin of which they feel themselves to have been guilty, and seem not able to find peace till they have been reconciled to those with whom they have been at variance, and spoken to those with whom they have been leagued in sin.[11]

Such scenes created great demands on the missionaries, who were sometimes forced to hold almost continuous services. Claydon observed that he had been working day and night for the past two weeks. He was not alone. John Mearns, a Methodist missionary also working in western Jamaica, had no doubt that it was a genuine revival; yet he was struck by its intensity.

> We have seen a large number struck down, and have heard them crying out in their agony; and then we have united with them in praising Him who sets the captives free. Our Chapel and Schoolroom have been filled – crowded for nights in succession, and the services have been continued until morning.[12]

In Kingston events took much the same course. A Methodist missionary there reported holding prayer meetings at 5 o'clock in the morning, at midday, and in the evenings; in some localities services continued day and night. The Methodist missionary in Montego Bay, John Corlett, recounted having to stop on his way home to hold a service by the side of the road. In this makeshift way Corlett baptised twenty people, married a couple, and received seven on trial.[13]

But some missionaries soon had doubts about the nature of the revival. One of the Methodists working in Brown's Town, St Ann, William Tyson, reported a worrying conversation about the revival with a recent convert. According to his parishioner, there were two spirits at work: one was that of Jesus, who helped him to find peace. However, the other was 'a violent spirit which when it seizes hold of the people, they become frantic and scarcely know what they do'. Tyson thought it likely that this was the spirit of the devil.[14]

Missionaries increasingly reported the triumph of 'fanaticism, disorder, and delusion'. In some cases those attending chapel made a mockery of the church. At one Methodist station the people

> got possession of the chapel, put the local preacher at defiance, men and women embracing each other, formed a circle and danced round and round in the House of God. . . . I found them congregated in a meeting house in the locality, and if ever a concourse of people had the appearance of demoniacal possession, these had.

Some were eating the earth, others behaved like animals prancing around on all fours, and still others were simulating sexual intercourse.[15]

Some of those most caught up in the revival joined together to spread the message. They went from place to place, calling meetings and assembling people in the woods at all hours of the day and night. Usually unconnected with any denomination, they helped to widen the impact of the revival but often at the expense of the missionary churches. Others, sometimes known as myal men, went about digging up obeah charms, symbols of sorcery which were often meant to harm individuals. Myal, a community-oriented African religion and one which counteracted the workings of obeah, was in the process of taking over the revival.[16]

As Philip Curtin has concluded, the Great Revival had turned African. In the end, Myalists captured the revival movement. Moreover, it is possible that several new Afro-Christian sects emerged during this period. Even more importantly from the point of view of events at Morant Bay, the revival greatly strengthened all forms of native religion. With these religions, and especially with the Native Baptists, came a particular political agenda and one which emphasized the plight of the blacks in post-emancipation society. The politics of the Native Baptists went far beyond the ballot box; theirs was a religion which 'provided a vehicle for cultural resistance, giving moral authority to an alternative world view'.[17]

For many observers this was a worrying development. Writing in the wake of the Morant Bay rebellion, one Methodist missionary, Jonathan Edmondson, commented on the large number of 'uneducated and I fear unprincipled men [who] have risen up as native Preachers, chiefly of the Baptist persuasion'. For Edmondson these preachers were not only incapable of promulgating the Gospel, but they were also potentially quite dangerous. Such preachers were likely to have 'dwelt much on the claims of *classes* and represented the blacks as an oppressed race who ought to defend themselves'. Edmondson had heard of a black preacher going further and preaching an early form of 'black power':

> You are black, and I am black, and you ought to support your own colour. The blacks are seven to one of the others and they ought to have the Island.[18]

There was also a more pragmatic political agenda adopted by some of the Native Baptists. We have already seen some of the effects of the electoral alliance in St Thomas in the East between George William Gordon and Paul Bogle. It is clear, for example, that Gordon owed his election to the Assembly in 1863 to the support of the Native Baptists in St Thomas in the East and to the work of Paul Bogle as his election agent. Moreover, as Robert Stewart has commented, 'Gordon's progression from Presbyterian to Native Baptist seemed calculated to bring his influence closer to the working class. It was a religious journey that Paul Bogle himself noted, and to which he gave his blessing . . . .' For Stewart, Gordon appropriated religion to politics in an almost deliberate manner and made use of his religion as a basis for political protest about the condition of the ex-slave population in St Thomas in the East and in Jamaica generally.[19]

Apart from electoral alliances, there were other forms of religio-political protest in the 1860s. Not surprisingly, the courts were sometimes the object of this protest. For example, there was a very strong reaction during and after the sitting of a court in Trelawny in 1864. The particular case involved people from a district known as Sawyers who had been charged with petty larceny. They were accompanied to the court house by a crowd of about three or four hundred supporters who responded to the sentences with a religious demonstration.

> [The crowd], after the passing of the respective sentences by the Justices, commenced a noise which beggars description, associated with indecent contortions of their bodies, with the loud singing of 'revival' hymns, and with wild and execrable vociferations in which, under the guise of prayer, the sacred name of the Creator was blasphemed.

In light of the intense feelings of the crowd, it seems likely that this protest could have become violent had the authorities responded more provocatively.[20]

There was also a potentially more revolutionary aspect of the impact of revival and of native religion. One example of this was a book describing the leaders of the 1831 slave rebellion as martyrs. According to Rev. Edward Key, an Anglican curate, this book was being circulated in Baptist schools in early 1864. It may have been the *Voice of Jubilee*, a book marking the fiftieth year of the Baptist mission in Jamaica. If so, it would have contained material venerating the memory of slaves who had died in the cause of religion, including Samuel Sharpe, the leader of the 1831 rebellion. Key thought that this martyrology of the rebellion was 'treasonable' and 'that it would do mischief among the people'.[21]

Even more problematic for the authorities was a vision of the millennium which would deliver blacks from their oppressors. It was expressed most vividly in the form of a placard found on a wharf gate at Lucea, Hanover in June, 1865:

> I heard a voice speaking to me in the year 1864, saying, 'Tell the sons and daughters of Africa that a great deliverance will take place for them from the hand of opposition', for, said the voice 'They are oppressed by Government, by magistrates, by proprietors, by merchants', and this voice also said, 'Tell them to call a solemn assembly and to sanctify themselves for the day of deliverance which will surely take place; but if the people will not hearken I will bring the sword into the land to chastise them for their disobedience and for the iniquities which they have committed. And the sword will come from America. If the people depend upon their arms and upon our Queen, and forget Him who is our God they will be greatly mistaken, and the mistake will lead them

to great distresses.' Shame or fear seems to have kept me back, but the Great Being who rules all things reminds me again to proclaim it aloud. The calamity which I see coming upon the land will be so grievous and so distressing that many will desire to die. But great will be the deliverance of the sons and daughters of Africa, if they humble themselves in sackcloth and ashes, like the children of Nineveh before the Lord our God; but if we pray truly from our hearts, and humble ourselves, we have no need to fear; if not the enemy will be cruel for there will be Gog and Magog to battle. Believe me.[22]

Signed 'A SON OF AFRICA', this document linked the revivalists directly with the politics of protest. Robert Stewart suggests that this placard also pointed to 'the existence of a connection between prophetism, politics, and Africa consciousness' that pre-dated Garveyism and Rastafarianism, both of which emerged in the twentieth century. In addition, there was potentially a coded warning in the placard: the allusion to the sword that will come from America. This may have referred to the Civil War in the United States and the fear of re-enslavement if American slaveowners expanded into Jamaica. Found four months before the outbreak of the Morant Bay rebellion, the document should have alerted the government to a radically different vision of society.[23]

Paul Bogle, the Maroons and the aims of the rebels

The growing strength of a highly politicized native religion was a significant development in the 1860s. As in the 1831 slave rebellion, the native churches, and especially the Native Baptists, provided a structure around which resistance could develop. This could take a variety of forms. For example, the black courts which sprang up in St Thomas in the East were often organized around religious communities. Many of the meetings held just before the Morant Bay rebellion took place in native chapels and were organized by class leaders or, as in the case of Paul Bogle, deacons. At some of these meetings Bogle preached about the social and political problems of St Thomas in the East and warned of the impending 'war' in the parish. But Bogle did more than harangue those attending the meetings. He also sought to create a black militia to counteract that of the whites. In addition, he worked to create an alliance with the one Jamaican group which could destroy his rebellion, the Maroons.

Bogle was aware of the Maroons' role in helping to crush the slave rebellion of 1831; they were excellent shots and skilled at tracking rebel forces. The Maroons were therefore greatly feared by the rest of the Jamaican population for their martial skills and for the violent manner in which they put down unrest. In making his plans for the rebellion at Morant Bay, Paul Bogle clearly wanted the Maroons on his side.[24]

About a month before the outbreak, Bogle travelled to Hayfield, one of the Maroon communities located in the Blue Mountains above Bath. He was accompanied by another leader of the rebellion, James Bowie, and three other people. According to James Sterling, a major of the Maroons, Bogle discussed various problems, including the low rate of wages paid on the estates and the high level of taxes.[25] Another account of the meeting provided by a Maroon captain, James Walters, suggested that Bogle was more specific in his requests. Walters recalled that Bogle discussed going to Moore Town, a large Maroon settlement in the parish of Portland. Bogle was

> in fear of the Maroon because they were going to Court to have a battle and he was afraid of the Maroons, and he was going to the Maroon Town to tell them not to interfere. Since Bogle was afraid of the Maroons, he wanted to go there and tell them not to interfere with what he wanted to do.

Bowie used even stronger language than Bogle; he maintained that 'we want to beat all the brown and white off the island, and we will find a place to secure Mr Gordon.'[26] But the Maroons were not responsive to the appeals of either Bowie or Bogle. They prayed with their visitors but offered them no encouragement.

Neither did a Maroon from Moore Town, Francis Dean, when approached about two weeks before the outbreak at Morant Bay by a man named Richard Fennison. Fennison asked Dean if the Maroons intended to fight against the whites, clearly expecting that they would do so. However, Dean responded that the Maroons could not entertain such a notion.[27]

While the exactness of this conversation is questionable, there is little doubt that Paul Bogle was worried about the Maroons and sought to win them over to his side. There also seems to have been a general belief among those involved in the rebellion that the Maroons would join them. Moreover, the discussion between Francis Dean and Richard Fennison reinforces the view that people expected a rebellion or an outbreak of some kind. Again, particular individuals were targeted on the day of the rebellion. George Adam Hague, a coloured collector of customs at Port Morant and Morant Bay, reported an encounter with a black man, Charles Mitchell, in his office on the day of the rebellion. Mitchell walked into his private office, and, pointing to Hague's chair, said

> That place is the place of a blackman, and if you don't quit it quietly we will have your head cut off as we intend to have that of the Baron, and of the Cooke's.[28]

Bogle was also aware of the likelihood of violence at Morant Bay on the day of the rebellion. He warned one of his supporters about the possible consequences of going to Morant Bay: 'maybe he might be dead or come safe, he did not know.'[29] It is important to remember that the first target of Bogle's forces at Morant Bay was not the court house where the vestry was in session but rather the police station. Although his supporters had some arms, they were seeking more weapons in order to confront the militia. The well-ordered march to Morant Bay and the attack on the police station reinforce the view that this was a carefully planned operation.

Yet there is evidence that Bogle hesitated on the way to Morant Bay. This is not surprising, since he would have known about the militia guarding the vestry. According to the deputy collector of debts in St Thomas in the East, Edward House, a man named Thomas threatened Bogle that he would take over Bogle's men. This was because Bogle 'was taking advice of buckras' side. From yesterday we would go and take the bay but you are backing us, and if you do not come I'll take away the men.' Bogle decided that 'before the men go away, they must go into the bay.' His forces then divided and marched to Morant Bay.[30]

Those men and women who came into Morant Bay on 11 October were not a disorganized rabble. There were captains and colonels in charge of various groups, and there was considerable drilling of these people in advance of the rebellion. One observer also noted a significant amount of blowing of shells and collecting of forces in the days immediately preceding the outbreak. On the morning of the 10th, for example, parties were seen leaving Stony Gut playing the fife and drum in the direction of Coley and Mount Lebanus and returning that evening with greatly increased numbers. These combined forces, along with others from Torrington and from places beyond Bath, joined together at Morant Bay.[31]

Following the massacre at Morant Bay, Bogle and his forces withdrew to Stony Gut. The service which Bogle held in his chapel on his return made it clear how satisfied he was at the outcome of events at Morant Bay. During the service he offered a prayer to 'thank God, that he went to do his work and God succeeded him in his work'.[32] Over the next few days he and others provided some evidence of their motivations and their expectations.

For instance, one of the leaders of the rebellion, George Craddock, spoke to the people at Stony Gut the day after the outbreak at Morant Bay. Craddock believed that the people would now take charge of the island. He proclaimed

> that this country would belong to them, and they were about getting it, to take possession, that they had been long trodden under sandals, and now they were about getting the country; it had long been theirs, and they must keep it wholly in possession.[33]

Bogle also addressed the crowd at Stony Gut, but warned them they should not go to work. If anyone flouted Bogle's advice and particularly if anyone chose to work for $1.00 per day or less, Bogle would appoint ten men who would be in charge of flogging that individual. If people wanted anything Bogle suggested

> they must go to an estate and take a cow out and kill it; and they must go off to Monklands, and tell Mr James Paterson to leave his place and go off the island, it is not his country.[34]

This idea that blacks would now take over was repeated over the next several days. Observers reported that, although there was considerable plundering of shops and houses, the crops and the estate buildings were generally left undisturbed. As the headwoman on Hordley estate noted, one member of the crowd said that 'as they broke out at Morant Bay yesterday already, they must have buckra life, and have the estate and be busha [overseer] and book-keeper themself'. Elsewhere there were warnings not to burn estate buildings as 'we want to make sugar for ourselves'. One man, Richard Cousins, who was involved in the murder of Augustus Hire at Amity Hall estate, maintained that 'it was not buckra people making the sugar all the time, it was black people making the sugar.' Cousins declared that the people were planning to harvest the crop the next week at the Garden River district. When asked what they would do with the sugar, Cousins responded that they would send it to England.[35]

There is some evidence that Bogle believed that no more whites should be killed after the outbreak at Morant Bay. A black policeman who was released the day after the events at Morant Bay claimed that Bogle had another solution for whites whom he captured: 'as fast as they catch them they would make them work in the cane fields'. The crowd at Manchioneal two days after the start of the rebellion had a very different idea of what they would do with the whites. According to a black shoemaker from the town, the crowd vowed to kill all the whites and all those who joined the whites. As a result, the Queen would be forced to send 'fresh gentlemen from England and we and those gentlemen will quite agree'.[36]

Whatever the intentions of the various groups involved in the rebellion, there was a war to be fought. In the days after the outbreak at Morant Bay, Bogle was seen at various places, usually marching with his forces. He was apparently prepared to fight against the soldiers, although dissuaded from doing so when the troops were in the vicinity of Font Hill. Bogle also had his men chop down trees to erect barricades across the roads and may have helped to organize earthworks which had the appearance of fortifications in the vicinity of Mount Lebanus. Five days after the beginning of the rebellion, Bogle, along with a number of his followers, returned to the Maroon community of Hayfield, probably seeking support. However, only the women in the village were there, as the men were guarding Bath.[37]

The following day, 17 October, Bogle and several of his associates including McLaren, signed a document which was a call to war. Bogle still had hopes that the Maroons would come to their aid and was still seeking the support of the people:

> It is time now for us to help ourselves. Skin for skin, the iron bars is now broken in this parish, the white people send a proclamation to the governor to make war against us, which we all must put our shoulder to the wheels, and pull together. The Maroons sent they proclamation to us to meet them at Hayfield at once without delay, that they will put us in the way how to act. Every one of you must leave your house, takes your guns, who don't have guns take your cutlisses down at once. Come over to Stoney Gut that we might march over to meet the Maroons at once without delay. Blow your shells, roal your drums, house to house, take out every man, march them down to Stoney Gut, any that you find in the way takes them down with there arms; war is at us, my black skin, war is at hand from to-day to to-morrow. Every black man must turn out at once, for the oppression is too great, the white people are now cleaning up they guns for us, which we must prepare to meet them too. Chear men, chear, in heast we looking for you a part of the night or before day break.[38]

Nothing was heard from Bogle again until he was captured by the Maroons six days later, although he may have been involved in a skirmish against the Maroons at Torrington on 19 October.[39]

Looking at the rebellion as a whole, it is apparent that Bogle and the other leaders of the rebellion planned a violent confrontation at Morant Bay. They marshalled their forces in the period leading up to the outbreak, and, as in many other rebellions, swore their followers to secrecy. As Native Baptists, the leaders of the rebellion were informed by a highly politicized religion, one which reinforced their sense of injustice. Aware of the dangers which the Maroons posed, Bogle sought their support in advance. When he and his forces marched to Morant Bay on 11 October, they proceeded directly to pillage the police station of its arms before confronting the militia. The chant of the crowd at Morant Bay, 'Colour for Colour', was also taken up in the days after the massacre. For the blacks it meant avenging any of their number who were killed by slaughtering browns and whites. To some of them it also signified the end of white dominance, at least in St Thomas in the East. The whites, however, equated it with the end of civilization and acted accordingly.[40]

Notes

1 JRC: Evidence of J.H. Williams, p. 154; JRC, Evidence of William Eccles Ward, p. 205.

2 JRC: Evidence of John McLaren, p. 246; Evidence of Francis Gordon, p. 133; Evidence of John Spence, p. 166; Spence's testimony at the trial of Alex Taylor cited in *The Colonial Standard and Jamaica Despatch*, 1 March 1866. The backlands referred to the provision grounds worked by blacks, usually on estate land which was not cultivated by the plantation owners; see Veront M. Satchell, *From Plots to Plantations: Land Transactions in Jamaica, 1866–1900* (Mona, Jamaica; Institute of Social and Economic Research, 1990), p. 64.

3 JRC, Evidence of Alexander Bothwell, pp. 131–2.

4 JRC, Evidence of George Thomas, pp. 1038–9.

5 JRC, Evidence of George Lake, p. 1036.

6 JRC: Evidence of William Anderson, p. 158; Evidence of Colonel Thomas Hobbs, p. 758.

7 JRC: Evidence of William Anderson, pp. 158, 165; Evidence of Colonel Thomas Hobbs, p. 758. See also William Law Mathieson, *The Sugar Colonies and Governor Eyre, 1849–1866* (London: Longman, Green & Co., 1936), p. 207.

8 JRC, Evidence of Rev. Samuel Ringold Ward, p. 555–6.

9 JRC: Evidence of Alexander Cameron, p. 154; Evidence of John Moody, p. 155.

10 Philip D. Curtin, *Two Jamaicas: The Role of Ideas in a Tropical Colony, 1830–1865* (Cambridge, Mass.: Harvard University Press, 1955), pp. 170–1; Robert J. Stewart, *Religion and Society in Post-Emancipation Jamaica* (Knoxville: University of Tennessee Press, 1992), p. 145.

11 BMS, Jamaica Sundries, Cuttings from *The Missionary Herald*, 1858–1862: 1 January 1861.

12 MMS 199, Mearns to the General Secretaries, 22 November 1860.

13 *Ibid.*: Edmondson to the General Secretaries, 22 April 1861; Letter of John Corlett, 8 December 1860.

14 *Ibid.*, Tyson to the General Secretaries, 23 April 1861.

15 *Ibid.*, Holdsworth to the General Secretaries, 7 March 1861.

16 BMS, Jamaica Sundries, Cuttings from *The Missionary Herald*, 1858–1862: 1 July 1861; 1 March 1861. For very useful discussions of Myal, see Monica Schuler, *'Alas, Alas, Kongo': A Social History of Indentured African Immigration into Jamaica, 1841–1865* (Baltimore: The Johns Hopkins University Press, 1980), ch. 3 and Stewart, *Religion and Society*, pp. 136–47.

17 Curtin, *Two Jamaicas*, p. 171; Schuler, *'Alas, Alas, Kongo'*, p. 104; Stewart, *Religion and Society*, pp. 146–47; Thomas C. Holt, *The Problem of Freedom: Race, Labor, and Politics in Jamaica and Britain, 1832–1938* (Baltimore: The Johns Hopkins University Press, 1992), p. 291.

18 MMS 199, Edmondson to the General Secretaries, 23 October 1865.

19 Stewart, *Religion and Society* pp. 162, 161, quote on p. 162. For further details on the electoral link between Paul Bogle and George William Gordon, see ch. 5.

20 *Ibid.*, p. 147.

21 *Ibid.*, p. 169; JRC, Evidence of Rev. Edward Key, p. 712.

22 JRC, Evidence of Joseph Williams, p. 849.

23 Stewart, *Religion and Society*, pp. 121–2; Schuler, *'Alas, Alas, Kongo'*, p. 160, note 29.

24 For more information on the Maroons, see chap. 3.

25 JRC, Evidence of James Sterling, p. 1031.

26 JRC, Evidence of James Walters, p. 1032.

27 JRC, Evidence of Francis Dean, p. 1033.

28 JRC, Evidence of George Adam Hague, p. 181.

29 JRC, Evidence of William Anderson, p. 159.
30 Papers, In the Court held under Special Commission, January, 1866: The Queen v. Bogle and others, Copyevidence for Mr Attorney General, Statement of Edward House, p. 437. See also BMS, 'Jamaica Affairs', vol. 2, p. 142: clipping from *The Morning Star*, 31 March 1866.
31 JRC, Evidence of J. Williams, p. 185; Report, p. 13.
32 JRC, Evidence of Joseph Muir, p. 797.
33 JRC, Evidence of M. Cresser, p. 144.
34 *Ibid.*
35 Papers, Deposition of Diana Blackwood, p. 67, subenclosure 4; Report, p. 16; JRC, Evidence of T. Cousin, p. 424.
36 JRC: Evidence of James Asher, p. 152; Evidence of William Rennie, p. 418.
37 Report, p. 17; Holt, *The Problem of Freedom*, p. 301; JRC: Evidence of Col. Thomas Hobbs, p. 770; Evidence of Adelaide Finlayson, p. 1034.
38 CO 884/2, Confidential Print, no. 2: Papers Relating to the Insurrection in Jamaica, October, 1865, Printed for the Use of the Cabinet, December, 1865, p. 23.
39 JRC, Evidence of George Bernard, p. 947. For more on the skirmish with the Maroons, see ch. 9.
40 Michael Adas, *Prophets of Rebellion: Millenarian Protest Movements against the European Colonial Order* (Cambridge: Cambridge University Press, 1987), p. 147; JRC, Evidence of Joseph Williams, p. 185.

Part III:

Suppression and aftermath

No one will ever believe the things that were done here in that mad bad time. And very few will ever hear of the tenth part of them – including some of the worst.

Governor John Peter Grant to Colonial Secretary, 23 July 1867

CHAPTER 7 | Panic and paranoia in Jamaica

Once the rebellion had broken out at St Thomas in the East, whites in Jamaica became convinced that they were dealing with a massive conspiracy. In their view, blacks were intent on killing whites and coloureds and taking over the island. For whites it was therefore essential that the outbreak be suppressed as quickly as possible. This was the line adopted by Governor Eyre in his first dispatch after the rebellion to the Colonial Office. Writing nine days after the events at Morant Bay, Eyre maintained that it had been necessary to put down the rebellion immediately. Otherwise, 'the insurrection would have been universal throughout the entire Island, and . . . either the Colony would have been lost to the Mother Country, or an almost interminable war and an unknown expense would have had to be incurred in suppressing it.'[1]

White repression after the rebellion

Eyre was clear about the existence of an island-wide conspiracy. He had no doubts that 'there had been an intercommunication between the negroes of the different parishes and an intention to act in concert for the destruction of the white and coloured inhabitants'. In his view some blacks outside of St Thomas in the East had advance warning of the outbreak, while others were waiting to see the outcome of the rebellion before taking action. Although there was no evidence of 'any actually organized combination to act simultaneously', Eyre was convinced that the whole island was in great danger.[2]

Along with many other whites, the Governor believed that the rebellion had broken out prematurely. A local incident had prompted Paul Bogle and his followers to take steps on their own at Morant Bay. This had made it possible for the local government to contain the outbreak and to prevent 'a general insurrection'.[3] There were various versions of the planned uprising. For example, one planter thought that 'the scheme was well laid, and of most consummate design drawn by a master intellect'. The rebellion was meant to begin at Christmas, when there would be a simultaneous massacre of whites from one end of the island to the other. The only exceptions were those named by George William Gordon as well as white women and their female children. All property in the hands of whites, and especially the sugar plantations and the great houses, was to be spared. Writing from Kingston, the planter concluded that 'the Morant Bay Meeting happily for us in this part of the country, but unhappily for those brave fellows who fell victims, broke the egg before it was hatched'.[4]

Nearly a month after the outbreak of the rebellion and long after it had been crushed, Eyre described Jamaica as still 'on the brink of a volcano'. Addressing a meeting of the Jamaican Legislature, he warned the legislators of the dangers they had faced and how close they had come to seeing Jamaica become 'a second Haiti':

> One moment's hesitation, one single reverse might have lit the torch which would have blazed in rebellion from one end of the island to the other; and who can say how many of us would have lived to see it extinguished.[5]

For Eyre, the danger was not limited to Jamaica. Responding to a memorial from St Vincent, where he had served as Lieutenant-Governor, Eyre suggested that there would have been rebellions in the other British West Indian colonies if the outbreak at Morant Bay had not been crushed. This was particularly the case for small and unprotected colonies such as St Vincent.[6]

Eyre was not alone in his views about the grave threat posed by the rebellion. Officials around the island were terrified by news of the outbreak. The custos of Vere, Lewis Mackinnon, regarded his parish as 'the powder magazine of the south side'; for Mackinnon it was only the repression of the rebellion which ensured the safety of his parish before troops arrived there. Gilbert Shaw, the clerk of the peace in the parish, was more graphic about the consequences of any delay in crushing the rebellion. He was 'convinced that 12 hours hesitation on [Eyre's] part would have resulted in the uprising of the rebels in Kingston and all along that Coast here and that long before this time, we would have been the food of John Crows'. Shaw thought that he owed his life to the Governor's actions.[7]

The custos of Trelawny, Robert Nunes, shared this view. He was certain that the rebellion had to be suppressed quickly. Had it lasted three more days Nunes believed there would have been a rebellion in Trelawny. Elsewhere in the island officials feared disturbances in the wake of Morant Bay. For instance, two justices of the peace from St Thomas in the Vale came to Kingston on 16 October to plead for troops to be despatched immediately to Linstead. They were certain of an outbreak that day. A few days later the government received news that disturbances were expected in Brown's Town, and there was also a demand for troops to be sent to Port Maria and subsequently to Westmoreland as well. In addition, the custos of St Elizabeth warned the Governor of 'the readiness of a large portion of the blacks to join an insurrectionary movement in this parish, if once commenced, and therefore of the necessity of a show of force'.[8]

Many people believed that Kingston was particularly vulnerable. There were reports that disturbances were expected on 14 October, followed by threats the following day to massacre the whites and to burn down the town on 17 and 18 October. These rumours were heightened by the arrival of refugees fleeing from St Thomas in the East and spreading horror stories about the rebels' intentions. A member of the Executive Committee, Henry Westmorland, reported that the government had established an office in Kingston which was besieged by people requesting protection. As Westmorland recalled, 'families were flowing into Kingston from all parts, and the excitement and alarm was intense'.[9]

As a result, the government took various precautionary measures. Since there was a large amount of powder stored in Kingston and since the government storehouses were full, the powder was transferred to a ship in the harbour. All of the cutlasses were collected from various depots and stored at the Ordnance. Westmorland recalled that all of these steps were designed to ensure that the rebels would not capture this weaponry. More ominously, private letters of suspected persons were opened, and passes were required for all persons travelling to and from the disturbed districts.[10]

The atmosphere in Kingston was clearly very tense. This was reflected in the account given by a coloured lawyer and member of the House of Assembly, Samuel Constantine Burke, to the Jamaica Royal Commission. Burke, who had been educated at Harrow and Cambridge and later served on the Legislative Council, hoped that he would never 'see such a state of feeling again'. First, there was the fear generated by the rebellion itself and then consternation at the nature of its suppression. Burke himself was continually under the impression that he was to be arrested at any moment.[11]

This feeling was not limited to Kingston. One magistrate, Fred Todd, informed the custos of St Ann that he was keeping a 'black list' of people using seditious language. When the Governor learned about this, he requested that Todd immediately produce his list and provide all the information he had. Those on Todd's list as well as other suspects would not necessarily be protected by the law. As in the case of George William Gordon, Eyre was prepared to have such people arrested and sent into areas under martial law rather than allow them to be tried in the usual courts.[12]

The experiences of Samuel Constantine Burke and Fred Todd in the aftermath of the rebellion point to a highly repressive atmosphere. Whites were afraid of the spread of the rebellion and were convinced that they were surrounded by sympathizers of the rebels. Yet the evidence suggests that this was not the case; on the contrary, most Jamaicans remained loyal to the government and were horrified by the events at Morant Bay.

All across the island blacks voiced their shock at the outbreak. In St David, which bordered on St Thomas in the East, a large group of black labourers requested that a Justice of the Peace, Richard Mothersill, appoint them as constables. Mothersill swore in over a hundred constables who vowed to destroy the rebels who came their way. Henry Clarke, a minister of the Church of England in Westmoreland, reported that his parishioners 'expressed great horror at [the rebellion]'. A Baptist missionary in St James, Edward Hewitt, described the feelings of 'great sorrow, dismay, and . . . horror' expressed by his people at the news of the rebellion. In Manchester the custos wrote to Eyre that the 'inhabitants generally feel very indignant at the atrocities committed in St Thomas in the East'.[13]

At the same time there were disturbing signs of discontent all over the island. Despite their protestations of loyalty, many blacks in Jamaica shared the grievances of the rebels in St Thomas in the East. While they did not respond in the same way, there were serious indications of protest in the wake of the events at Morant Bay.

Threats against court houses, and anonymous letters

The court houses in Jamaica were one of the targets of the protesters following the rebellion. At Morant Bay the court house had been destroyed during the rebellion, partly because it was the symbol of an oppressive judicial system. In the weeks which followed the outbreak there were threats against court houses in various parts of the island.

The most serious threat took place in Savanna-la-Mar. A meeting of the circuit court was scheduled to take place there on 30 October. However, less than a week after the outbreak of the rebellion there were rumours of an imminent attack on the Savanna-la-Mar court house. The problem grew out of a case, the Queen v. Tait, which was to be tried during the sitting of the court. William Tait had allegedly wounded a trespasser who had destroyed some fences on Tait's property in an attempt to gain access to water. According to several parish officials, it was likely that a large number of people would be brought to Savanna-la-Mar at the opening of the court. The custos, Benjamin Vickers, was therefore afraid of the possibility of a riot.[14]

Worse was yet to come for the authorities. Vickers subsequently reported that nightly meetings were being held in the parish, and that the people were threatening to burn down the court house if the verdict went in favour of Tait. Moreover, Tait had received an anonymous letter threatening to murder him if he were acquitted. As Vickers noted in an express letter to the Governor's secretary, these rumours alarmed the inhabitants of Savanna-la-Mar, particularly since the town was also threatened with destruction by fire.[15] The custos was worried as well, because Savanna-la-Mar itself and the parish generally were largely unprotected. He assembled the volunteers in the parish and asked that a ship which had docked in town, HMS *Steady*, be detained in port for a few days. In the meantime, Eyre was also taking steps to defend the town. He issued an order to the senior naval officer in Jamaica, Captain de Horsey, to dispatch a man-of-war to Savanna-la-Mar. The Governor's instructions made it clear that the ship should arrive in advance of the meeting of the circuit court and remain there until the risk had passed. Moreover, Eyre requested that a considerable military force sail on the ship and be landed once it had arrived in port. Finally, in light of the threat to the circuit court, Eyre asked that the man-of-war accompany the court as it met in various localities in the island.[16]

This was not the only threat against court houses or meetings of the court in the island. Brown's Town was another potential source of trouble for the government. Eyre reported that he had learned of a prevailing spirit of 'disloyalty and sedition' in the town and 'that the most threatening language is openly indulged in . . . .' According to the custos of St Ann, people in Brown's Town were threatening 'to rise in insurrection' on 2 November, which was the next meeting of the court. In support of this allegation a local magistrate, Fred Todd, had learned that people were saying that 'the next Court day will be our day' and that 'they are only waiting for a commencement' of the court to take action. As in the case of Savanna-la-Mar, Eyre was prepared to act quickly. He immediately ordered a ship to be chartered to take troops to Dry Harbour, the closest port to Brown's Town.[17]

In at least one parish, Clarendon, there was an attempt to burn down a court house. Almost as soon as news of the rebellion reached the parish, someone tried to destroy the court house. According to the custos of the parish, Francis Lowe, one of the offices had been saturated with kerosene oil, and matches as well as the remains of some burnt rags had been found when the office had opened. A fire had apparently started but had not spread.[18]

Elsewhere there were different kinds of threats, again often related to the courts. Edward B. Lynch, a parish official in St Catherine, received an anonymous letter threatening to burn down Spanish Town 'if we don't get justices in this October Court'. The letter also threatened a riot at the next meeting of the court:

> and we have 1,500 men consent to raise a riot at the Court-house, October the 23 of this month, and Monday we looking out to see what trial will be; then we will be commence. *Lif* for *lif* will be taken that day at the Court-house, for we don't fare, and that day of October, for we is well *armdid* with cutlass and gun appeas and that day besides women to help us, 400.

The letter was signed 'No name' and ended on an even more threatening tone: 'Powder we have plenty, as much as to kill hold town.'[19]

There were many other anonymous letters found all over Jamaica in the aftermath of the rebellion. Like the one from 'No name', several letters expressed a concern about the lack of justice in the island and a desire to attack the court house or the parish officials. For example, a letter addressed to the Town of Lucea and the Gentlemen of the parish concluded by suggesting that 'it was a good thing that the Court House was shut up or it might have ended by this but it is not too late for it as yet'.[20]

Letters found in St Thomas in the Vale also referred to meetings of the court; in this case, a doctor practising in the district, Jasper Cargill, was warned not to attend the next circuit court. The message was that Cargill's father, who was the presiding judge, was hated by the people, and that there would be a serious disturbance at the court. Another anonymous letter found in the parish directly threatened the clerk of the magistrates, John H. Hall: 'Old man, 37 men have sworn to murder you, you are closely watched; for your wife and child's sake be careful, you are to be waylaid and shot and chopped.' In light of these threats the meeting of the circuit court was postponed, and Governor Eyre dispatched troops to Linstead.[21]

Many anonymous letters threatened to burn down various estates and continue the war which had begun at Morant Bay. One such letter, referring to an area south of Montego Bay, claimed to be written by Daniel Watson:

> My name is Daniel Watson take notice, I going raise War I will be a Second Paul Bogle and will take fire and burn down Kew Park house and kill all the white man, I Daniel Watson say so. Bring Black soldier come we will kill them too and I will burn down Copse Estate. I Daniel going raise War this very night.[22]

An equally menacing letter was written by someone signing his name 'Thomas Killmany, and intend to kill many more'. In the letter dated 17 October, 'Killmany' vowed to destroy the town and the inhabitants of Port Maria: 'The fire-burn in St Thomas in the East, that is nothing; but when we commence with Port Maria it will be from top, to bottom . . . It will be now life and death. You shall see blood running through the bay like river.'[23]

In neighbouring St George, an overseer of Spring Garden estate, W.G. Ramsay, received a letter threatening to kill him. Like other letters, it also raised the prospect of fire, but this one pointed to a specific grievance: the problem of pay on the plantations.

> Walter Ramsay, you sure better take care of yourself how you paying money, you damn thief. I were having at you a long time, for in a short time there will be fire, and fire enough in Spring

Garden Plantation, for when I come down I not going too burn task-house alone, for I going to burn from still-house, boiling-house, and your house and self too, for I means to cool all of you St George's fellows, for all the solders in the camp can't cool me, for my troops are solders too.[24]

The writer of this letter, Joseph Rooster, did not remain anonymous for long: he confessed, was tried, and sentenced to be hanged, although the sentence was apparently not carried out.[25]

Like Rooster's letter, others also complained about particular problems. In the case of a letter signed by 'Anancy Green' and sent to the custos of St Mary, the issue was the high level of taxes:

by those new laws what is making in the House of Assembly, by oppressing the poor people in the island with horse tax, canoe tax. I am a fisher myself. Take warning, warning, warning, take it, this is it. Our cutlass is now ready. Your swords we do not care about. Your firearms we don't care about. It must be life or death between us before we should live in such a miserable life, because we cannot pay, we have not the means of paying.[26]

'Anancy Green' was not alone in pointing to the problem of taxes. In the letter found in Lucea, the anonymous writer warned that 'if Taxes be not reduce it will be like Gog and Magog to battle . . . .' The writer warned that his people would not be 'so foolish' as those in St Thomas in the East: 'we will get brimstone and fire and we will luminate the town in a moment and then when are finish we do not care what become of us after as to say that a War will broke out you may rest assure it will broke out if no alteration . . . .'[27]

As at Morant Bay, land was also an important issue for the anonymous letter writers. The rector of the parish of St Andrew, Rev. William Mayhew, received a letter the week after the outbreak at Morant Bay threatening to kill him. The letter compared Mayhew to Baron von Ketelhodt, the custos of St Thomas in the East who was killed at Morant Bay. It went on to suggest that, like the Baron, Mayhew oppressed the people because he made them pay rent for church-owned land.[28] Like Mayhew, Gilbert McLean, a coloured merchant at Port Maria, was warned about some land. In McLean's case it was land that he wished to sell, but a placard posted in the town of Port Maria advised people not to pay for the land but to keep it. If McLean persisted in trying to sell the land, his store would be burned down. McLean was also one of the targets of an anonymous letter found over a month after the outbreak at Morant Bay. The letter, which threatened to burn down a store and two estates in St Mary, may have emanated from Goshen estate, the scene in 1848 of a serious riot over taxes.[29]

Kingston also had its share of anonymous letters, and several of them expressed specific grievances. One very strong complaint was about the importation of ready-made goods, which was reminiscent of some of the resolutions at the Underhill meetings earlier in the year. In a letter to the police magistrate, Henry Bicknell, the anonymous writer complained particularly about manufactured boots, shoes and shirts. There was also a concern in the letter about the situation of the poor in Kingston: 'Rob no black; pay your way well; servants well pay; in fact, doo good to all men, to the poor more so. If you don't doo as we say in everything the solders will be no yous to the land, for fire to the east, to the west, to north and south of the land. Judgment, judgment.'[30]

Another letter, this time sent to the custos of Kingston, Lewis Bowerbank, suggested a common cause among blacks, browns and poor whites. The writer was angered by the arrest of blacks living in Kingston and their subsequent removal to Morant Bay to stand trial under martial law: ' . . . it is lives for lives, and as black and brown and poor whites, so we don't care for burn, lose lives, so bring them back and let them go . . . Death! Death for all!' As in the letter to Henry Bicknell, the anonymous writer raised the plight of the poor, especially in light of George William Gordon's execution.

> As Mr G.W. Gordon is gone, the poor man's friend, for in the house not a man remember the poor man. Well, we will burn down the town down to the ground, and kill you and kill ourselves, if you don't bring back every man you take away from Kingston. We don't care of our lives, or your lives or property. Not all the soldiers or men-of-war ships can do good. We will bring judgment to Jamaica at once, at once.[31]

Not all the anonymous letters found in the island threatened the authorities or promised revenge for the suppression of the rebellion. Several had a different purpose: they were warnings of the need to take action against potential rebels. For example, 'a Friend to the Public' in a letter to the custos of Manchester urged him to send soldiers or volunteers to the border of St Ann and Manchester. The writer believed that the people in that district were 'now ready to go on side of any rebel that will fight against the whites in the Island and I do beg the Public to send either soldiers or Volunteers to stop the riot at once'.[32] Another anonymous letter found in Westmoreland and dated 4 November expressed great anxiety about the forthcoming Christmas period. Although many people believed that Westmoreland was calm, the letter writer maintained that 'many myself included fully know what *is to be* attempted against during Xmas. Let this be the warning to our worthy Custos . . . Strong and efficient guards must be placed well armed in *this Town* and *country parts*'.[33]

A similar letter was sent to the clerk of the peace for St James, Thomas Brown. In the letter dated 24 October, the writer warned about 'seditious whisperings' in his district. He believed that 'were the slightest disturbance (which God forbid) to arise, his honour the Custos, as well as the rest of the whites, would *fair* off no better than those at Morant Bay'. Precautions were therefore necessary. In this case, Thomas Brown was aware of the writer's identity but realized that the writer was afraid of signing his name.[34]

These anonymous letters were significant. As in eighteenth-century England, they were a form of social protest by people who, if identified, would have been subject to arrest and possible execution. These letters emerged in the aftermath of the Morant Bay rebellion; in the case of some of them only news of the outbreak would have been available. For others the severity of the repression incited the writers to respond. Although many of the letters are addressed to specific individuals, they point toward collective grievances: taxes, justice, wages, land.[35]

The letters also have a ring of authenticity, in part because they expressed grievances which were felt all over the colony. While there were undoubtedly a few 'crank' letters among them, they were the work of people who had no other literary or political outlet to express their anger. Edward Thompson has described the anonymous letter writers of eighteenth-century England as people who 'cannot articulate their grievances openly, who cannot form their own organizations or circulate their own pamphlets and press, whose voices break out anonymously with intemperate force'.[36] In the wake of the Morant Bay rebellion, this applies to the writers of anonymous letters in Jamaica.

These anonymous letters were addressed to people in authority: the gentlemen of Hanover, the custos of St Mary, the rector of St Andrew, a police magistrate, the clerk of the peace. Unfortunately, it is not possible to provide information on the authors of the letters; apart from the occasional individual, such as Joseph Rooster, they remain truly anonymous. Their targets are clearer: the majority mention arson, some against towns, others against estates. Particular individuals are threatened with murder and a few of the letters promise to continue the war begun at Morant Bay. Some of the anonymous letters highlight the problems of the poor, and one suggested a linking of class rather than colour. It united blacks, browns and poor whites, a combination which might well have worried the authorities. Ultimately, these anonymous letters expressed the views of people who identified with the rebels at Morant Bay but were unable to follow their example. Perhaps surprisingly, there were also people who were prepared to state such views verbally rather than in writing.

Verbal threats and white paranoia

In the aftermath of the rebellion many people wanted to emulate the rebels at Morant Bay. For example, a head man on an estate in Vere openly declared his wish to seize the weapons of the police and 'begin the row in Vere'. Another man on the same estate talked about joining the rebels, if they came to Vere. He also had the idea of attacking the police station for guns, although his plan was to burn down the building. Elsewhere, a group of men in St Thomas in the Vale were prepared to 'rise like those in St Thomas in the East'.[37]

Others hoped that the rebellion would spread to their parish. People in St Ann were heard publicly expressing this view. In other parishes people were clear about what they would do if the rebellion reached their district. Thomas Campbell, who lived in St George, was charged with saying that if the rebels came there, he would use the occasion to kill two prominent white officials. A middle-aged woman in the parish, Mary Harris, expressed the same wish. But according to a planter in St George, Mary Harris went much further. She allegedly proclaimed to people in Annotto Bay, 'Rise, rise, you ought to rise here the same as they do in St Thomas in the East.' Like many others, Harris declared that if the war extended to St George, she would 'join the black people'.[38]

Several people expressed strongly pro-black or anti-white views in the wake of the rebellion at Morant Bay. Like Thomas Campbell or Mary Harris, some were anxious to attack specific whites. In Trelawny, a shop-keeper, Richard Cressett, predicted that the rebels would soon arrive in his district, and he would then shoot all the white men there. Interestingly, there were two whites living in the area who were at the head of his list. He also targeted the browns, although he was prepared to spare a local coloured planter. In St James a man was indicted for predicting that the war would break out there, even if it were suppressed in St Thomas in the East. Moreover, the man was said to have asked another black man whether ' "if the war should break out here, would you, being a black man, not join the black people; what are you, sir, are you not a black man?" ' The statement earned him a twelve months' prison sentence.[39]

As in the case of the anonymous letters, several people addressed specific points. One of these was low pay. Three days after the outbreak at Morant Bay, Andrew Buchanan reportedly said in a shop in St Mary that ' "the white people do too much; when you work they cut your money, if they (black people) cut off their heads and throw them in the bush, what about it?" ' Two days later Buchanan was discussing the rebellion and concluded that 'if the black people do so they have a right, for when they work the white people won't pay them.' Buchanan was tried by a court-martial and received fifty lashes. In St Elizabeth Joseph Miller complained about the police who deserved to be killed because 'they were too damned fast and . . . they took more liberties than Buckra gave them . . . .' He indicated that he would like to chop off the heads of the local police, following the lead of what he thought was happening at Morant Bay. There was also support for George William Gordon, especially after it became known that Gordon had been hanged at Morant Bay. When Edward Robinson learned about Gordon's execution in a shop in Lucea, he proclaimed that it would cause a revolution in the island. Moreover, he would be on Gordon's side and predicted that 'it would be a revolution of slashing'. Robinson was arrested and placed in custody.[40]

The authorities believed that some of these threats were made at meetings held at night. In St Elizabeth the Rev. Basset Key reported that several men had been arrested 'for holding meetings, whereat schemes of murder and plunder were canvassed . . . .' Rev. Key also believed that there were well-attended meetings held in the mountains of Manchester which were very suspicious, partly because of descriptions of 'rebellious shell-blowing' on these occasions. These accounts were not unique. Several magistrates in the area of Kew Park south of Montego Bay were alarmed by nightly meetings of blacks in the district. The meetings were bad enough, but, in addition, blacks 'have been seen in the early morning as if undergoing a drill – that conversations of a most rebellious nature have been very recently overheard and reported to us'. As in St Elizabeth, the local minister, Rev. Mr Anderson, noted that something worrying was clearly going on, since there had been a good deal of shell and horn blowing all night near his home.[41]

There were reports of blacks drilling elsewhere in the island. In Westmoreland Benjamin Vickers received accounts of blacks involved in drilling on 19 October, which coincided with the problems over the court case of William Tait. One description of this activity put the number of men undergoing drilling at 250. Across the island in St Dorothy, the Inspector of Police at Spanish Town had arrested some men who were drilling and found firearms and some bullets hidden in their homes. In a dispatch to the Colonial Office, Eyre concluded that these practices seemed to be almost universal in the colony.[42]

It was not just drilling which worried government officials. The continuation of revivalist meetings, which had begun earlier in the decade, was a source of some concern. A Wesleyan missionary in Lucea did not regard these meetings as dangerous in themselves, but believed that they provided 'material for evil disposed persons to work on and that their religious fanaticism might soon be changed to rebellious furor'. In the parish of St Elizabeth the discovery of a large number of spears and the knowledge that they were owned by people who had secret meetings caused considerable alarm. The Inspector of Police investigated the matter and discovered, in addition to the spears, 'a large quantity of stones, a loaded Gun and a paper signed "Bogle", with several unintelligible sentences, such as the War to begin at Lucea on the 7th August, and Buckras and Brown men to be killed also their animals and Beasts'. The police arrested more than a dozen people and brought them to Black River to be tried. It appears that over one hundred of these spears or spikes were found; they were made of hard wood and were about eight or nine feet long.[43]

Eyre took these reports very seriously. He had already dispatched men-of-war and troops to Savanna-la-Mar, Brown's Town and Linstead in response to appeals for protection. Following up these earlier requisitions, Eyre ordered fifty troops stationed in Black River and another fifty in Lucea. Writing in early November to the officer commanding troops in Jamaica, Major General O'Connor, Eyre emphasized the importance of these troops being sent to these particular destinations. This was especially the case since the meeting of the island legislature was about to commence, and many of the leading parish officials would be absent from their districts. In addition, Eyre had requested imperial troops from Barbados and Nassau; when these arrived, the number of troops in Jamaica was increased from about 1,000 to 1,700.[44]

A month later Eyre was expressing a different kind of concern. As Christmas was approaching and as there had been intimations of possible disturbances during that period, the Governor informed O'Connor that men-of-war would be stationed at Morant Bay, Montego Bay, Savanna-la-Mar, Port Antonio, Lucea, Black River and Carlisle Bay. By this time there were also troops in Port Maria, Brown's Town, Falmouth, Mandeville, Golden Grove and Manchioneal in addition to the ports where the men-of-war would be located.[45]

In sending these troops and ships to so many locations Eyre could be accused of overreacting to developments around the island. Much of the drilling, for example, seemed harmless in retrospect. When Benjamin Vickers held a magisterial investigation of the drilling in Westmoreland, 'the utmost statement that could be obtained, even from the most excited of the witnesses, was that 10 or 12 persons had been drilled with wooden guns'. Similarly, in the case of St Dorothy, the police reported that they had seen twenty-four men drilling with red cloth on their caps and arms. The head constable had arrested seven of them, but the leader of the group 'voluntarily stated that he got the men together and drilled them for amusement and to enable them to join the Old Harbour Volunteers'. Rather than acting as a threat, these men seemed to be supporting the authorities. However, another inspector of police, Thomas Mitchell, cast a different light on the drilling he had witnessed in Trelawny. Mitchell heard that the men in that parish believed that they would be exempt from taxes, once they had achieved a certain level of proficiency in drilling. It was certainly the case that the volunteers had their taxes reduced by £2.[46]

As for the revivalists in St Elizabeth, there is evidence that the sticks found in their homes were used as part of their rituals. An analysis of revivalist movements in Jamaica a century later is suggestive about the ceremonial use of ornamental sticks. Moreover, upon investigation one of the sects in St Elizabeth seemed more devoted to its own particular practices than to promoting resistance. For example, one of the men arrested was named McPherson alias 'John the Baptist'. Formerly a fairly prosperous small landholder, 'John the Baptist' had been severely beaten by his sect for transgressing an important rule. In this group men were not supposed to work their own grounds under any circumstances. 'John the Baptist' had been flogged for violating this rule, even though he claimed to be starving and had nothing to eat. Yet despite being emaciated and reduced to begging, he was arrested. While in prison, 'John the Baptist' would say nothing except that he would give himself 'up to the Lord who knows all things'.[47]

There were also reasons to doubt the reliability of some of the verbal threats expressed after the outbreak of the Morant Bay rebellion. In the case of Edward Robinson, for instance, who said he would support Gordon's party, the justice of the peace who ordered his arrest also pointed out that Robinson had been drinking. The man sent to gaol for twelve months in St James for supporting 'the war' made his comments in a store where rum was sold.[48] The statements of these two men, then, are questionable on the grounds of intoxication while others may well have been exaggerated. Similarly, at least one of the anonymous letters may have been a fabrication. It has been suggested that the letter found in Linstead was written by a volunteer seeking to enhance his pay by being called up for service.

On balance, then, the evidence does not support Eyre's vision of communication between the blacks from St Thomas in the East and the rest of the island. But as Catherine Hall has suggested, Eyre's view of blacks meant that it was almost inevitable that he saw the rebellion as he did. For Eyre, blacks were 'savages' and 'barbarians' who could never rise to the level of western civilization. It was therefore up to whites to maintain mastery and control of the blacks. The outbreak of the rebellion at Morant Bay was 'the preordained fulfillment of [Eyre's] worst fantasies, in which the whites of Jamaica faced extinction and all manner of torment'.[49] In reality, there is nothing to substantiate the idea of a black conspiracy to kill all the whites and coloureds in the island.

Yet the volume of the evidence as well as its tone suggests a profound sense of grievance among many people all over Jamaica. Their complaints were similar to those of the rebels at Morant Bay: high taxes, an unfair judicial system, limited access to land, and a strongly-entrenched white power structure. The rebellion at Morant Bay and the nature of white paranoia in its aftermath helped to bring these protests to the surface. The subsequent repression in the island ensured that these grievances would ultimately remain frustrated.

Notes

1 CO 137/393, Eyre to Cardwell, 20 October 1865, no. 251.

2 JRC, Evidence of Edward Eyre, p. 1006.

3 Papers, Trench to Myers, n.d., p. 52.

4 CO 137/398, Eyre to Cardwell, 23 November 1865: Jamison to Carter, 24 October.

5 CO 137/394, Speech to the House of Assembly.

6 CO 137/399, Storks to Cardwell, 8 February 1866, no. 23.

7 Papers, Mackinnon to Myers, n.d., p. 51, subenclosure 4; PRO 30/48/42, Cardwell Papers, Shaw to Mackinnon, n.d.

8 JRC: Evidence of Robert Nunes, p. 830; Evidence of Henry Westmorland, p. 864; Letter of John Salmon, custos of St Elizabeth, in Evidence of Henry Westmorland, p. 866.

9 JRC: Evidence of Major-General L. Smythe O'Connor, p. 679; Evidence of Henry Westmorland, p. 860.

10 JRC, Evidence of Henry Westmorland, p. 865; PRO, 30/48/44, Cardwell Papers, 'Jamaica' by Lewis Q. Bowerbank, proofs of article, p. 10.

11 Gad J. Heuman, *Between Black and White: Race, Politics, and the Free Coloreds in Jamaica, 1792–1865* (Westport, Conn.: Greenwood Press, 1981), p. 63; JRC, Evidence of Samuel Constantine Burke, p. 1021.

12 CO 137/394, Eyre to Cardwell, 7 November 1865, no. 271: Todd to Solomon, 27 October; Hall to Royes, 28 October; Eyre to the Senior Naval Office, 28 October.

13 JRC: Evidence of Richard Mothersill, p. 887; Evidence of Rev. Henry Clarke, p. 1022; Evidence of Rev. Edward Hewitt, p. 784; Evidence of Henry Westmorland, p. 865.

14 JRC: Evidence of Henry Westmorland, letter of Benjamin Vickers, 17 October, p. 862; Evidence of Benjamin Vickers, pp. 610, 612.

15 JRC, Evidence of Henry Westmorland, letter of Benjamin Vickers, 19 October, p. 862. See also *The Falmouth Post*, 27 October 1865.

16 CO 137/394, Eyre to Cardwell, 7 November 1865, no. 271, Vickers to Jordon, 23 October; *Ibid.*, no. 270, Eyre to Captain de Horsey, 23 October.

17 CO 137/394, Eyre to Cardwell, 2 November 1865, no. 261, Eyre to O'Connor, 28 October 1865; *Ibid.*, 7 November 1865, no. 271, Todd to Solomon, 27 October.

18 JRC, Evidence of Francis Lowe, pp. 515–16.

19 CO 884/2, Confidential Print, no. 2, Papers Relating to the Insurrection in Jamaica, October, 1865, Printed for the Use of the Cabinet, December, 1865, p. 28, Enclosure 48 in no.1 [Eyre to Cardwell, 20 October 1865, no. 251], Communication addressed to Mr Lynch.

20 CO 137/394, Eyre to Cardwell, 7 November 1865, no. 271, Letter found in Lucea, forwarded with Lyon to Jordon, 30 October 1865.

21 JRC, Evidence of Dr Jasper Cargill, pp. 450–1.

22 CO 137/395, Eyre to Cardwell, 23 November 1865, no. 302.

23 JRC, Evidence of Edward Eyre, anonymous letter to Messrs. J.B. Goffe & Co., 17 October 1865, p. 993.

24 CO 884/2, Confidential Print no. 2, Papers Relating to the Insurrection in Jamaica, October, 1865, Printed for the Use of the Cabinet, December, 1865, Enclosure 47 in no. 1 [Eyre to Cardwell, 20 October 1865, no. 251], Guscott to Hosack, 15 October, p. 27.

25 JRC, Evidence of Horatio Guscott, p. 588.
26 JRC, Evidence of Edward Eyre, anonymous letter to Honourable A.J. Lindo, 17 October, p. 993.
27 CO 137/394, Eyre to Cardwell, 7 November 1865, no. 271, Letter found in Lucea, forwarded with Lyon to Jordon, 30 October.
28 JRC, Evidence of Rev. William Mayhew, p. 552.
29 JRC: Evidence of Gilbert McLean, p. 590; Evidence of Elias Lopez, p. 594; CO 137/395, Eyre to Cardwell, 23 November 1865, no. 302, Maclean (sic) to Carr, 14 November.
30 JRC, Evidence of Edward Eyre, letter to Mr Bicknell, p. 1009.
31 CO 137/394, Anonymous Letter to the Custos of Kingston. A printed version appears in JRC, Evidence of Edward Eyre, p. 1009.
32 CO 137/395, Eyre to Cardwell, 23 November 1865, no. 302, anonymous letter to Mr Hollingsworth.
33 CO 137/396, Eyre to Cardwell, 8 December 1865, no. 310, anonymous threatening letter, 4 November, Westmoreland.
34 JRC, Evidence of Thomas Brown, pp. 615–16.
35 E.P. Thompson, 'The Crime of Anonymity', in Douglas Hay *et al.*, *Albion's Fatal Tree: Crime and Society in Eighteenth-Century England* (London: Allen Lane Press, 1975), pp. 255, 273.
36 *Ibid.*, pp. 273, 279 (quote, p. 279).
37 Papers, Mackinnon to Myers, n.d., p. 51, subenclosure 4; JRC, Evidence of Robert Grant, p. 905; CO 137/394, Extract from a letter of one Roman Catholic Priest to another, 26 October 1865 (the printed version is in JRC, Evidence of Edward Eyre, p. 999).
38 CO 137/394, Eyre to Cardwell, 7 November 1865, no. 271, Statement of Mr Parry; Papers, Stewart to Eyre, 19 January 1866, p. 44; JRC, Evidence of Thomas Creed, p. 597.
39 Papers, Mitchell to Myers, p. 55, n.d.; JRC: Evidence of Thomas Mitchell, p. 694; Evidence of Thomas Brown, p. 616.
40 Papers, Stewart to Eyre, 19 January 1866, p. 44; CO 137/394, Extract from a letter of one Roman Catholic Priest to another, 26 October 1865 (the printed version is in JRC, Evidence of Edward Eyre, p. 999); JRC, Evidence of Edward Eyre, Statement of John Dawson Cort, 23 October 1865, p. 997.
41 Papers, Key to Myers, 6 January 1866, p. 59, subenclosure 4; CO 137/394, Eyre to Cardwell, 3 November 1865, no. 264, Brett to Whitfield, 1 November 1865, no. 2, To Col. Whitfield or the officer in command of the Troops at Montego Bay at a meeting of the magistrates; *Ibid.*, 7 November 1865, no. 271, Coke to Vickers, 30 October 1865.
42 JRC, Evidence of Benjamin Vickers, p. 611; CO 137/396, Eyre to Cardwell, 21 December 1865, no. 338.
43 CO 137/394, Eyre to Cardwell, 7 November 1865, no. 271, Hutchinson to Lyon, 30 October; CO 137/395, Eyre to Cardwell, 23 November 1865, no. 302: Lawrence to Salmon, 16 November; Finlason to Salmon, 16 November.
44 CO 137/394, Eyre to Cardwell, 4 November 1865, no. 266, Eyre to O'Connor, 3 November; CO 137/400, Storks to Cardwell, 19 February 1866, no. 23, enclosure: Eyre to Cardwell, January, 1866.
45 CO 137/396, Eyre to Cardwell, 22 December 1865, no. 399: Eyre to O'Connor, 7 December; O'Connor to Eyre, 12 December.
46 JRC, Evidence of Edward Eyre, Vickers to Jordon, 23 October 1865, p. 995; CO 137/396, Eyre to Cardwell, 21 December 1865, no. 338, Ramsay to Jordon, 11 December; JRC, Evidence of Thomas Mitchell, p. 693.
47 George Eaton Simpson, *Religious Cults of the Caribbean: Trinidad, Jamaica and Haiti* (Río Piedras, Puerto Rico: Institute of Caribbean Studies, University of Puerto Rico, 1980 [orig. pub. 1965]), p. 183; CO 137/395, Eyre to Cardwell, 23 November 1865, no. 302, Finlason to Salmon, 16 November.

48   JRC: Evidence of Edward Eyre, Statement of John Dawson Cort, 23 October 1865, p. 997; Evidence of Thomas Brown, p. 616.

49   Catherine Hall, 'Imperial Man: Edward Eyre in Australasia and the West Indies, 1833–1866', in *The Expansion of England: Essays in the Cultural History of Race and Ethnicity*, edited by Bill Schwartz (forthcoming), pp. 29–30.

CHAPTER 8 | The military suppression: The troops in the field

Eyre first learned of possible trouble at Morant Bay on Wednesday, 11 October. Early that morning the Governor received a letter from Baron von Ketelhodt written the previous evening. In the letter, von Ketelhodt warned the Governor that serious disturbances were expected at Morant Bay and requested that troops be sent immediately. After consulting with his executive committee, Eyre ordered one hundred troops to be sent to St Thomas in the East. The senior naval officer at Port Royal, Captain Algernon de Horsey, was notified that a man-of-war was needed to take the troops to Morant Bay. By that evening the troops were embarked on de Horsey's own ship, HMS *Wolverine*; at dawn the next morning they set sail.[1]

On Thursday afternoon, while at his country residence, Eyre was informed that the rebellion had broken out. A letter from a magistrate in St David made it clear the blacks had risen in rebellion and had killed some of the leading officials in Morant Bay. Even more worryingly, 'it was

Fig. 4   HMS Wolverine

113

expected the rebels were coming along the line of the Blue Mountain Valley to destroy the Properties contiguous thereto and to murder the white and colored inhabitants.' Eyre therefore requested further reinforcements for Morant Bay and hastily travelled to Kingston for consultations with the general commanding the forces in the island, L. Smythe O'Connor. An Irishman, O'Connor had spent his army life in the West Indies and in Africa; he had been wounded in action in Africa and had served as Governor of the Gambia. General O'Connor ordered one hundred men to be sent on board a gunship, the *Onyx*, and Eyre requested troops from the garrison at Newcastle to be despatched immediately. These troops were to march eastward to St Thomas in the East and thereby block the threatened advance of the rebels.[2]

Eyre also met with his officials and, just before midnight, with members of the Privy Council. They agreed that it was essential to establish martial law, and a council of war confirmed that view the next morning, the 13th. In justifying this decision, Eyre maintained that proclaiming martial law was 'the only means of meeting so grave an emergency'. The council of war unanimously agreed, and martial law was declared for the entire county of Surrey, except for the city and parish of Kingston.[3] Later that morning, Eyre boarded a chartered French ship, the *Caravelle*, to take him as well as a further detachment of fifty troops and several officers of the militia and volunteers to Morant Bay. Travelling along with the Governor was the newly-promoted Brigadier-General Abercrombie Nelson, formerly a colonel and Adjutant General who had seen considerable experience in Afghanistan and in India. Nelson would command the troops in the field and would himself report to the commander-in-chief, General O'Connor, who was in overall charge of the military forces. As Governor, Eyre issued general orders, but General O'Connor and his officers were responsible for specific troop movements.[4]

In the meantime, the first body of troops on board the *Wolverine* had arrived at Morant Bay. They consisted of one hundred men of the 1st West India Regiment, a force of black troops first established in 1795, and twenty of the Royal Artillery.

Captain de Horsey described the scene:

> I immediately landed the troops and the field gun and occupied the square, where the still burning Court House, and the bodies of the murdered men in all directions evinced but too clearly the results of the previous day. Many ill looking persons were loitering about the town but the armed insurgents had retired.[5]

The troops buried the bodies and also served as escorts for those wounded in the rebellion and for the people in the area who wanted to shelter on the *Wolverine*. De Horsey believed that there would be another attack on

Morant Bay that night, the 12th. However, it never materialized and troops were sent the next day to Bath to collect further refugees.[6]

De Horsey was also concerned about the spread of the rebellion and decided to return to Kingston for reinforcements, bringing the refugees with him. On the way to Kingston the *Wolverine* met Eyre's chartered ship. Boarding the *Wolverine*, Eyre learned at first hand about the events at Morant Bay. Perhaps inevitably, the initial stories about the rebellion were highly lurid and inaccurate accounts of the massacre. For example, the island curate, Rev. Victor Herschell was supposed 'to have had his tongue cut out whilst still alive, and an attempt is said to have been made to skin him'. One of the volunteers was wrongly described as having been 'pushed into an outbuilding, which was then set on fire and kept there until he was literally roasted alive'. Others allegedly 'had their eyes scooped out; heads were cleft open, and the brains taken out'.[7]

These scenes were compared to the atrocities of the Indian mutiny eight years previously, an image which was to recur and which may help to explain the ferocity of the soldiers. It was significant that some of the British troops were veterans of the mutiny and hardly likely to be characterized by 'a liberal temper'. But even those who had not served in India had absorbed the hardening racial attitudes of the mid-nineteenth century and, as in the suppression of the Indian mutiny, were intent on 'a war of racial revenge'.[8]

Eyre arrived at Morant Bay on Friday evening. He inspected the troops already at Morant Bay and ordered some of them to Easington, just across the south-western border of St Thomas in the East. These troops were to liaise with the soldiers from Newcastle. Later that evening Eyre travelled to Port Morant, where several blacks were captured, a court martial was held, and one was hanged. Returning to Morant Bay on Saturday morning, the Governor boarded the *Wolverine* which had brought troop reinforcements. The weather that day was atrocious; it was unusually wet, even by the standards of the rainy season, and made conditions for the troops extremely difficult.

Returning to Port Morant, Eyre observed the refugees who had by that time made their way from Bath and the Plantain Garden River district to the port. The troops had escorted about one hundred people, most of whom were women and children, to Port Morant. Some of them were only partly clothed, and many had spent several nights in the cane fields or the woods. They were boarded onto the *Onyx*, whose commander recalled that 'the women were in a most wretched state, some of them nearly dead, some with little children who had been in the bush three or four nights; they were fainting when carried on board'. The boat took them to Kingston.[9]

The troops who had brought in these women and children joined the *Wolverine*, which travelled up the coast to Port Antonio. Arriving on Sunday, the 15th, Eyre wrote home that they had come 'just in time to save this Settlement from the Rebels, who were burning buildings and destroying property about twelve miles to the eastward and had already threatened to come in and destroy Port Antonio this very day'. The troops were then disembarked and, by noon, one hundred men from the 2nd battalion 6th regiment and the 1st West India regiment were marching toward Manchioneal to confront the rebels. They were under the command of Captain Lewis Hole.[10]

Captain Hole's troops and the march to Manchioneal

Hole's instructions were to reach Manchioneal with as little delay as possible. Writing to Hole before he departed, Brigadier-General Nelson also expressed concern about protecting the whites in the area. As for prisoners, Hole was expressly directed not to bring any in, unless they were leaders of the rebellion. As Nelson put it, those 'found in arms [were] to be shot on the spot'.[11] On his march south Hole was accompanied by two local magistrates, Arthur Warmington and Christopher Codrington, and a lieutenant in the volunteers, Henry Bunting. Dr Morris was the medical officer accompanying the troops, and Ensign Francis Cullen was in charge of the 1st West India regiment.[12]

Their first major stop on the way to Manchioneal was the village of Long Bay. There, Hole reported, the troops 'found the huts full of plunder' and Hole had all the houses in which stolen goods were found burned down. In the process, twenty people were killed, many of them shot while running away from the troops. By the time his troops reached Manchioneal on the 16th, Hole estimated that more than sixty people had been killed. According to Henry Bunting, over one hundred houses had been destroyed, although he later testified that several houses were left standing where no plunder was found. Once at Manchioneal, Hole dispatched a small party of troops to rescue whites in the vicinity. He clearly regarded Manchioneal as an important base for military action against the rebels, since in his terms, it was 'in the heart of the rebellion'.[13]

Brigadier-General Nelson was clearly pleased with Hole's progress. Writing to Major-General O'Connor on the 17th, Nelson noted that Hole had arrived in Manchioneal. In the dispatch Nelson commented that Hole's 'proceedings were temperate, decided, and judicious; all the rebels captured having tried [he] had had instantly executed'. For Nelson, Hole had 'in every way carried out [his] orders, and has proved himself not only an excellent officer, but what is still more valuable, an officer of sound sense and judgment'.[14]

Yet even in the context of martial law, it was obvious that legal niceties were not being observed. On 19 October, Hole reported that three black soldiers of the 1st West India regiment had got ahead of the troops. Acting on their own, they went as far as the Plantain Garden River district and reported seeing many rebels in the district. The troops shot ten people, all without trial, three of whom they believed were involved in the murder of Augustus Hire at Amity Hall estate. They also brought back two wagons filled with possessions which they claimed had been taken from the homes of whites. Since the whole area was considered very dangerous, Hole was surprised that only a few men could accomplish so much. In his dispatch, Hole concluded that 'these men [had] done good service'.[15]

Another case in which suspects were shot before being tried involved a black soldier, Drummer Phillips. In one instance an officer put Phillips in charge of a prisoner in his absence. When the officer returned and asked about the suspect, Phillips had already hanged him. A shopkeeper in Long Bay, David Meine, observed that Phillips had shot six prisoners, also without a trial. These prisoners were to have been sent to Manchioneal for trial, and Phillips was to have taken them there with the help of some constables. However, Phillips told one of the constables that he carried 'no prisoner, all I meet on the road I shoot; I have orders to shoot, not to carry prisoners'. This was not all. On the way to Manchioneal he came across four additional prisoners being sent for trial. Again, he shot them all. When questioned about Phillips, Captain Hole indicated that he had only learned about these events by accident. Certainly no court of inquiry was ever held to investigate Phillips.[16]

It was not only troops who were involved in shooting suspects without trial. Dr Morris was alleged to have had three prisoners shot in this manner on the way from Golden Grove estate to Manchioneal. Although there is contradictory evidence in this instance, it seems likely that three prisoners were brought to the troops by special constables, and that Ensign Cullen ordered them to be flogged. However, Morris countermanded the order and instead had them shot. There was also other testimony against Morris. He was accused of shooting another man, William Gray, without a trial and of treating prisoners badly. One who had been flogged one hundred times, John Ricketts, claimed that after he had been whipped Morris had forced him 'to bow down before him and say, "I am much obliged to you, sir." '[17]

The reports of the victims were particularly revealing about the brutality of the soldiers. Jane Wilson, a black woman who was recently widowed, recalled the soldiers coming to her house in Long Bay and Codrington ordering them to burn it down. Although one of her children had died and was lying in the house and another was sick, she was ordered to bring a fire-stick to Codrington to burn the house. Wilson managed to pull out the body of her dead child and the sick one as well, but remembered how the soldiers tore up her mourning clothes and left her destitute. When she cried, a soldier had said, 'If you bawl, I will shoot you, much less your house to set it on fire.'[18]

Wilson's case highlights a problem about the identification of goods stolen from the whites during the rebellion. According to Wilson the soldiers had not searched the house and had just set it on fire. She claimed that one of the soldiers did not believe that a black person could have as many clothes as she had. For the soldier, 'a black person have all these; they must be the white clothes'. Since her husband was a clerk in the church as well as a schoolmaster, her claim that the clothes belonged to her was quite plausible. However, in their fury to pillage and plunder, the soldiers did not examine individual cases with any care. They pulled out her husband's riding saddle and her clothes and took them away. Similarly, when they discovered a box containing three silver spoons and several rings in Wilson's house, the soldiers assumed that these items could not belong to a black woman living in Long Bay.[19]

Loyalty to the whites during the rebellion did not necessarily prevent abuse and mistreatment by the troops. Charles Nelson, a black man who looked after the stock and helped to run Mulatto River estate, suffered at the hands of the troops. When the great house at Mulatto River caught fire while it was being pillaged on the night of 13 October, Nelson did all he could to salvage the owner's possessions. He also gave evidence against some of those involved in the destruction of the great house. Yet on 16 October, troops burned his house and took away all his goods. Nelson observed that Christopher Codrington was with the troops and that Dr Morris was the officer in command; neither of them charged him with being involved in the rebellion, but his house was none the less destroyed and his clothes removed.[20]

Another black man, George Hamilton, who lived at Manchioneal, had proof of his good character and lack of involvement in the rebellion but also to no effect. Hamilton described Dr Morris searching his house and threatening to shoot him, in spite of not finding any stolen goods. A constable was asked about Hamilton and said, 'The man is no rebel, but he always tries to work honestly for his bread, and does nothing'. Yet Morris had the house burned down as well as a shop where Hamilton sold provisions. All of Hamilton's money, which totalled £82, was taken.[21]

Many people who were ill or obviously unable to take part in the rebellion still suffered. Henrietta Piercy, a black woman married to a blind man, recounted how her house had been burned down. The first two waves of troops had spared the home on the grounds of her husband's obvious infirmity. However when the magistrate, Arthur Warmington, approached the house, he told the soldiers he was accompanying them, 'Haul out the blind man, and put fire to the d——d house.' Piercy lost everything.

Similarly, Isabella Francis, a black woman living with Andrew Clarke at Manchioneal Bay, remembered the shooting of Clarke. Clarke had been ill for three months and was clearly incapable of being involved in the rebellion. As in the case of Henrietta Piercy, one group of troops was satisfied with Clarke's innocence but three other soldiers shot Clarke, on learning that the house belonged to an alleged leader of the rebellion. Clarke was killed and the house destroyed.[22]

Local magistrates and volunteers travelling with the troops were often extremely brutal. According to Esther Williams, a black woman from Manchioneal, Christopher Codrington set her house on fire while she was in childbirth. Another black woman, Ann Wilson, appealed to Henry Bunting, a lieutenant in the volunteers, to save her house. She claimed to have done nothing in the rebellion, but Bunting responded that 'as everybody's house was to be burnt, he would burn it to please him, to please him, his own generosity'. Furthermore, since Bunting's own house had been destroyed in the rebellion and his wife did not have a home, Esther Williams should suffer equally.[23]

This vindictive behaviour on the part of magistrates extended to heavy flogging and also, on occasion, to dispensing with even the minimum forms of justice. For instance, Christopher Codrington was involved in the whipping of two men, one of whom was named Johnson Speed. As Speed was receiving one hundred lashes, the whip broke. While another was being prepared, a bystander indicated he had seen Speed in one of the great houses which had been destroyed. A soldier took up his rifle and killed him. Codrington then advised those who had witnessed this shooting that they should 'take warning by that man shot on the tree, or else you will get the same'.[24]

Women as well as men suffered severe whipping. Codrington indicated that many women were flogged, because he believed that they were often worse than the men and incited the men to plunder homes and shops. There is evidence that women were not only whipped but also had salt brine rubbed into their wounds immediately after the flogging. One black woman from Long Bay, Charlotte Scott, alleged that she was whipped for having walked into David Meine's shop at Long Bay. Meine gave no reason for ordering her to be whipped, apart from observing that 'by the time it was all over he would give [her] a damn good catting'. Two weeks later she was flogged again, this time after she greeted James Codrington, a shopowner and planter. Codrington sent a constable after her who stripped and whipped her, even though martial law was over.[25]

Not all of the victims of the suppression suffered punishments without trial. Courts martial were held in many cases, although these varied considerably. A white man, John Wighan, who witnessed some of them, indicated that those held at Port Antonio were better conducted than the ones at

Manchioneal. The officers at Manchioneal, such as Dr Morris and Ensign Lewis, were quite young and inexperienced. In all, thirty-three people were executed at Manchioneal and seventy-three flogged. In these cases, as opposed to the activities of the troops in the field, there was at least an attempt to provide evidence against the prisoners. But those shot or flogged as a result of the courts martial were a small fraction of the number killed and flogged by the troops in the field. Tragically for the people of St Thomas in the East, this was only one field of operations for the troops.[26]

The forces of Colonel Thomas Hobbs

The other major theatre of operations for British troops was the western part of St Thomas in the East. Troops from the barracks at Newcastle located in the hills above Kingston were sent across the island as soon as news of the rebellion reached Kingston. They were under the command of Captain Spencer Field and were to proceed to Mahogany Vale, the home of a retired Indian army officer, General Forbes Jackson. The commander at Newcastle, Colonel Thomas Hobbs, subsequently reinforced these forces and then, at dawn on Saturday, 14 October, travelled himself to take charge of the troops. An apparently religious and humane man, Hobbs had served at the siege of Sebastopol in the Crimean War.[27]

On arriving at Arntully, on the St David side of the border with St Thomas in the East, Hobbs was immediately confronted with reports of the very disturbed state of the surrounding area. General Jackson, who apparently expected to take charge of the troops, warned Hobbs that there were large numbers of armed rebels prepared to block his entry into St Thomas in the East. At the same time the refugees and magistrates in the area urged Hobbs to advance to Monklands, a village which was to become Hobbs' base. They assured him that 'every man in the district had risen in open rebellion' and urged him to shoot them all. On Sunday, the 15th, Hobbs with his force of 120 men and six officers, pushed on to Monklands; they encountered no opposition but had to deal with the atrocious weather which the other troops in the field also reported. Writing to General O'Connor on Sunday evening, Hobbs was by now convinced that 'the rebellion is much more serious and more regularly organized than any we had at all expected'.[28]

For Hobbs there was considerable evidence of a serious rebellion. He observed that

> all labour was suspended, that the negroes had taken to arms; and
> I saw signals flying over all the commanding hills, and flags of
> various colours and heard occasional shots, and I found the house

of Mr Paterson, which they had broken into, completely smashed, and the doors broken up, and his shop — he kept a store — completely gutted and numerous other indications, such as horns blowing and impromptu drums in the houses, and the houses all deserted, and a number of indications which it is impossible to mistake.[29]

Urged on by the local magistrates, Hobbs proceeded eastward to the villages of Ross Isle and Mount Lebanus. Both were deserted, but the magistrates travelling with the troops were able to point out the homes of the leading rebels. The troops burned some of these houses, although in defending his actions, Hobbs pointed out that the presence of anyone in the house usually saved it from destruction. At Mount Lebanus the forces surprised some of the villagers, who escaped up a nearby hill. Believing them to be rebels, Hobbs had his troops fire at them. He later claimed that some of them wore swords and had on a uniform of some sort. However, the people never returned the troops' fire.[30]

On Tuesday, 17 October, Hobbs and his troops marched to Somerset, a prosperous village which was also deserted. The constables and magistrates accompanying the troops maintained that Somerset 'was in a more advanced stage of rebellion, and that everyone in the place had risen in rebellion'. In the hilltops beyond the village, Hobbs could see small groups of people watching them and waving flags from one hill to another. He also found powder horns and new cutlasses, all of which he believed were to be used in the rebellion or in a military manoeuvre. Later that day, as his forces were returning to Monklands, they were apparently attacked by a group of about seventy people. However, only one or two of the attackers actually fired at the troops, who advanced on them and killed several of them.[31]

During this time, Hobbs had been receiving instructions from Major General O'Connor. Like those from Brigadier-General Nelson to Captain Hole on the other side of the parish, the orders were not always very explicit. For example, O'Connor wrote to Hobbs on 16 October, concluding that he 'can give you no instructions and leaves all to your own judgment'. On the 18th, O'Connor ordered Hobbs and his forces to take Stony Gut, the home of Paul Bogle. However, in the dispatch, John Elkington, O'Connor's Deputy Adjutant-General, discouraged Hobbs sending in any prisoners. He also described how the other forces were proceeding:

> Hole is doing splendid service with his men all about 'Manchioneal' and shooting every black man who cannot account for himself (60 on line of march.) Nelson at Port Antonio hanging like fun, by Court-martial. I hope you will not send in any prisoners. Civil law can do nothing . . . Do punish the blackguards well.[32]

As a result, Hobbs proceeded to Stony Gut, leaving Monklands at midnight on the 18th. The torrential rains continued, and Hobbs reported that the march from Monklands to Stony Gut was one of the most difficult he had ever experienced, due in large part to the swollen rivers the troops often had to cross and recross. On the way, the troops stopped at Chigoe Foot Market, a small settlement consisting of a few houses, a shop and a smith's forge. There, a group of special constables brought in eleven prisoners, whom they claimed were involved in the massacre at Morant Bay. Hobbs was in favour of leaving the men until he returned from Stony Gut, but the constables who had brought in the prisoners 'begged I would not, or [the prisoners] would be rescued, as the district was full of rebels and all the houses there were smashed to pieces'. Assembling a drumhead court martial, Hobbs had these men tried, shot and hanged. Reflecting on the trials and the punishments several months later, Hobbs regretted that the trials had been held in such a summary fashion. However, he believed it was necessary to make an example of these prisoners, and he had also been guided by his instructions not to take any prisoners.[33]

Despite not having faced any opposition, Hobbs was still very concerned about being outnumbered by rebel forces. Writing to Major-General O'Connor just before embarking on the march to Stony Gut, Hobbs expressed his concern about the 'thousands of rebels all around us' and the possibility that they might seize Monklands in his absence. In the event, he reached Stony Gut, only to find that a group of sailors and soldiers under Lt Oxley had already arrived there. Before marching back to Monklands, Hobbs gave orders 'that this rebellious settlement [Stony Gut] be utterly destroyed'.[34]

Returning through Chigoe Foot Market, Hobbs assembled a court martial to deal with over seventy prisoners who had been taken on the march. Twenty-seven of them were found guilty and were divided into groups, each to be executed in their own villages. Nine were shot and hanged at the Native Baptist chapel at Font Hill and a further eighteen prisoners were shot at Coley, two of whom escaped death when the musket balls cut their ropes and they ran away. Two leading prisoners, Arthur Wellington and his secretary, McLaren Graham, were shot at Monklands in a stage-managed execution. Allegedly an obeahman and a murderer, Wellington was placed on a hillside above Monklands so that his death could be witnessed by the large group of prisoners at Monklands. Since Wellington had claimed to be invulnerable to bullets, Hobbs wanted him shot in this very public fashion.[35]

Back at Monklands Hobbs tried and executed more prisoners who had been assembled there. In these actions he was guided by another directive from Major-General O'Connor, emphasizing the need to deal with prisoners summarily. As O'Connor put it in a letter dated 19 October and which Hobbs received on his return to Monklands a day later, 'you should deal in a more summary manner with [the rebels], and on no account forward prisoners to this place'. In all, Hobbs calculated that either sixty-three or sixty-four prisoners had been executed under his jurisdiction.[36]

Before returning to Newcastle, Hobbs and his troops made a last sweep through Somerset to the villages of Garbrand Hall and Spring. He left Monklands on 27 October and arrived at Newcastle without the loss of a single man. Ironically, six men died subsequently due to fevers contracted while in St Thomas in the East. A day before he left for Newcastle, Hobbs wrote to Major-General O'Connor that he felt he could now withdraw his troops 'after a very successful day's work'.[37] In assessing his campaign before the Royal Commission, Hobbs added after a long interrogation that he had 'exercised the best judgment [he] was possessed of to put down the revolt'.[38] Others proved to be highly critical of that judgement.

As with the people in the Manchioneal area, those who had to face Hobbs and his troops had a very different perspective. One problem for the populace was whether to flee or to stay in their homes, especially since the troops' instructions were to shoot people if they ran away. One of the sergeants in the 2nd battalion 6th regiment, William Neale, put it succinctly:

> The orders I had were that any people who stayed in their houses were not to be molested, and that any people who deserted their houses and were found any distance away in the bush were to be fired on, but if they came up to the soldiers they were not to be molested.[39]

Yet a black woman, Sophia Davis, clearly did not believe anything of the kind. As she observed, 'we heard that if the soldiers saw any man in the house they would shoot him'.[40] The evidence of what actually happened decidedly supports her view.

At Mount Lebanus, for example, Rebecca Telford, whose husband had a shop and two houses on about fifty acres, recalled how the soldiers had been physically threatening her. Her father-in-law, who lived nearby, came out of his home and, without any warning, 'just as they saw the old man, they shot him down, and he dropped, and I ran up the hill'. The troops subsequently destroyed her two homes and shop.[41]

At the neighbouring settlement of Barracks the troops continued their rampage. Joshua Francis, an old man who served as sexton of the parish church, was shot as he was leaving the church. A black man, Edward Reid, witnessed the shooting:

> [Francis] was coming out of the church, and locked the door, and had the keys in his hands, and he came out of the gate and locked the gate, and was going up the road, and the soldiers met him and they shot him here (cheek) and here (elbow).[42]

Reid also described the killing of a young man, John Shand, who was lame and had been ill for several years. Shand was sitting in his house when the soldiers shot him. Shand's mother sought to ward off the troops:

> I rise up and say, 'Sir, it is a sick person; it is a son that is sick', and against as I say so, the other one fire off, and the young man drop down, and they said they were truly sorry, it was an innocent person; but they can't help it, it was done already; them doing their duty.[43]

As in Manchioneal, obvious physical disabilities did not protect innocent people. Roderick McLaren watched the shooting of an old blind man in the village of Somerset: he reported that the soldiers shot the man as he was sitting in his house.[44]

Sheltering the troops was no guarantee of protection. Grace Cherrington recalled that her husband had given the troops dinner, dry clothes and a place to sleep in their home at Font Hill. Yet the next morning two soldiers shot her husband and then pillaged the house of nearly all its possessions, including her ring. Only the arrival of a constable who insisted that Cherrington had been a good man prevented the soldiers from burning the house.[45]

Other women from Font Hill suffered at the hands of the troops. For example, Sophia Davis was forced to give up her ring to save her life. Soldiers also ransacked her house and burned it.[46] Another woman from the village, Chloe Munroe, was raped by a soldier. As she described it, four soldiers took everything out of her house as well as her ring. However, one of them returned and told her to lie on the bed. When she refused,

> he fix me against the wall and drop his breeches and pulled my clothes. I called to my mother; him fix me on the wall, and I took my knee and shove him off; he tore up all my front. I can't pea for two days.[47]

The actions of the troops were not the only form of brutality against the people in this district. Many were subjected to having their land and their crops confiscated. Colonel Hobbs appointed a black schoolmaster, Mathew Joseph, to appropriate rebel property and collect the coffee in the district. Following his instructions, Joseph took possession of properties in the name of the Crown and kept them for over two months. After deducting his expenses, Joseph handed over £27.16s. to Hobbs 'for coffee picked off rebel grounds in Somerset and Mount Lebanus' until the middle of November. When Thomas Harvey and William Brewin toured this part of St Thomas in the East in early 1866, they concluded that taking away the people's crops 'had a strong tendency to drive them to a wild life in the woods, and to plunder as a chief means of subsistence. The political wisdom of the course pursued was on a par with its humanity.'[48]

There was worse to come. The courts martial conducted by Hobbs did not provide even a semblance of justice. A proprietor from Manchester who travelled with the Newcastle troops, John Sawers, described the speed of the trials held at Chigoe Foot Market on 19 October. Since the troops were attempting to reach Stony Gut that morning, Hobbs was unable to inquire into each prisoner's case individually. There was no time to question each man and they were all shot, without being given time for prayers. Even more seriously, the men may have been innocent. According to a black carpenter, James Munroe, the executed men were all labourers on the Blue Mountain estate who had been working on the day of the massacre at Morant Bay.[49]

There was also a problem about those who were tried at a more leisurely pace at Chigoe Foot Market the next day. Two brothers, James Graham and William Francis, who were found guilty and sentenced to death, claimed that they were not properly tried. Graham, a sawyer, recalled that the soldiers 'never tried me at all; they never ask me anything at all'. His brother observed that when he tried to speak, 'the soldiers said I must shut my mouth'. Both narrowly escaped death at Coley when the shots of the firing squad failed to kill them, and they were able to escape.[50]

The witnesses at some of these trials were not necessarily impartial. For example, William Anderson had himself been spared execution so that he could guide Hobbs' forces to Stony Gut. Anderson's evidence in the courts martial at Chigoe Foot Market consisted largely of his pointing out people who were marching with the rebels. He did not know the names of all those against whom he gave evidence. In the trials held at Monklands, a young woman, Eliza Ford, testified against George Anthony. But Anthony had once asked Ford to live with him, and although she refused, it is possible this relationship affected her testimony. Anthony claimed that she gave false evidence against him, nearly resulting in his death.[51]

Some of the evidence was also quite flimsy. Evelina Williams was frequently the only witness against the prisoners. Williams was the maid for Mrs Paterson, the wife of the owner of Monklands. A black labourer from New Monklands, Moses Williams, observed the trials at Monklands and claimed that her evidence alone condemned many men to execution. Yet it consisted of her being asked if she saw the men at Monklands 'and upon that they took them out and shot them'.[52]

Prisoners were often treated badly. In addition to being flogged, many men and women had their heads shaved. One black woman, Elizabeth M'Intosh, had her plaits cut off and was also humiliated for allegedly verbally abusing two women, Mrs Smelley and Miss Fowles.

they put a piece of string round my head, and stuck fowls feathers in it, all round; and when them done, they mix up a pudding with some lime, and some fat, and put it on my head; then Mr Smelley said, some of my constables should take up to beg Mrs Smelley's pardon, and then go up to Arntully and beg Miss Fowles' pardon.[53]

Even the execution of the obeahman, Arthur Wellington, had a macabre twist to it. After he was shot, a soldier cut off Wellington's head and placed it on a stump. Ironically, heavy rains that night washed away Wellington's head, and it could not subsequently be found.[54]

Further troop movements

Apart from the forces of Hobbs and Hole, there were two other major troop movements directed at containing the rebellion. The first consisted of a group of seventy-four seamen and thirty-one marines attached to the *Wolverine* who had landed at Morant Bay on 12 October. Two days later, under the command of Lt Charles Oxley and accompanied by the Provost-Marshal at Morant Bay, Gordon Ramsay, who was a veteran of the Crimean War and had participated in the Charge of the Light Brigade, they marched to Easington, just across the parish border in St David. On the way, Oxley's troops captured several prisoners and shot three people. One was a prisoner who was seeking to escape and the other two would not stop when ordered to do so. As elsewhere in St Thomas in the East, British troops were shooting people without even interrogating them first.[55]

After remaining in Easington for three days, Oxley's forces returned to Morant Bay and were immediately ordered to take Stony Gut. They arrived there on 18 October and 'found the village completely deserted, and everything left in confusion, the rebels evidently having heard of our intended advance'.[56] The troops were fired on by a single marksman in the village, but he escaped. When Hobbs reached Stony Gut the next morning, he ordered Oxley to destroy the upper part of the village. Questioned later about its destruction, Oxley maintained that he had only obeyed orders. After burning down the village, Oxley departed for Morant Bay and subsequently reoccupied Easington.[57]

The other force put together to contain the rebellion consisted of a variety of different units. One was organized by Henry Ford, a Kingston merchant who also had a business and a home in Bath. He travelled to Morant Bay nearly a week after the rebellion had broken out and found a considerable number of bookkeepers there from the Plantain Garden River district. Mostly destitute and out of work because of the uprising, they enlisted as volunteers under Ford with the intention of reoccupying the Plantain Garden River district. They were joined by a group of twenty other men, also from the district, who had escaped to Kingston and then returned to Morant Bay. In addition, the force consisted of another ten men, Captain Astwood's Mounted Kingston Volunteers, and ten British troops under the command of Lt Adcock. In all, sixty men made up the unit which left Morant Bay for the Plantain Garden River district on 21 October.[58]

On the way, the force stopped at Leith Hall estate, where some prisoners had been collected. Several were cursorily tried and flogged and one, who had been wounded at Morant Bay, was sentenced to be shot. As a coloured resident of Bath summarized the proceedings:

> [the troops] asked [the prisoner], 'how came you by that wound', he said he went to Morant Bay the day of the fight to buy medicine for his sweetheart, and suddenly he felt something here, and when he looked he saw he had received a wound. They said, 'Oh, this is one of the Morant Bay men; shoot him', and he was put out.[59]

Henry Ford was given the order to execute the prisoner and had a group of his volunteers carry it out. When examined several months later about this execution, Ford adopted the same line as Lt Oxley: he had merely obeyed orders. Although he ordered his men to fire, he was acting in 'a subordinate capacity'.[60]

Another summary execution took place at Harbour Head. There, the force arrested Charles Mitchell, a bowl maker and schoolmaster, at his home. Tied to a tree, Mitchell was given fifty lashes for having been involved in the rebellion. As Lt Adcock described the scene, a group of officers then examined the case more closely and Mitchell was shot.[61] He was accused of having threatened the lives of Sigismund Depass, an overseer who worked for James Duffus, and Duffus himself. Depass claimed that Mitchell came to Bowden's wharf on the morning of 11 October, the day of the outbreak at Morant Bay and, motioning to the goods on the wharf, said:

> 'All these are for the black people, we will have all this; all these premises . . . will belong to the black people.'

According to Duffus, Mitchell also threatened 'to have [his] head chopped off'. The next day Mitchell repeated these threats to both men.[62]

As in the case of the man wounded at Morant Bay, this execution raises a number of questions. Neither man was tried properly. Witnesses were not sworn and no record was kept of the proceedings. Mitchell does not seem to have been questioned at all or warned of his impending death. Moreover, his neighbours regarded him as slightly mad, and one of the justices killed at Morant Bay had recommended a year earlier that Mitchell be put in the lunatic asylum. There is also evidence that Mitchell had been to Bogle's chapel at Stony Gut, and a receipt was found in his coat linking him with Bogle. It seems likely, therefore, that Mitchell was killed as much for his political ideas as for the threat he posed to the lives of Depass and Duffus.[63]

Once the force reached Golden Grove estate it was joined by about forty troops of the 1st West India Regiment under Lt Cullen and Dr Morris. The combined troops made a variety of sorties in the Plantain Garden River district and collected a large number of prisoners. Many of them were flogged and some were hanged, although only after a court martial. Lt Adcock returned to Morant Bay on 24 October, leaving Henry Ford in command of the district. Ford's volunteers were finally disbanded on 1 November, most of them returning to their estates.[64]

Soon after arriving at Golden Grove, Henry Ford wrote to his brother describing martial law. As he saw it, 'the soldiers enjoy it, the inhabitants have to dread it'.[65] The soldiers, whether in Golden Grove, Manchioneal or Monklands, met almost no opposition and were able to pillage and plunder their way through the parish. Following the lead of General Nelson, they believed that all of St Thomas in the East was their enemy, and they behaved accordingly.[66] Edward Underhill accurately described the situation:

> . . . this part of the island was treated as an enemy's country in time of war, and subjected, with scarcely a pretence of discrimination between guilt and innocence, to military execution . . . .[67]

But if the soldiers inspired fear among the populace, then the other major group which helped to suppress the rebellion, the Maroons, aroused sheer terror.

Notes

1   CO 137/393, Eyre to Cardwell, 20 October 65, no. 251; CO 137/397, Report of Captain de Horsey, 22 October 1865: Riots in Jamaica.
2   CO 137/393, Eyre to Cardwell, 20 October 1865, no. 251; Sidney Lee, ed., *Dictionary of National Biography* (London: Smith, Elder & Co., 1894), vol. 41, p. 405; Geoffrey Dutton, *The Hero as Murderer: The life of Edward John Eyre, Australian Explorer and Governor of Jamaica, 1815–1901* (Sydney and Melbourne: Collins and Cheshire, 1967), p. 284.
3   JRC, Evidence of Edward Eyre, p. 990.
4   CO 137/393, Eyre to Cardwell, 20 October 1865, no. 251; Papers, O'Connor to Eyre, 29 December 1865, p. 271, subenclosure in no. 4; W.F. Finlason, *The History of the Jamaica Case: Being an Account of the Rebellion of the Negroes in Jamaica . . .* 2d ed., (London: Chapman and Hall, 1869), p. 7. But, in its report, the Jamaica Royal Commission complained that many problems associated with the suppression of the rebellion

'might have been avoided if clear and precise instructions had been given for the regulation of the conduct of those engaged in the suppression . . . .' See JRC, Report, p. 39.

5 CO 137/397, Report of Captain de Horsey, 22 October 1865: Riots in Jamaica. For information on the formation of the West India Regiments, see Roger Norman Buckley, *Slaves in Red Coats: The British West India Regiments, 1795–1815* (New Haven: Yale University Press, 1979), ch. 2.

6 JRC, Evidence of Captain William Ross; CO 137/397, Report of Captain de Horsey, 22 October 1865: Riots in Jamaica.

7 CO 137/393, Eyre to Cardwell, 20 October 1865, no. 251. John Gorrie denied that these atrocities had ever occurred: see his *Illustrations of Martial Law in Jamaica: Compiled from the Report of the Royal Commissioners, and Other Blue Books Laid Before Parliament*, Jamaica Papers no. 6. (London: Jamaica Committee, 1867), p. 3.

8 James Morris, *Heaven's Command: An Imperial Progress* (London: Faber & Faber, 1973), p. 310; Bernard Porter, *The Lion's Share: A Short History of British Imperialism, 1850–1970* (London: Longman, 1975), p. 30.

9 *Ibid.*; JRC, Evidence of Lt Herbert Brand, p. 652.

10 CO 137/393, Eyre to Cardwell, 20 October 1865, no. 251.

11 JRC, Appendix: Military Orders and Documents, Memo for Captain Hole, p. 1124.

12 JRC, Evidence of Capt. Lewis Hole, p. 714.

13 JRC: Appendix: Military Orders and Documents, Hole to Nelson, 17 October 1865, p. 1129; Evidence of Thomas Bunting, p. 204.

14 Nelson to O'Connor, 17 October in *The Colonial Standard and Jamaica Despatch*, 19 October 1865.

15 JRC: Appendix: Explanations of Officers under the Requisition of the Secretary of State, Hole to Nelson, 19 October 1865, p. 1130; Evidence of Capt. Lewis Hole, p. 718.

16 JRC: Evidence of John Collins, p. 257; Evidence of David Meine, pp. 583–4; Evidence of George Bryan, p. 212; Evidence of Lewis Hole, p. 719.

17 JRC: Evidence of Abraham Donaldson, p. 1053, but see the contradictory evidence of Ensign Francis Cullen, p. 1042; Evidence of Robert Deacon, p. 575; Evidence of John Ricketts, p. 579.

18 JRC, Evidence of Jane Wilson, p. 146.

19 *Ibid.*, pp. 146–47; JRC, Evidence of James Codrington, p. 584.

20 JRC, Evidence of Charles Nelson, p. 151.

21 JRC, Evidence of George Hamilton, p. 570.

22 JRC: Evidence of Henrietta Piercy, p. 572; Evidence of Isabella Francis, p. 575.

23 JRC: Evidence of Esther Williams, p. 564; Evidence of Ann Wilson, p. 534.

24 JRC: Evidence of Christopher Codrington, pp. 581–2; Evidence of George Bryan, p. 215.

25 JRC: Evidence of Christopher Codrington, p. 582; Evidence of George Bryan, p. 214; Evidence of Charlotte Scott, p. 461.

26 JRC: Evidence of John Wighan, pp. 585–6; Evidence of Capt. Lewis Hole, p. 717.

27 JRC: Evidence of Col Thomas Hobbs, pp. 746–7; Appendix, Military Despatches and Orders, Hobbs to O'Connor, 15 October 1765, p. 1120; Dutton, *The Hero as Murderer*, p. 284.

28 JRC: Evidence of Col Thomas Hobbs, p. 747; Appendix, Hobbs to Deputy Adjt-Gen., 30 December 1865, p. 1129; Hobbs to O'Connor, 15 October 1865, p. 1120.

29 JRC, Evidence of Col Thomas Hobbs, p. 747.

30 *Ibid.*, p. 748.

31 *Ibid.*, pp. 751–2.

32 JRC: Appendix: Military Despatches and Orders, Memo for Col. Hobbs, 16 October 1865, p. 1120; Elkington to Hobbs, 18 October 1865, p. 1120.

33 JRC, Evidence of Col Thomas Hobbs, pp. 754–5.

34 JRC, Appendix: Military Despatches and Orders, Hobbs to O'Connor, 18 October 1865, p. 1121; *Ibid.*, 19 October 1865.

35 JRC, Evidence of Col Thomas Hobbs, pp. 758–61.

36 JRC: Appendix: Military Despatches and Orders, Elkington to Hobbs, 19 October 1865, pp. 1121–2; Evidence of Col Thomas Hobbs, p. 765.

37 *Ibid.*, pp. 765–7; JRC, Appendix: Military Despatches and Orders, Hobbs to O'Connor, p. 1123.

38 JRC, Evidence of Col Thomas Hobbs, p. 771.

39 JRC, Evidence of Sergeant William Neale.

40 JRC, Evidence of Sophia Davis, p. 249.

41 JRC, Evidence of Rebecca Telford, p. 500.

42 JRC, Evidence of Edward Reid, p. 931.

43 *Ibid.*; JRC, Evidence of Charlotte Ross, p. 933.

44 JRC, Evidence of Roderick McLaren, p. 912.

45 JRC, Evidence of Grace Cherrington, pp. 272–3.

46 JRC, Evidence of Sophia Davis, p. 250.

47 JRC, Evidence of Chloe Munro, p. 932.

48 JRC: Evidence of Roderick McLaren, p. 912; Evidence of Mathew Joseph, pp. 107–8; Thomas Harvey and William Brewin, *Jamaica in 1866: A Narrative of a Tour Through the Island, with Remarks on its Social, Educational and Industrial Condition* (London: A.W. Bennett, 1867), p. 12.

49 JRC: Evidence of John Sawers, p. 224–6; Evidence of James Munroe, p. 366.

50 JRC: Evidence of James Graham, p. 298; Evidence of William Francis, pp. 935–6. As Graham reported the event, he and his brother were tied up with the other men facing the firing squad. When the shots were fired, Graham realized that the bullets had missed him and instead cut the ropes in which he was tied. He escaped. His brother was injured, but pretended to be dead; he later crawled away.

51 JRC: Evidence of William Anderson, p. 165; Evidence of George Anthony, p. 438.

52 JRC, Evidence of Moses Williams, p. 499.

53 JRC, Evidence of Elizabeth M'Intosh, p. 939.

54 JRC, Evidence of Richard Sherrington, p. 240.

55 CO 137/397, Oxley to de Horsey, 21 October 1865; Dutton, *The Hero as Murderer*, p. 284; JRC, Evidence of Lt Charles Oxley, p. 668.

56 CO 137/397, Oxley to de Horsey, 21 October 1865.

57 JRC: Evidence of George Pollard, p. 670; Evidence of Lt Charles Oxley, p. 669.

58 JRC, Evidence of Henry Ford, pp. 392–3.

59 JRC, Evidence of John March, p. 253.

60 JRC, Evidence of Henry Ford, p. 400.

61 JRC: Evidence of Lt Adcock, p. 703

62 JRC: Evidence of Sigismund Depass, p. 293–4; Evidence of James Duffus, p. 187.

63 Gorrie, *Illustrations of Martial Law in Jamaica*, p. 79; JRC: Evidence of William Porter, p. 190; Evidence of Ann Mitchell, p. 104; Evidence of James Duffus, p. 188.

64 JRC, Evidence of Henry Ford, pp. 395–7; CO 137/397, Adcock to Nelson, 25 October 1865.

65 JRC, Evidence of Henry Ford: Henry Ford to James Ford, 22 October 1865, p. 399.

66 JRC, Evidence of Brigadier-General Nelson, p. 690.

67 Edward Bean Underhill, *The Tragedy of Morant Bay* (London: Alexander and Shepheard, 1895), p. 12.

CHAPTER 9

The military suppression: The Maroons, the floggings and Morant Bay

The Maroons

Once the Jamaican government learned of the outbreak at Morant Bay, it sought to ensure that the Maroons in the eastern parishes would stay loyal. For one of the members of the executive committee, William Hosack, this was vital, in part because the Maroons controlled some of the most important roads across the island. Hosack was therefore concerned about a rumour that the Maroons would side with the rebels. A planter who had an estate in St George near one of the Maroon settlements, he knew many of the Maroons personally and did not believe that they would oppose the government. Hosack proved correct: as soon as the Maroons heard that there was some doubt about their position, they sent a deputation to see Hosack. The Maroons not only proclaimed their loyalty but also indicated that they were prepared to support the government in whatever form was required.[1]

Eyre was also aware of the Maroons' potential role in putting down the rebellion. When he travelled to Morant Bay two days after the outbreak, the Governor took along the former commander of the Maroons, Colonel Alexander Fyfe. A white man, Fyfe had led the Maroons in helping to suppress the 1831–2 slave rebellion and was a highly respected figure among them. In addition, he was a stipendiary magistrate, the custos of Portland and a member of the Legislative Council.[2]

Fyfe met about 200 Maroons assembled at Port Antonio when he arrived there on 15 October with Governor Eyre. At that point, the Maroons were poorly armed and consequently unable to be of immediate service to the government. However, when the *Wolverine* returned to Port Antonio four days later with a supply of weapons and ammunition, the military authorities could consider deploying them. In a memorandum to Colonel Fyfe on 19 October, Brigadier-General Nelson ordered the Maroons to patrol various routes out of St Thomas in the East. As in the case of the British officers marching from Port Antonio and from Manchioneal, Nelson authorized Fyfe 'to follow his own judgment' in making use of the Maroons.[3] This latitude was of considerable importance to Fyfe. In his discussions with Nelson before leaving Port Antonio, Fyfe pointed out the main military advantage of the Maroons. For Fyfe, it lay in 'the suddenness and the rapidity of their movements', and it was therefore critical that he be allowed to proceed as he thought best.[4]

The Maroons under Fyfe's command left Port Antonio on the 19th, stopped at their home in Moore Town overnight and marched to Bath the next day where they found another sixty Maroons. There, they learned that the rebels were waiting for them at Torrington, a village just north of Stony Gut. According to Fyfe the insurgents 'had left a challenge to the Maroons to come up, and that they had a fort from which they could kill 100 men at a time'.[5] As an advance party of the Maroons approached the village, one of them, Thomas Burton, heard a voice say, 'Yes, come on, we are prepared to meet you. Turn out the men; let them commence firing.' Shots were then fired at the Maroons, wounding one of them before they were able to regroup. One witness claimed that he saw Paul Bogle among the attackers. However, in response, the Maroons killed at least seven of the rebels. The Maroons then entered the deserted village, burning all the houses, but sparing a small outbuilding in each case to house the women and children.[6]

During the subsequent few days, Fyfe and the Maroons searched the considerable area from Wheelersfield in the Plantain Garden River district to Whitehall, west of Torrington. They discovered a good deal of plunder and also found a terrified populace. Fyfe reported that everything was quiet, 'the people subdued and surrendering to me fast for some days'.[7] When Fyfe ordered the people living in the hills above Torrington to surrender within twenty-four hours, all appear to have complied except for one man who was shot. Fyfe told the people that they would have to travel to Bath on a particular day; if they did not, Fyfe made it clear that 'the Maroons would find them and give them no quarter'. In response, 'they said they would come whenever [Fyfe] sent for them'.[8]

Apart from the skirmish at Torrington, Fyfe and the Maroons met no resistance. As he reported to Eyre, his problems did not come from the rebels but rather from the appalling weather and the dangerously high rivers he had to cross.[9] During his scouring of the area around Torrington, Fyfe learned from an informer that Paul Bogle was hiding in the vicinity. On 23 October the Maroons, 'moving with their usual silence after a hard day's work', caught Bogle unarmed coming out of the bush on the road between Torrington and Stony Gut. A Maroon captain, Joseph Briscoe, recalled Bogle's reaction when arrested. Bogle asked Briscoe whether he had seen three of his associates, Craddock, Bowie and Bailey, and insisted that they hang with him. According to Briscoe, Bogle would not say any more about other conspirators, because 'if I tell you, St Thomas in the East will be ruined'.[10]

In dealing with the people of St Thomas in the East, Fyfe was informed by some of the same ideas as Brigadier-General Nelson. For Fyfe almost every black in the parish was 'by act or connivance an accessory' to the plot to massacre whites and coloureds. He believed that some innocent people would be caught up in the retribution but that this was unavoidable. For more impartial observers of the situation, however, this was hardly a satisfactory excuse for Maroon violence toward the populace of the parish.[11]

The Methodist missionaries in the area around Bath, for example, passed a strong resolution against the activities of the Maroons. The missionaries reported that one of their best members had been killed by the Maroons, despite being 'harmless, loyal and well-behaved'. He had been bound, 'his clothing pillaged, his house burnt, himself shot, and his widow and fatherless children left through Maroon lawlessness in utter destitution to mourn their irreparable loss'. In a letter home, one of the missionaries, William Murray, summarized the atrocities committed by the Maroons as a 'tale [which] would scarcely be credited in enlightened and Christian England'. When Murray protested in writing to Fyfe about the Maroons, he and his wife were subsequently accosted on the streets of Bath by the Maroons and their lives threatened.[12]

The people of Torrington and the neighbouring settlements also described the actions of the Maroons. James Stewart, a small settler from Torrington, recalled the Maroons coming into the village, burning houses as they advanced. He also saw them shoot three old men and a young woman in the village. According to Stewart, the men were all shot in their homes. In the case of one of the men, William Treffick, the Maroons called out to him, ' "Old man, come out here," and they shot him as he came'. A rural constable in the village, Joseph Osborne, observed the shooting of another old man, William M'Farlane, who was afflicted with sores. Osborne counted 136 houses burnt at Torrington, effectively the entire village. The young woman who was shot was sixteen years old; she was hiding in the bush with her mother when the Maroons mistakenly took her for a man.[13]

There were other reports of wanton destruction of life. At Stony Gut a constable, Thomas Davis, witnessed the shooting of a man named Frenderson: a group of five Maroons executed him. Davis also found the body of Duncan Grant, who was killed at the doorway of his home. In the case of Grant, the Maroons said they had an order from Morant Bay to shoot him, but there was no evidence of a court martial or a trial of any kind. At York, a village close to Stony Gut, the Maroons shot John Milliner, who was guarding a great house in the district. Milliner's wife saw the Maroons shoot her husband, just as they had told him to march ahead of them.[14]

The story was repeated at Middleton, another settlement close to Stony Gut. There, David Valentine, a resident of Middleton, observed the Maroons shooting one of his neighbours, a sick young man whom they pulled out of his house. The Maroon captain, Joseph Briscoe, said, ' "Four men fall out and blow brains", and they shot him'. The Maroons also burned down

Valentine's house and took away his clothes. When Valentine asked them what he had done, the Maroons' response was that 'what the rest had done I must pay for, for one rotten sheep spoiled the whole flock'. Even Colonel Fyfe admitted to shooting one man without trial at Stony Gut. Fyfe found the man in possession of Baron von Ketelhodt's ring, which had been removed from his body after the massacre at Morant Bay. As Fyfe put it, 'finding [Ketelhodt's] ring with this man I thought of his mutilated hand and the missing finger, and I ordered the man to be shot without a court martial'.[15]

Closer to Morant Bay, at the settlement of Nutts River, the Maroons continued to shoot people without hesitation. Thomas Duncan, a labourer from Port Morant, described the slaughter of his father-in-law, an old African man who had been ill for many years:

> [The Maroons] ordered him out of the house, and he said he could
> not go, and they shoved open the door, and took him out, and took
> this rope (witness produced a rope), and bound his hands, and
> bound him to a tree, and shot him, and left word with Mr Woodrow
> [a magistrate] that they must not interfere with the body.[16]

When a constable asked the Maroons why they had killed Noble, they said that they shot all the men. Henrietta Bailey, also a resident of Nutts River, confirmed that this was the case. The Maroons came into her house and shot her son, who was lying in bed with fever. They then saw her husband and ordered him to 'put your face to me'; he turned around, and the Maroons shot him.[17]

There is evidence that the Maroons also used their power to settle old scores. At Nutts River they took a young man, Hamilton Harris, out of his home and tied him to a tree. One of the Maroons, John White, accused Harris of saying that he saw White 'sleep with a horse'. The Maroons then shot Harris.[18] Even in the context of martial law, these actions obviously exceeded their brief. Yet there was no one to stop them. As a witness to the Maroons' pillaging and burning of homes put it: 'The Maroons were so powerful that they would not give time to say a word. They went in and did as they liked . . . .'[19]

Floggings and forced labour

The Maroons were not just used to help suppress the rebellion. In the early stages of the outbreak the Maroons from Hayfield, a village close to Bath, were called on to guard the town. According to William Kirkland, a magistrate and merchant in Bath, the people who were plundering Bath fled from the town as soon as they realized that the Maroons were entering it. He calculated that there were over sixty Maroons who helped to protect it, until

Colonel Fyfe arrived in Bath on October 20. The Maroons had other duties as well. They arrested a large number of prisoners whom they brought to Bath and sometimes had a role in trying these people. In addition, they transported those thought to have committed more serious crimes from Bath to Morant Bay.[20]

As the only magistrate in Bath, Kirkland received instructions from Brigadier-General Nelson and Gordon Ramsay, the Provost-Marshal at Morant Bay. Kirkland's responsibility was to deal with minor cases, such as plundering, but to send those charged with more serious crimes to Morant Bay for trial. Kirkland himself decided how the prisoners should be treated; he maintained that those found with stolen property were whipped but that others with no evidence against them were freed.[21]

However, there were problems about the evidence and also about the procedures adopted by Kirkland. Kirkland admitted that prisoners were not allowed to call witnesses to prove that a particular piece of property belonged to them. In his view, there was no time to allow the accused this opportunity. One man who was flogged, James Turner, recalled appearing before Kirkland, who ordered him to be whipped. Turner was flogged along with the rest of his gang who worked on Golden Grove estate, numbering about one hundred people. Yet according to Turner there was no evidence against him, and Kirkland 'did not pick and choose any one of us, but he ordered them to flog us, and let us go'.[22]

There was also little doubt about the severity of the whippings. Kirkland ordered a black soldier who was a bandmaster, Peter Bruce, to take charge of the floggings. At first, the whippings were done with cats made with ordinary twine, but Kirkland insisted that these were regarded as 'trifling' by the people. Subsequently, Bruce threaded wire into the cats to make the punishments more severe.[23]

Large numbers of people suffered from these floggings. John Hamilton, a coloured carpenter from Bath who witnessed the whippings, counted more than 300 people who had to endure them. Approximately fifty of these were women. Other estimates put the figures much higher: two Quakers visiting Jamaica in 1866 suggested that 600 people had been whipped, 200 of them women. The man in charge of the whipping, Bruce, was unable to say how many he had flogged, but he often began at 6 a.m. and continued flogging until 6 p.m., 'until [he] could not see [his] way'. His instructions from Ramsay were to flog the plunderers well, but those involved in the massacre at Morant Bay were to receive 100 lashes before being sent for trial. A missionary noted that the majority of those flogged were Africans rather than creoles. These were people who had been brought as indentured labourers to work on the estates of the Plantain Garden River district and had settled in villages nearby.[24]

The scale of the floggings was often overwhelming. Lydia Bruce, the wife of the chief flogger, described the whippings as 'terrible'; she had never seen anything like it, despite having witnessed many floggings in the army. She could not personally bear the cruelty and recalled that it also badly affected her husband. He fainted, became very ill and needed medical treatment.[25]

Another observer, the Methodist missionary William Murray, was present almost every day at Bath. On one occasion he witnessed two pregnant women being flogged. Another day he sought to intervene on behalf of a boy named Stephens. While he was being flogged, Stephens cried out loudly but then became quiet, and Murray could only hear the sound of the whipping and the number of lashes being counted.

> . . . when they counted 50 I rushed up to the place where they were flogging him, and asked Bruce who was superintending, 'How many lashes do you intend to give to this boy?' He said, 'As many as he could take.' 'Well,' I said, 'if you give him another lash, you will kill him. The boy has fainted.'

Murray was verbally abused by the magistrate, William Kirkland, but the flogging of Stephen ceased.[26]

In meting out the punishments, the soldiers treated men and women differently. According to a coloured volunteer, Robert Jacobs, men were flogged with the wire cats, while women were punished with cats made of twine. Women also had to suffer far fewer lashes, usually averaging from six to twelve at any one time. However, a large number of men received fifty lashes, and around a dozen men had to endure one hundred. Even Colonel Fyfe, the commander of the Maroons, regarded the wire cats as improper and unnecessarily cruel. When he realized they were being used he stopped it immediately.[27]

Kirkland and Fyfe also administered another form of punishment. According to John Gorrie, a barrister who represented the Jamaica Committee before the Jamaica Royal Commission, the two men sentenced people to forced labour. For instance, Peggy White, whose husband was executed, reported that she was 'bound to the Maroons' and required to work on the road to Portland for two months. She received no pay and her own property was confiscated.[28]

But Peggy White was not alone. Kirkland confirmed that over forty men and women were put to work on the Portland road without pay and with only an allowance of salt fish provided by the authorities. When asked whether these people were properly tried, Kirkland responded that there was 'no regular court. I was the only magistrate, and Colonel Fyfe was the only officer'. Yet this abuse of power as well as the floggings at Bath, although brutal and often sickening in their intensity, paled by comparison with the horror of the repression at Morant Bay.[29]

Martial law at Morant Bay

During the course of martial law, which lasted from 13 October to 13 November, nearly 1,000 prisoners were brought to Morant Bay. Out of this total just under 200 were executed and another 200 flogged. The man in charge of martial law, Gordon Ramsay, an inspector of police who was given the title of Provost-Marshal, estimated that there were almost 400 prisoners under his jurisdiction at the height of this period. In these circumstances and in light of the repression elsewhere in St Thomas in the East, the atmosphere at Morant Bay was predictably brutal.[30]

One official from the parish of Vere, halfway across the island, expressed great concern about the nature of martial law in Jamaica. Lewis Mackinnon, the custos of Vere, described it as the 'most dreadful' martial law he had ever encountered. For Mackinnon the British soldiers were 'very fierce men of war', comparable to uncontrollable bloodhounds. He observed that the soldiers 'flog people for looking sulky or for speaking a hasty word or for nothing at all. In short, the dogs of war are let loose and there is no holding them in.'[31]

This was especially the case at Morant Bay under the administration of Gordon Ramsay. For example, prisoners were tortured to extract confessions, not always with the consent of Ramsay. The missionary, William Murray, witnessed a prisoner receiving this sort of treatment. Five days after the outbreak of the rebellion on 16 October, he saw a prisoner brought in to Morant Bay and flogged until he admitted taking an oath to join the rebels.

> The officer next asked, 'Who gave the oath to you?' The man made no answer, but somebody in the police station I distinctly heard whisper the name 'Bogle', and the man caught (sic), and said that Bogle gave him the oath. He was asked, 'What Bogle?' and he was being flogged as the questions were being asked, 'What Bogle?' He made no answer, and I heard Paul Bogle named, and the man caught the words, and said 'Paul Bogle gave me the oath.'

Gordon Ramsay walked in at this moment and ordered the man to be set free, with the injunction that, 'You will kill these brutes and they won't tell the truth.' Yet Murray reported that another prisoner was about to be whipped and possibly face a similar ordeal, although he did not see it.[32]

Ramsay did not always adopt such a protective attitude toward the prisoners. The coloured nephew of George William Gordon, Joseph Smith, saw several men brought in from Easington to face Ramsay. According to Smith, Ramsay flogged them without even asking their names. Subsequently, Ramsay had five of the prisoners tied up and a rope placed around their necks. He demanded that they ' "shall well and truly state what G.W. Gordon has to do with the rebellion", and between each part of this a sailor came down with the whip over their shoulders'.[33]

Other prisoners complained that Ramsay ordered them to be flogged without any charge or trial. A cooper from Font Hill, Joseph Hall, was imprisoned for over three weeks at Morant Bay and subsequently received seventy-five lashes on Ramsay's orders. The only rationale for the whipping was that Hall came from Font Hill, a place which had 'a bad character'.[34] Some prisoners were flogged for being on the road without a pass and could receive fifty lashes for this offence. If prisoners were thought to have been involved in the murders at Morant Bay or in the outlying areas, they were whipped when they were brought in before being imprisoned to await trial. One of the rebel leaders, Scipio Cowell, was flogged on two separate occasions before being hanged.[35]

Many of those who were flogged had to face further abuse by the soldiers and sailors. Upon release and after having been whipped, prisoners had to run a gauntlet of soldiers armed with stones or sticks. As the prisoners ran through the line of soldiers, they were stoned and often clubbed. To make matters worse, the sentry at the end of the line sometimes beat the prisoners with the butt end of their rifles. However, there is some evidence that this practice was stopped on the orders of Ramsay and of Brigadier-General Nelson, once they learned of it.[36]

Prisoners who remained in captivity were forced to watch the executions which took place at Morant Bay. Joseph Hall reported that Ramsay ordered the prisoners to the parade to witness the hangings. Even when some prisoners sought to avoid watching the executions, soldiers were present to force them to do so. Soldiers were also sometimes brutal in pushing the prisoners into line; in addition, prisoners had to bury the people who had been executed. It was the usual practice for the bodies to be left on the gallows overnight and for the prisoners to bury them the next day. One leading rebel, E.K. Bailey, who had sought unsuccessfully to evade detection by enlisting as a constable, never reached the hanging ground: he was shot while trying to escape from imprisonment at Morant Bay.[37]

The procedure at the executions was relatively simple. The condemned prisoners were marched onto a board placed over two barrels; they stood on the board with their hands and feet tied and the rope around their neck. When the board was pulled away the noose tightened. A black politician from Kingston, William Kelly Smith, described the scene:

> All the military officers were there . . . and a number of other gentlemen, and after that the Provost-Marshal, as I found it to be usual with him, took his watch out of his pocket and placed it to his ear, and gave the order to be hanged. Just as the plank upon

which they were was drawn, their bodies swung, and a few seconds after that the sailors went one by one to them as they were kicking and drew down the noose tight, knocking it down, laid hold of each of their necks, and broke the neck and, after that, if they were kicking again, they would lay hold of their legs and drag the legs.[38]

Some of the condemned prisoners were said to have cried out 'innocent death!' repeatedly at the gallows. One prominent prisoner allegedly blamed George William Gordon for causing his death, but there is some doubt about this claim.[39] According to a military eye-witness, Paul Bogle went calmly and bravely to his death. He was hanged on 25 October, along with several other leaders of the rebellion: Bowie, McLaren and Bogle's brother, Moses. Fourteen others were hanged with them.[40]

Seven women were hanged at Morant Bay. The first execution of a woman took place on 14 October, just three days after the outbreak of the rebellion. A court sentenced Sarah Francis to life imprisonment, but General Nelson ordered her to be hanged. His rationale was that one of the planters in the parish had informed him that 'the women were worse than the men in inflicting atrocities'. Mary Ward was hanged with her father on 20 October and, five days later, Mrs Letitia Geoghegan suffered the same fate alongside one of her sons. She had led the stone-throwing at the court house on 11 October. On 27 October, Mary Ann Francis was executed at the same time as her father and, the next day, Ellen Dawkins and Judy Edwards were hanged. The last woman to be hanged was Justina Taylor on 1 November; together with Mary Ward, she was implicated in the murder of Charles Price at Morant Bay. One of the women was pregnant.[41]

At the courts martial held at Morant Bay, the procedure of dealing with the alleged rebels varied considerably. The police magistrate in Kingston, Henry Bicknell, maintained that those he witnessed were conducted carefully and fairly. Although Bicknell was surprised by the speed of the trials, he believed witnesses were properly examined and given every opportunity to cross-examine.[42] Yet someone who experienced a court martial, George Clarke, had a very different view. A parish politician and vestryman, Clarke was the son-in-law of Paul Bogle. When he was court martialled he was not even aware of the charge against him. Questioned before the Royal Commission, Clarke described his ordeal:

> Was any written notice of the charge served against you? – No.
> Were you told at any time what the charge was? – Not at all, not
> a note; there was no charge against me . . . Then they did not tell
> you what you were charged with? – No, not at all. Were you
> called to plead anything? – Nothing at all. Were you asked whether
> you were guilty or not guilty? – No. Never? – No, they never

asked me whether I was guilty or not; no persons at all were asked those questions at these Courts. I have seen six, eight, 10 persons taken up before the court martial, and in less time they were put right in the condemned cell.[43]

Clarke also impugned Gordon Ramsay's handling of witnesses before the courts martial. When witnesses did not give satisfactory evidence in Ramsay's view, they could be flogged until they did so. In one instance which Clarke observed, the witness, Manfield Panton, provided evidence against his own son and another young man. Since it was not good enough, 'Ramsay brought him down from upstairs, put him down, and gave him a dozen lashes; and after he went back he gave evidence, and they were all hung', including the witness himself. This was apparently not unusual. George Clarke mentioned several witnesses who were hanged along with the individuals they helped to convict.[44]

This was one indication of a very serious problem with the administration of martial law at Morant Bay: Gordon Ramsay himself. The evidence suggests that Ramsay often behaved dictatorially and also highly erratically. His treatment of prisoners and also of magistrates varied considerably and gave rise to the view, even at the time, that it was not simply a case of a man whose power had gone to his head. Apart from a possible problem with alcohol, Ramsay appears to have had serious mental difficulties.

This pattern of behaviour became clear during the course of martial law. For example, John Grant, a stillerman at St Albion Estate in St David, was arrested by soldiers on 15 October and taken to Morant Bay. While tied to a cart, Grant saw Ramsay approach him. Grant then 'just turned [his] eyes this way and looked at [Ramsay], and he said, "Oh, you look at me, give him 25"; and they laid hold of me and gave me 25 lashes'.[45]

A collector of customs, George Hague, had a series of even more bizarre encounters with Ramsay. Seeking a pass during martial law, Hague went to Ramsay's office. Ramsay took out a piece of paper, wrote 'Pass' on it, and asked for Hague's name. After Ramsay had written out the name, he 'stopped suddenly, he looked me in the face, got up and pitched the piece of paper on the ground, [and] said, "That be d——d!" and walked out of the room'.[46] On another occasion Hague was present when Ramsay inquired about a woman who had been sent to the police station. When asked why the woman was there, Hague responded:

> 'For having been with the rebels on the 12th, with a knife in her hand, and with having been seen on the wharf with a knife, calling out the men in general to go on and cut the throats of every damned Mulatto in the place.' That's what I told him. Ramsay said, 'Did she say that?' I said, 'She did'. Then Ramsay called out to the policeman, 'Let that woman go – it was devilish well said.'

Hague left the police station, but a few moments later was asked to see Ramsay. As Hague recalled the scene, he 'found Ramsay in a frightful state of excitement'. He was not certain whether Ramsay was drunk, but he was certainly unwell: 'he ground his teeth, and was in a terrible way'.[47]

Ramsay's anger could be sparked off by relatively trivial incidents. Mary Ann Thomas, a baker from Morant Bay, was at the baker's shop one night when it was raining. Ramsay requested her to bring him a fire-stick, but she refused because of the rain. In response, Ramsay threatened to shoot her with his pistol; even after she had obtained the fire for Ramsay, he still held the pistol to her head as if to shoot her. Yet all he required was a light for his pipe. In another case Ramsay asked James Barnet, who was in charge of a bakery, to get him a mule and harness. Barnet's reply was that he would be pleased to do so if Ramsay could tell him where to find them. Ramsay then had Barnet arrested, and when he protested, the Provost-Marshal ordered that Barnet be given a dozen lashes.[48]

Even a retired soldier had to face Ramsay's wrath. Picked up for being without a pass, the soldier, John Green, was brought to Morant Bay because the constable was under orders to arrest anyone 'who was walking about the place'. Ramsay blamed the police for bringing in an old soldier, but he none the less had Green placed under the gallows. According to Green, Ramsay then badly assaulted him and ordered him to be given fifty lashes.[49]

Ramsay was particularly abusive to the prisoners who had been active in Jamaican politics. Known generally as political prisoners, they were brought from Kingston to Morant Bay during the martial law. One of them, William Kelly Smith, described Ramsay's turning on two of the men and ordering each to receive a dozen lashes. Another prisoner, Rev. J.H. Crole, was sweating and using a handkerchief to wipe his face.

> Mr Ramsay said, 'That man is winking at his fellow prisoner, take him out and give him a dozen.' [Crole] said, 'I was not doing anything.' Ramsay said, 'Give him another dozen for saying that.'[50]

Magistrates and prominent local people were not exempt from Ramsay's abuse. At least two people saw Ramsay drag Mr Kirkland from his shop, with his hands around Kirkland's throat. One of the witnesses, George Hague, described Kirkland as 'a very quiet, law-abiding, God-fearing man'. In this instance, Hague was able to inform Brigadier-General Nelson of Kirkland's fate, and Nelson immediately ordered him to be released. Another storekeeper, Daniel Marshalleck, was arrested and sent to gaol, despite being a magistrate. When he lodged a complaint, Nelson personally examined the case. Nelson's conclusion was that Ramsay had 'exceeded his powers', and he proceeded to censure the Provost-Marshal. In a memo to Ramsay written on 6 November, Nelson also banned all summary punishments at Morant Bay. In addition, he made it clear that all serious cases should be referred to him.[51]

But Nelson's order came too late to prevent Ramsay from acting arbitrarily and even summarily during most of the martial law period. For example, Charles King, a black labourer from Manchioneal, was arrested and brought first to Bath and then in a large group to Morant Bay. As King arrived at Morant Bay, Ramsay took away one of his fellow prisoners and had him hanged. According to King there was no trial.[52] In a more notorious incident, Ramsay ordered a prisoner who was being flogged, George Marshall, to be hanged immediately. Again, it was a case of execution without trial.

Governor Eyre subsequently heard about this case and wrote to Ramsay for an explanation. In reply, Ramsay claimed that Marshall was a dangerous prisoner and, while being flogged, had actually threatened his life. As Ramsay explained:

> I did not know how many lashes he had received at the time but as the other prisoners were muttering and expressing sympathy I ordered him to be taken down. He then shook his fist and growled at me again saying words to the effect he would do for me – there was no Court Martial likely to sit for some days and considering that his remaining in the yard with other prisoners would be dangerous I ordered him to be hanged.[53]

Some other witnesses confirmed Ramsay's account; others denied that Marshall had ever said anything or that he posed a problem for the authorities. What is striking, however, is that the man in charge of martial law could order the execution of a prisoner without any trial at all. Moreover, Marshall had been given nearly fifty lashes and was unlikely to be in a condition to pose a threat either to Ramsay personally or to law and order generally.[54]

But it was not only at Morant Bay that Ramsay considerably exceeded his powers. When he accompanied the sailors and soldiers who went to Stony Gut, Ramsay threatened to execute a woman, Polly Levingston, found in the village. Levingston was first badly flogged and then a rope placed around her neck. A policeman who was present remembered Ramsay saying to her, 'If you don't tell he where [Bogle and his party] are gone and take me there, I will hang you.' Although she was not killed, Levingston was kept tied up outside in the rain for two days.[55]

Ramsay also travelled with the soldiers to Easington on 14 October. A woman who lived at a village on the way, Penny Aikin, saw Ramsay that morning. He told her that 'he was the King of Jamaica' and that he had just shot a young man and would shoot her if she 'interfered with him'. Later that day Ramsay shot another man, Archy Francis, as he emerged from his yard at White Horses to meet the troops. Moreover, Ramsay ordered that Francis not be buried 'but must remain there as an example to the rest'.[56]

Yet Ramsay had his defenders. A black junior sergeant of police who was stationed at Morant Bay, Romeo Drysdale, witnessed the floggings and the treatment of prisoners generally. Drysdale maintained that Ramsay 'did his duty straightforward'. Lieutenant Brand, commander of the *Onyx*, believed that Ramsay had carried out his responsibilities very well. Other soldiers also supported Ramsay's handling of martial law.[57]

Perhaps more revealing was the account of Augustus Lake, a reporter for *The Colonial Standard*, who had written that Ramsay was 'the right man in the right place'. When questioned about this description, Lake recanted and claimed that he had written in this vein to save himself from being flogged or arrested. Lake was not alone. As another observer concluded, nearly everyone was truly frightened: 'the times were such that no man could open his mouth, you were almost afraid to hear your own breathing, such was the state of things.'[58]

For blacks in St Thomas in the East, it was 'The Killing Time'.[59] They had to confront Maroon atrocities. In addition, there was the barbaric treatment of prisoners in Bath and at Morant Bay. British troops and Jamaican auxiliaries also went on the rampage. Since many of the worst offences took place after the rebellion had been effectively quelled, it was clear that the authorities were not just putting down a rebellion. Governor Eyre did issue an amnesty on 30 October, but it did not include prisoners who were already in custody awaiting sentence or those found guilty of murder or arson. More significantly, the amnesty had no effect on martial law, which continued until 13 November.[60] This was further evidence that the government was intent on establishing its authority and on stifling black political expression of any kind. At Morant Bay there was a political as well as a military dimension to the suppression.

Notes

1 JRC, Evidence of William Hosack, p. 924.
2 CO 137/393, Eyre to Cardwell, 20 October, 1865, no. 251; JRC, Evidence of Alexander Fyfe, p. 894.
3 JRC: Evidence of Alexander Fyfe, p. 894; Appendix: Military Orders and Documents, Memo for Col Fyfe, 19 October 1865, p. 1125.
4 JRC, Evidence of Alexander Fyfe, p. 894.
5 *Ibid.*
6 JRC: Evidence of Thomas Burton, p. 902; Evidence of George Bernard, p. 947; CO 137/394, Eyre to Cardwell, 8 November 1865, no. 272: Fyfe to Eyre, 22 October 1865.
7 CO 137/394, Eyre to Cardwell, 8 November 1865, no. 272: Fyfe to Eyre, 28 October 1865.
8 *Ibid.*, Fyfe to O'Connor, 25 October 1865.

9   *Ibid.*, Fyfe to Eyre, 28 October 1865.
10 *Ibid.*, Fyfe to Eyre, 29 October 1865; JRC, Evidence of Joseph Briscoe, p. 1029.
11 JRC, Evidence of Alexander Fyfe, p. 896.
12 MMS 199, Report of the Religious State of the Societies in the Bath Circuit for the year ending 31st December 1865; *Ibid.*, Murray to Hoole, 23 December 1865.
13 JRC: Evidence of James Stewart, p. 212; Evidence of Joseph Osborne, p. 487; Evidence of Hannah Aspitt, p. 485; Evidence of Robert Rennock, p. 904.
14 JRC: Evidence of Thomas Davis, p. 453; Evidence of Cecilia Stewart, p. 540; Evidence of John Miles, p. 974.
15 JRC: Evidence of David Valentine, p. 455; Evidence of Alexander Fyfe, p. 898.
16 JRC, Evidence of Thomas Duncan, p. 528.
17 *Ibid.*, p. 942; Evidence of Henrietta Bailey, p. 969.
18 PRO 30/48/44, Cardwell Papers, 'Jamaica' by Lewis Q. Bowerbank, p. 11; JRC, Evidence of Thomas Bennett, p. 975.
19 JRC, Evidence of Charles Benjamin, p. 467.
20 JRC: Evidence of William Kirkland, p. 266; Evidence of Arthur M'Queen, p. 486.
21 JRC, Evidence of William Kirkland, p. 266.
22 *Ibid.*, p. 269; Evidence of James Turner, p. 574.
23 JRC, Evidence of William Kirkland, p. 266.
24 Thomas Harvey and William Brewin, *Jamaica in 1866: A Narrative of a Tour Through the Island, with Remarks on its Social, Educational and Industrial Condition* (London: A.W. Bennett, 1867), p. 13; JRC: Evidence of John Hamilton, p. 483; Evidence of Peter Bruce, p. 76; Evidence of William Murray, p. 530.
25 JRC, Evidence of Lydia Bruce, p. 315.
26 JRC, Evidence of William Murray, p. 530.
27 JRC: Evidence of Robert Jacobs, p. 233; Evidence of John M. Gray, p. 169; Evidence of Alexander Fyfe, p. 897.
28 John Gorrie, *Illustrations of Martial Law in Jamaica. Compiled from the Report of the Royal Commissioners, and Other Blue Books Laide Before Parliament.* Jamaica Papers, no. 6 (London: Jamaica Committee, 1867), p. 59; JRC, Evidence of Peggy White, p. 528.
29 JRC, Evidence of W.P. Kirkland, p. 268. Kirkland was not the only magistrate who made use of forced labour; another magistrate, John Woodrow, did so as well. See JRC: Evidence of James Minot, p. 471; Evidence of Strawberry Johnson, p. 468.
30 JRC, Evidence of Gordon Ramsay, p. 930.
31 PRO/48/42, Cardwell Papers, Mackinnon to Sheldon, 20 October 1865.
32 JRC, Evidence of William Murray, p. 529.
33 JRC, Evidence of Joseph Smith, p. 364.
34 JRC, Evidence of Joseph Hall, p. 241.
35 JRC: Evidence of Augustus Lake, p. 274; Evidence of Joseph Hall, p. 242.
36 JRC: Evidence of Charles Robertson, p. 141; Evidence of John March, p. 253; Evidence of William Porter, p. 190.
37 JRC: Evidence of Joseph Hall, p. 242; Evidence of Arthur Beckwith, p. 123; Evidence of W.G. Astwood, p. 265.
38 JRC, Evidence of William Kelly Smith, p. 196.
39 JRC: Evidence of Alexander Phillips, p. 345; Evidence of Lt Herbert Brand. See also the evidence of Henry Clyne before the JRC, p. 735, which contradicts Brand's claim about prisoners' blaming Gordon for their deaths.
40 *The Morning Journal*, 8 November 1865; BMS, 'Jamaica Affairs', vol. 2, p. 142, clipping from *The Morning Star*, 31 March 1866.
41 *The Colonial Standard and Jamaica Despatch*: 20 October 1865, 26 October 1865; Gorrie, *Illustrations of Martial Law in Jamaica*, pp. 77–9, quotation on p. 77.

42 JRC, Evidence of Henry Bicknell, p. 340.
43 JRC, Evidence of George Clarke, p. 130.
44 *Ibid.*, p. 131.
45 JRC, Evidence of John Grant, p. 55.
46 JRC, Evidence of George Hague, p. 182.
47 *Ibid.*, p. 183.
48 JRC: Evidence of Mary Ann Thomas, p. 191; Evidence of James Barnet, p. 172.
49 JRC, Evidence of John Green, p. 385.
50 JRC, Evidence of William Kelly Smith, p. 195.
51 JRC: Evidence of George Hague, p. 183; Evidence of Francis M'Kay, p. 220; Evidence of Daniel Marshalleck, p. 51; Appendix: Military Orders and Documents, p. 1118.
52 JRC, Evidence of Charles King, p. 384.
53 CO 137/399, Storks to Cardwell, 18 January 1866, confidential: Ramsay to Jordon, 6 January 1866.
54 JRC: Evidence of Edwin Gentle, p. 65; Evidence of George Clarke, p. 128; Evidence of George Levy, p. 814; Evidence of Alfred Penny, p. 774.
55 JRC: Evidence of William Fuller, p. 82; Evidence of Robert Jones, pp. 91–2; Evidence of Polly Levingston, p. 350.
56 JRC: Evidence of Penny Aikin, p. 111; Evidence of James Loague, p. 430.
57 JRC: Evidence of Romeo Drysdale, p. 203; Evidence of Lt Herbert Brand, p. 661; Evidence of William Astwood, p. 264.
58 JRC: Evidence of Augustus Lake, p. 282; Evidence of Francis M'Kay, p. 221.
59 *The Morning Star*, 13 February 1866, Letter from our special correspondent [John Gorrie], 24 January 1866. I am grateful to Bridget Brereton for this reference.
60 PRO 30/48/44, Cardwell Papers, 'Narrative of the Rebellion in Jamaica, October, 1865 taken from the official Despatches', Confidential: Printed for the use of the Cabinet, 14 December 1865.

CHAPTER 10

The political suppression: The political prisoners

George William Gordon's arrest and court martial

In the wake of the rebellion, Governor Eyre as well as his executive committee expressed great concern about the role of politicians and others outside of St Thomas in the East in fomenting the uprising. For example, the organizers of the Underhill meetings across the island came under almost immediate suspicion. This was also the case for editors and writers working for newspapers which had been highly critical of the government. But the man whom Eyre immediately identified with the rebellion was his most virulent political opponent, George William Gordon.

On his return to Kingston from St Thomas in the East on the morning of 17 October, Eyre was surprised to learn that Gordon had not been placed under arrest. Although this had clearly been considered by members of the government, the officer in charge of the troops in Jamaica, General L. Smythe O'Connor, had ruled it out. O'Connor believed that Gordon's arrest could lead to further disturbances, especially in Kingston, at a time when his troops were fully stretched elsewhere in the island. However, Eyre disagreed, maintaining that it was essential Gordon be arrested to ensure that other areas of the colony did not follow the example of St Thomas in the East. According to the custos of Kingston, Lewis Q. Bowerbank, the general was still hesitant, but Eyre 'took a sheet of paper and wrote a warrant upon it for G.W. Gordon's immediate arrest, directing the same to myself'.[1]

Gordon himself first heard of the government's intentions a few hours later from his doctor and friend, Alexander Fiddes. On learning of the warrant for his arrest, Gordon immediately drove with Dr Fiddes to army headquarters. There, General O'Connor made it clear that he could not arrest Gordon; however, before Fiddes and Gordon could leave, Eyre and Bowerbank arrived to see the general. As Bowerbank described the scene

> On seeing the Governor enter, Mr Gordon turned towards him and said, 'Oh! your Excellency.' The Governor replied, 'I regret, Mr Gordon, I can hold no communication with you.' On which Mr Gordon said, 'Why?' His Excellency replied, 'Because you

are a prisoner.' Mr Gordon answered, 'What for?' The Governor gave no answer, but turned to me. I immediately arrested Mr Gordon in the name of the Queen on a charge of treason. As I laid my hand on his shoulder he got very pale and trembled much.

Gordon was then taken to see his wife in another part of Kingston and put on board the *Wolverine* which was preparing to return with the Governor to Morant Bay.[2]

In this manner Gordon was transferred from Kingston, which was under civil jurisdiction, to Morant Bay and the prospect of a drumhead court martial. It was not surprising that Gordon believed he would die later that day. On board the *Wolverine*, Gordon was kept in the stern of the ship separate from the other prisoners. Although he was not held in chains, he was denied access to a solicitor, William Wemyss Anderson, who was travelling on the ship. Anderson subsequently wrote to Gordon, advising him how to proceed during his trial. However, Brigadier-General Nelson refused to allow Gordon to see the letter and had it destroyed.[3]

Gordon arrived in Morant Bay on the morning of Friday, 20 October. He was incarcerated in the Morant Bay police station overnight before his trial on Saturday and was apparently the object of considerable abuse by soldiers and sailors in the town. According to a reporter on *The Colonial Standard*, Gordon was kept tied up at the police station. A group of sailors held up a whip and asked him if 'he would like a taste' of it. ' "He'll soon get it", said another; and a third said, "We'll get a rope for you, you haven't long to remain here." ' A member of the Assembly who observed Gordon's trial, Andrew Lewis, recalled that Gordon looked very ill; he had a blanket on him rather than a coat and 'he appeared to me very debilitated and sick'. As it was an open court, the room was packed and quite hot.[4]

The court martial was presided over by three young and relatively junior officers. The president of the court, Lieutenant Brand, was commander of the gunboat *Onyx* and had served as a lieutenant for less than seven years. The other two men were Lieutenant Errington, an officer on the *Wolverine* and a lieutenant for under four years and Ensign Kelly of the 1st West India Regiment, who had held the rank of ensign for less than a year. When asked why he had chosen these men for the court martial, Brigadier-General Nelson pointed out that the more senior men available were members of the House of Assembly and therefore inappropriate. However, Lieutenant Herbert Brand might also have been considered problematical. Although Brand denied the charge, he was accused of having said that he 'had the pleasure of hanging the first damned rebel . . . but nothing would give me greater pleasure than the hanging of this d– – –d son of a b– – –h [George William Gordon]'.[5]

Gordon was charged on two counts: 'high treason and sedition' as well as 'having complicity with certain persons in the insurrection at Morant Bay on the 11th October 1865'. The prosecution evidence was based on the oral testimony of several witnesses and written depositions as well as documents submitted by the provost martial. For example, one of the witnesses, John Anderson, testified that Gordon travelled to Stony Gut and 'told Paul Bogle to get Volunteers and get the back lands; if the lands were not got, all buckras will die'.[6]

Although Gordon was not given any chance to prepare his case and had no legal adviser, he was able to cross-examine each witness. In the process, Gordon asked Anderson whether other people were present when he had visited Stony Gut. Gordon continued: 'did they hear what you say I said to Bogle, and were all present; and did I say that publicly in presence of all parties? (Witness) Yes.' Following this testimony, Gordon requested the use of pencil and paper to take notes of the evidence. After clearing the court to consider this request, the court agreed to Gordon's application.[7]

During the trial the Provost-Marshal, Gordon Ramsay, submitted several depositions. One from a dying prisoner, Thomas Johnson, claimed that Gordon had held meetings next to his house and that he had heard the rebels talking about war. Another deposition came from Vere and was an account of Gordon's speech at the Underhill meeting there. It confirmed his alleged admonition to the people of Vere to follow the example of Haiti, coded language signifying the overthrow of white domination. Confronted with this evidence, Gordon claimed that 'he never thought of it; and my Heavenly Father knows it'. A further piece of written evidence came from a wounded prisoner, George Thomas. In his statement he emphasized that Gordon was 'the head of the rebellion [and] he put up the Bogles to do it'.[8]

Not all the prosecution witnesses gave evidence which implicated Gordon. One of the leaders of the rebellion who served as Paul Bogle's secretary, James McLaren, denied that Gordon had anything to do with the outbreak. McLaren confirmed Gordon's political and religious connections with Paul Bogle. However, when Gordon cross-examined McLaren, the witness agreed that Gordon had never told the people 'not to pay for lands or to incite them to any improper acts'.[9]

In his defence Gordon called a storekeeper from White Horses, Thomas Testard. Gordon asked Testard to testify that he had visited Gordon two weeks previously in Kingston and found him unwell. But Testard was unable to say whether Gordon had been ill or not. Gordon also sought to examine Dr Major on the state of his health; for Gordon, this would explain why he had not been at the vestry meeting at Morant Bay on 11 October. But the president of the court responded that Dr Major was not in court or readily available in the town.[10]

Gordon then made a long statement denying involvement in the rebellion and attacking the witnesses against him. He suggested that his whole upbringing and associations made a rebellion unthinkable. As an extensive landholder, 'a rebellion would be the last thing [he] would wish to see'. Although there was circumstantial evidence against him through his links with Paul Bogle, Gordon swore that he knew nothing about the rebellion. The only reason he had not attended the vestry meeting was because of ill health. Gordon went on to criticize the evidence of the various witnesses and claimed he had only visited Stony Gut on one occasion; moreover, that was a sabbath evening when only religious matters would have been discussed. His correspondence with Bogle and others concerned business and political matters, but there was nothing in it which could not be seen by the court or by the public at large. Finally, he had expected that he would have been tried in Kingston if there were charges against him rather than at Morant Bay; after all, he had not been arrested in any act of rebellion or in a district under martial law.[11]

During his speech Gordon was clearly nervous and also unprepared. Speaking almost immediately after the prosecution had finished its case, Gordon delivered the statement in an often hesitant manner. The president of the court, Lieutenant Brand, noted that Gordon had sometimes come to a complete stop during his speech. Yet Gordon persisted, indicating that he wished to continue. When Gordon had concluded his statement the trial ended, and he was taken back to the cells to await the court's verdict. The trial had lasted about six hours.[12]

But there were serious irregularities in the procedure and in the evidence at the trial. For example, the court failed to obtain Dr Major's testimony to prove or disprove Gordon's allegations about his health. This was an important piece of evidence, because much hinged on Gordon's non-attendance at the vestry meeting on the day of the outbreak. When Major was questioned about the state of Gordon's health several months later, he testified how unwell Gordon had been. Major's view was that Gordon would not have lived for another twelve months. Reflecting on this point, Augustus Lake believed that the court should have allowed more time to find Dr Major. This would not have been very difficult, as Dr Major was in St Thomas in the East; indeed, he appeared at another court martial the following day.[13]

The evidence itself was also flawed. Much of the prosecution's case rested on depositions taken by people who could have been brought to Morant Bay to provide oral testimony. Since these statements were taken in Gordon's absence, they were inadmissible as evidence against him in any English court, whether civil or military. Moreover, none of the evidence was conclusive. The representative of the Jamaica Committee, John Gorrie, observed that no witness accused Gordon of being present or participating in the rebellion at Morant Bay. After a thorough review of the case, the

Jamaica Royal Commission concluded that 'the evidence, oral and documentary, appears to us to be wholly insufficient to establish the charge upon which the prisoner took his trial'.[14]

However, the court found George William Gordon guilty and sentenced him to be hanged. Brigadier-General Nelson, who approved of the sentence, saw no military reason to carry out the execution on the Sunday and delayed it until Monday morning. He sent a dispatch to General O'Connor containing the proceedings of the court who, in turn, forwarded them to Eyre. On Sunday evening at 6 p.m., the Governor wrote to Nelson concurring 'in the justice of the sentence, and the necessity of carrying it into effect'. Nelson received the letter before Gordon was executed.[15]

Gordon himself was not told of the sentence until early Monday morning. He had been kept by himself at the Morant Bay police station on Saturday night and Sunday. On Monday Bridagier-General Nelson informed Gordon of his fate. Gordon then asked to see a Wesleyan minister, but Nelson regarded this as 'inexpedient'. When Gordon requested paper to write to his wife, Nelson acceded on the grounds that the letter would be handed to him. Nelson's account of Gordon's final words to him was revealing:

> G.W. Gordon said to me, 'I am innocent, sir.' My reply was, 'It is not for me to judge, hourly communications induce me to think your words caused the riot.' He replied, 'I never intended.' 'Perhaps not, such has been,' was my response, and I left him.[16]

Gordon was executed at 7.10 a.m. on 23 October. He was hanged on the centre arch of the court house, and seventeen others were hanged below him. According to George Clarke, who witnessed it, Gordon first took off his hat and then, as he was about to be executed, his glasses. Although there is some evidence that he was manhandled at the time, it appears more likely that he was treated considerately. His body was left hanging for twenty-four hours before being brought down.[17]

Gordon's final letter to his wife proclaimed his innocence but also made it clear that he was ready to die. The document was suffused with the mixture of religious and political ideas which were the hallmark of Gordon. On the one hand, then, he believed that he did

> not deserve the sentence, for I never advised or took part in any insurrection: all I ever did was to recommend the people who complained to seek redress in a legitimate way, and if in this I erred or have been misrepresented, I don't think I deserve this extreme sentence.

At the same time, Gordon wrote that

it is the will of my Heavenly Father that I should thus suffer in obeying his command to relieve the poor and needy, and to protect, so far as I was able, the oppressed; and glory to be His name, and I thank him that I suffer in such a case.

Gordon contradicted the evidence against him and denied knowledge of Bogle's intentions. He had expected a fair trial if there were any charges against him. But it was too late and all that remained was to send greetings to his family and friends and conclude that 'may the grace of our Lord Jesus Christ be with us all'.[18]

Robert Bruce and Sidney Levien

Gordon was not the only political dissident whom Eyre regarded as responsible for the outbreak at Morant Bay. He identified two other men, Robert Bruce and Sidney Levien, as dangerous figures. Bruce was a Scotsman, a doctor and the coroner of Vere while Levien, who was Jewish, owned and edited the *County Union* newspaper in Montego Bay. Writing to the Colonial Office in November, 1865, Eyre reported that evidence had come to light during the rebellion implicating Bruce and Levien. Like Gordon, they were men of 'better position and education [who] had been engaged in misleading the negro population by inflammatory speeches or writings, telling them that they were wronged and oppressed and inciting them to seek redress'.[19]

Bruce had come to the attention of the government because of his role in helping to organize the Underhill meeting in Vere. In addition, letters from him were found among Gordon's correspondence; moreover, the custos of Vere believed that Bruce was likely to create a serious disturbance in the parish. On these grounds, Eyre had him arrested and transported from Vere to Morant Bay. Bruce spent sixty days as a prisoner and was only released because of an application for *habeas corpus*.[20]

In a petition to the government Bruce complained bitterly about his treatment. His imprisonment for two months in Morant Bay had transformed him from a healthy man to one facing the prospect of death. Writing to the missionary, James Reid, Bruce reaffirmed his innocence and lack of complicity in the outbreak at Morant Bay. Had it not been for Sidney Levien, Bruce maintained that he would have starved in prison. Unlike Levien, all of Bruce's cash was taken from him when he was arrested, and the daily diet provided in gaol consisted of a loaf of bread worth 3d.[21]

Levien was a more prominent figure in the island. However, his arrest was as sudden as that of Bruce's. According to Eyre, Levien was seized because of a letter he had written to Bruce after the Vere Underhill meeting.

In the letter, Levien had described his editorials seeking to shield Bruce from the charges of 'anarchy and tumult' which would follow the meeting in Vere. For Eyre the letter was proof that there was 'a combination between him and Dr Bruce and others to stir up the people, with the full knowledge of what the result would be'.[22]

Since Levien was not arrested until 1 November, well after the rebellion had been suppressed, it is equally plausible that Eyre was intent on silencing one of his harshest critics. Levien's editorial on 17 October, just after he had learned about the rebellion at Morant Bay, was evidence of his strong feelings about Eyre. Effectively, he blamed the Governor for the outbreak. Levien recalled repeatedly warning Eyre of the consequences of raising taxes and ignoring the views of the people.

> But when the Governor and his advisers take upon themselves to make their will the law of the land, and that law is cruelly obnoxious to the people – when the Governor and his advisers run riot in their abandonment of practice and propriety – the lower classes become equally callous on their part and riotous in their way. A Government that sows the wind must expect to reap the whirlwind.

Levien also attacked the Governor personally, writing that 'more is needed from [Eyre] than the mere rearing of chickens at Flamstead [his country retreat], or studying economy over his one barrel of potatoes . . . ' Reflecting on that editorial four months later, Levien saw no reason to change his opinion.[23]

Levien was arrested by about thirty marines who came to his home at Montego Bay. Refused permission to see his children, he was marched under gunpoint to a waiting ship for transfer to Morant Bay.[24] From 2 November until 7 December, he was kept a prisoner at Morant Bay, without access to the outside world. Although martial law ended on 13 November, Levien remained a prisoner. As he described his incarceration:

> The personal indignities to which I was subjected – the mental agony I endured surrounded as I was by death in public executions without number – the sufferings of my family in ignorance of my fate during the frightful period – I am unable to portray. The horror of my situation intensified by a recurring daily fever may be imagined – it cannot be realised on paper.[25]

Levien was bitter about his arrest and imprisonment. He maintained that he had been apprehended because of his attacks against Eyre rather than for any substantive reasons. As Levien pointed out, no charge was ever brought against him while he was a prisoner; when he went to Spanish Town to appear before the chief justice under a writ of *habeas corpus*, he was released without bail. For Levien, his letter to Bruce, which was the apparent cause of his arrest, 'was such as any gentleman would write to another, finding his friend unjustly accused'. He wanted that letter made public.[26]

Levien and Robert Bruce were both arrested on the orders of Governor Eyre. The two men were kept in gaol at Morant Bay long after the expiration of martial law. But their ordeal was not over when they were released from gaol. Governor Eyre instituted legal proceedings against Levien and Bruce, who were then arrested and charged before a court of special commission. Bruce was accused of conspiring with George William Gordon, Paul Bogle and others to foment rebellion while Levien faced an additional charge of seditious libel. Although the two men were acquitted of conspiracy, Levien was found guilty of seditious libel for his remarks in the *County Union* on 17 October. He was sentenced to prison for twelve months.[27]

Further dissidents

Gordon, Bruce and Levien were the principal thorns in the side of the government, but there was also a larger group of dissidents, most of whom were black or brown. Governor Eyre and the members of the executive committee believed that these men were inciting the black population of the island. Although less prominent than Gordon, many of them were involved in the Underhill meetings which took place in the spring and summer of 1865. Some were members of the Underhill Convention, which formed a vocal part of the opposition to the Eyre administration.

Among this group was William Kelly Smith, a black politician from Kingston. Smith had been prominent in the Underhill meetings in Kingston and Spanish Town; moreover, he was editor of *The Watchman*, a newspaper once owned by George William Gordon and one of the most radical in the colony. On 18 October, a week after the outbreak of the rebellion, the inspector of police closed the offices of the newspaper. Early the next morning he arrested Smith who was brought to Up Park Camp, a military base in St Andrew under martial law.[28] Two days later Smith, along with about fourteen other prisoners, was taken under heavy military escort to the wharf and eventually onto the *Aboukir* in Port Royal harbour. There, Smith and the others were placed in irons.[29]

On 2 November, Smith and some of the other political prisoners were transferred to the *Cordelia* and taken to Morant Bay. There they were the object of considerable abuse. For example, as they were being marched by soldiers to the police station, the prisoners asked what had become of the thirty-five men transferred earlier from Up Park Camp to Morant Bay on the

Cordelia. The soldiers assured them that those prisoners had already been hanged and that 'we should go off shortly afterwards'. Smith witnessed the hangings and the flogging which lasted for the next eight days; after the end of martial law he was transferred to the Morant Bay district prison and then released on a writ of *habeas corpus*.[30]

Two other black politicians, Emanuel Joseph Goldson and Samuel Clarke, were also arrested about the same time. Both had taken an active part in the Underhill meetings. Goldson was a former sergeant in the police force while Clarke was a carpenter and a vestrymen from St David. The two men were imprisoned with William Kelly Smith on the *Aboukir* and subsequently on the *Cordelia*. Apart from the usual insults from the soldiers and sailors, Goldson reported the behaviour of the Provost-Marshal, Gordon Ramsay, once they reached Morant Bay. After Goldson had given his name to Ramsay, Ramsay went away and then turned back, saying, 'What are you looking at? Take him out and give him a dozen.' But Ramsay was apparently not satisfied. When Goldson had put on his clothes, Ramsay asked, 'Isn't this Goldson, the late sergeant of police?' When this was confirmed, Ramsay said, 'The d– –d electioneering brute, set him down in the book to be flogged for insubordination.' After a few days at Morant Bay Goldson became ill with fever and vomiting and remained so until he was released on *habeas corpus* on 26 December.[31]

Samuel Clarke was not so fortunate. The custos of St David, William Georges, regarded Clarke as a political opponent and one who sided with the people against the parochial authorities. According to Georges, Clarke sometimes acted as a 'lawyer' on behalf of the people, especially in the petty courts. Clarke also grew some cane and was a carpenter. The differences between Georges and Clarke had widened considerably after the publication of the Underhill letter. Clarke had helped to organize the Underhill meeting in St David and took part in the meeting at St Thomas in the East. He had also severely criticized 'The Queen's Advice', maintaining that neither the Queen nor the Secretary of State for the Colonial Office, Edward Cardwell, knew anything about it. Once at Morant Bay, Clarke was singled out by Georges and then tried by a drum head court martial. He was found guilty and hanged.[32]

At his trial it emerged that Clarke had given himself up, once he knew that he was wanted by the authorities. Speaking in his own defence, Clarke added: 'I have always been a loyal subject, and when this contention arose I was in St David's, and I declared I would use my endeavours and do all I could.' As Charles Buxton commented in a debate in the House of Commons, 'there was not so much as the faintest hint of his having been connected in any way with the recent riots, and yet . . . he was sentenced to be hanged for words used months before.'[33]

Samuel Clarke's brother, George Clarke, narrowly escaped hanging. A member of the vestry in St Thomas in the East, Clarke was the son-in-law of Paul Bogle. He was a carpenter and also had land at Spring Garden, about a mile from Stony Gut. Appearing before the Royal Commission, Clarke testified that he had quarrelled with Bogle and therefore left Stony Gut.[34]

On 7 October, the day when there was a scuffle at the Morant Bay court house, Clarke was in Morant Bay but took no part in the proceedings. Moreover, he openly stated that the people had been wrong in attacking the police. He was not involved in the rebellion, but when it broke out four days later, Clarke believed that he was in danger from the rebels and fled to St David for protection. Clarke subsequently volunteered to provide the authorities with information about the people who had marched to Morant Bay; instead, he was arrested and brought to Morant Bay.[35]

Once at Morant Bay, Clarke had to face the wrath of Ramsay, who had little doubt about Clarke's fate. Ramsay told him, ' "You are Mr George B. Clarke that the justice gives such a good character of," or "who has such a good character." I said, "Yes, sir." Then he said, "Oh, you will be hung." ' Clarke eventually faced a court martial, but there were insufficient witnesses against him and his case was put off. When Clarke sought Ramsay's help in producing witnesses, Ramsay threatened to shoot him. Later, Ramsay had Clarke whipped because he was talking to a constable who could testify on his behalf.[36]

Clarke remained in prison until martial law was over. He was treated like the other prisoners: he had to clean out the toilets, sweep the streets and dig graves for those who were hanged. When he was finally discharged, Ramsay ordered him not to appear in any vestry, public meeting or even Morant Bay. Although not found guilty of any wrongdoing, Clarke was prevented from any future political activity.[37]

In reviewing the cases of the political prisoners, Brigadier-General Nelson concluded on 4 November that they should not be brought before a court martial. In Nelson's view, Smith, Goldson, Levien, Bruce and others may have uttered seditious sentiments prior to the rebellion; however, this was not sufficient grounds for them to face a military court. Moreover, there was no evidence of actual involvement or complicity in the outbreak. General O'Connor agreed, and Eyre believed that Nelson had acted wisely in coming to this conclusion. However, this decision came too late for Samuel Clarke.[38]

The authorities were not just concerned about the activities of a group of black activists; they were also alarmed by the politics of several non-white ministers. There were three men in particular whom the government arrested along with the other political prisoners: Rev. James Roach, Rev. James Crole, and Rev. Edwin Palmer. Roach was a black Barbadian and an independent Wesleyan who had lived in Jamaica since the 1840s. Crole was a Native Baptist parson attached to George William Gordon's Tabernacle in

Kingston, and Palmer was a black Baptist pastor connected to the Baptist Union.[39] All three were linked to the other political prisoners because of their involvement in the Underhill meetings, and they suffered much the same treatment. Perhaps because of his connections with the Baptist Union and the British Baptist church, Palmer's case received the most attention.

Palmer was arrested on 20 October and taken to Up Park Camp where his hair was cut; the following day he was put in irons on board the *Aboukir*. While on the ship he was abused and threatened. For example, one of the officers asked him, 'What are you?' Palmer responded that he was a Baptist. The officer said, 'Then because you are a Baptist I will hang you for that.' On board the *Aboukir*, Palmer developed a fever but the doctor who attended him suggested that the best medicine for Palmer would be 'about 18 inches of rope'.[40] With the other political prisoners, Palmer was taken to Morant Bay on board the *Cordelia*. When he arrived there on 2 November he was 'instantly marched by a company of marines to the police station, and on my way thither, amidst the taunts and jeers of the marines, was shown the gallows, ropes, etc. all prepared for my execution at seven o'clock the following morning'.[41]

While in prison, Palmer was forced to witness the daily flogging and executions, scenes which he later characterized as beyond all description. His treatment at the police station was savage:

> For twelve days I was at the police-station, lying on the bare floor, and fed like a pig, unable to speak a word to my fellow-prisoners, policemen guarding with loaded guns and fixed bayonets night and day, and daily did I look for my execution, although wholly innocent of having done anything constitutionally wrong against the Government of her gracious Majesty the Queen.

During this time Palmer was never charged with any offence. At the end of martial law he was transferred to the Morant Bay district prison, where he was very sick. Palmer believed that if he had not been released on a writ of *habeas corpus* he would have died. As he wrote later, he left prison severely ill, having suffered from 'fever, ague, vomiting, spitting of blood, dysentery – in short, everything that bad air, bad food, bad water, and bad treatment are calculated to produce on a frame not very robust . . . .'[42]

Like some of the other political prisoners, his ordeal was not yet over. He was brought before the court of special commission charged with using seditious words at the Underhill meeting held in Kingston, found guilty and sentenced to two months' imprisonment. Along with a group including Levien, Bruce, Smith, Goldson, Roach and Crole, he was found not guilty of conspiracy. Two other men, Thomas Harry, a shoemaker and Isaac Vaz, the proprietor of *The Watchman*, were also tried unsuccessfully on this charge.[43]

For the authorities these were clearly the most important political prisoners in the colony. But there were many others who were also arrested. Some of them had spoken at Underhill meetings in various parts of the island. For example, Alexander Phillips was black and, in his own terms, a gentleman. He had been secretary of the Underhill meeting in Vere and had previously been connected to *The Watchman*. Brought to Morant Bay, he was ordered to receive 100 lashes. As Phillips knelt over to receive them, the officer forced him to say

> 'God Bless the Queen!' I did so; he said, say 'D– –n every black man,' and I said so; he said, 'Rise now, and take up your clothes, and take your pass and go away; and I hope that after this you will never interfere with politics. You ought to be thankful to the Queen; if it were not for the Queen you would have been hung this day.'[44]

Any connection with George William Gordon aroused suspicion. William Foster March, a coloured reporter, also worked as a clerk for Gordon preparing bills for the Assembly. When he was arrested in Kingston, the inspector of police informed him that 'the mere fact of my having been employed by Mr Gordon was sufficient to justify the government in having me arrested'. March was among the prisoners, brought to Morant Bay on the *Cordelia*. He was discharged on 14 November, the day after the expiration of martial law. Like many other prisoners, he was very ill at Morant Bay with fever and dysentery and was still unwell four months later.[45]

Others were arrested on equally flimsy grounds. Maximillian Benuzzi, an Italian who taught languages and drawing in Kingston, was detained by the authorities on the basis of a report by a Catholic priest. The priest claimed that Benuzzi was 'uttering speeches and sentiments calculated to excite the discontented portion of the community'; however, the allegation turned out to be false. None the less, Benuzzi spent thirty-five days at Up Park Camp and was treated as a condemned prisoner. In another case, a coloured Native Baptist minister, Rev. George Truman, was travelling to one of his congregations in St Andrew on 21 October when he was seized by a planter and brought first to a police station and then to Up Park Camp. When one of the officers at the camp identified him as a Baptist parson, he said, 'You are very dangerous people and you will be hung.' Truman was held overnight, but was released when his wife interceded and obtained a letter from the custos of Kingston, Lewis Q. Bowerbank, authorizing Truman's discharge.[46]

Similarly, a black American independent minister living in St David, Rev. John Menard, was arrested without warrant in Kingston. The clerk of the peace in St Andrew, H.J. Kemble, described Menard as president of a debating society in St David, a highly intelligent person and potentially 'very mischievous'. Menard believed in a form of black separatism; he apparently had a 'deep hatred to the ruling class' of the United States. Brought to Morant Bay, he was subsequently deported from the colony. When the United States consul examined the case, he could 'find nothing to justify even a suspicion of his having taken any part in any conspiracy against the authorities of the Island'. By March, 1866, Menard was employed as a clerk in New Orleans, but his wife and new-born child were still in Jamaica in destitute circumstances.[47]

Among the most bizarre of the arrests was that of a group of Haitian exiles living in Kingston. They included the ex-emperor Soulouque as well as others who were involved in an attempt to overthrow the government of Haiti. One of the Haitians, General Lamothe, had chartered a schooner, the *Oracle*, to convey supplies for the insurgents in Haiti. The ship foundered off the Portland coast and had landed in Port Antonio for provisions and water on 24 October. As this was during the height of the rebellion and the ship contained a considerable amount of gunpowder, the authorities at first assumed that the ship was meant to supply the rebels in Jamaica. Lamothe and the Haitian crew were arrested.[48]

On examining General Lamothe's papers, it soon became clear that the Haitians were not involved in the Morant Bay rebellion. None the less, Eyre decided to deport them and the other Haitians living in Kingston. He had learned from police reports that the Haitians had been in contact with William Kelly Smith and Emanuel Goldson. Indeed, the Haitian consul in Kingston reported that one of the Haitians, General Salomons, 'is a person likely to avail himself of the services of any disaffected persons out here to forward his own views . . . .'[49]

Accordingly, on 8 November, Eyre ordered the Haitians to leave Jamaica on the grounds that they had abused the hospitality of the British government. Justifying this decision, Eyre noted that, however the Haitians may have felt about the rebellion in Jamaica, 'several of the chief agitators and stirrers up of sedition in Kingston were in frequent and apparently confidential communication with the Haytiens and that G.W. Gordon himself held up the example of Hayti as one which the Jamaicans ought to imitate.' The Jamaican government also ordered a German, Noel Crosswell, who had been living in Jamaica for thirty years to be deported. It was his ship which the Haitians had chartered.[50]

Eyre and Crown Colony government

The political repression in the aftermath of the rebellion was not solely directed at individuals. Governor Eyre had a wider agenda as well. Since he had come to Jamaica, Eyre had held the view that the House of Assembly was helping to ruin Jamaica and that it should be abolished. The Colonial Office shared this attitude; in July, 1865, the head of the West India section, Henry Taylor, wrote a minute welcoming any changes along this line. Taylor believed that, 'if the majority of the Assembly could be induced to pass enactments in amendment of its own constitution, HM's government would be ready to give those enactments its most attentive and favourable consideration.'[51]

The Morant Bay rebellion provided Eyre with the opportunity he was looking for. Writing privately on 23 October to the Secretary of State for the Colonies, Edward Cardwell, Eyre indicated that members of the House would now be prepared to support the government in whatever measures seemed necessary. He believed that

> there is nothing like striking whilst the iron is hot or if we are to get a change of constitution thro' the medium of the Assembly itself, now is the time to do it when everybody is in a state of the greatest alarm and apprehension and looking to the Gover[i] for everything.[52]

The Governor's strategy, elaborated in a dispatch the following day, was to encourage members of the House to create a unicameral chamber, with half of the members to be nominated and the other half elected. When he finally addressed members of the House, he suggested a wholly nominated legislature. There was opposition to this plan: the planters wanted to retain an elected element in the legislature, although with a high franchise requirement. As this would have effectively excluded most of the black and coloured population from the vote, a small group of coloured and Jewish representatives in the House argued against any change in the system. However, the majority of Assemblymen favoured a unicameral legislature and, in the end, they accepted a proposal from the Colonial Office indicating that the Crown was prepared to take full responsibility for the colony. This meant Crown Colony government with a nominated Council, consisting of six officials and three unofficial members and the abolition of the two hundred-year-old House of Assembly.[53]

Eyre was also prepared to take less drastic but none the less highly repressive steps in the wake of the rebellion. Concerned about Underhill's letter and also about the Baptist missionaries in the island, the Governor and his executive committee authorized the interception of mail to some of these missionaries. Eyre quoted a passage from one of the letters: in it, Underhill wrote that 'in Jamaica, the people seem to be overwhelmed with discouragement and I fear that they are giving up in despair their long struggle with injustice and fraud'. For Eyre this was encouragement to the people of Jamaica to demonstrate disaffection and disloyalty. The Governor maintained that if nothing can be done to stop at home the pernicious writing such as I refer to, and if Ja is to be retained at all, it will be necessary to pass a law in the Colony authorising the deportation of all persons who leaving their proper sphere of action as Ministers of Religion become political demagogues and dangerous agitators.[54]

The reaction in Jamaica to the intended legislation was hostile, especially among the missionaries. John Mearns of the Methodist Missionary Society regarded it as 'a disgrace to any Christian legislature' and, even in an amended form, 'only equalled in tyranny by the laws enacted in Ja. before the abolition of slavery'. It was strongly opposed by local missionaries as well as the home societies and was eventually withdrawn. None the less, the bill suggested the tenor of the times and mindset of Eyre and his government.[55]

In the wake of the rebellion and of the military and political suppression, then, people were frightened for their lives. One Methodist missionary writing home from St Thomas in the East two days before Christmas, 1865 warned that his letter must not be made public. Although his statements were made 'in moderation and admit of no refutation, [they] might in the present state of this Country lead to the arrest and imprisonment of your Missionary . . . .' A barrister and future member of the Legislative Council, Samuel Constantine Burke, hoped 'never to see such a state of feeling again'. First there had been the fears about the size of the rebellion and then about the nature of the repression. He had himself been repeatedly told that he would be arrested.[56]

The political repression was clearly substantial. It resulted in the arbitrary arrest and imprisonment of the leading opponents of the government and the death of several of them. The government was able to destroy the opposition and to frustrate black political activism in the island. Moreover, the constitutional change from a representative system to Crown Colony government had a similar effect: it blocked the development of black and brown politics in Jamaica. The political and constitutional consequences of the rebellion would therefore last well into the twentieth century.

Notes

1   PRO 30/48/44, Cardwell Papers, 'Jamaica' by Lewis Q. Bowerbank, p. 8.

2   BMS, 'Jamaica Affairs', vol. 1, p. 133, *The Daily News* (n.d.), letter to editor from Alexander Fiddes, Kingston, 16 January 1866; PRO 30/48/44, Cardwell Papers, 'Jamaica' by Lewis Q. Bowerbank, p. 9; JRC, Evidence of Captain de Horsey, p. 206.

3   PRO 30/48/44, Cardwell Papers, 'Jamaica' by Lewis Q. Bowerbank, p. 9; JRC: Evidence of William Wemyss Anderson, pp. 794–5; Evidence of Brigadier-General Nelson, p. 795. While on board the ship, Gordon wrote a long letter to his wife about the management and

liquidation of his business affairs. The letter was retained by the authorities for two months; in the meantime, Gordon's creditors seized all his property and goods. See Rev. David King, *A Sketch of the Late Mr G.W. Gordon, Jamaica* (Edinburgh: William Oliphant and Co., 1866), p. 14.

4 JRC: Evidence of Augustus Lake, p. 280; Evidence of Andrew Lewis, p. 838; Evidence of Lt Herbert Brand, p. 656.

5 Baptist Wriothesley Noel, *The Case of George William Gordon, Esq. of Jamaica* (London: James Nisbet and Co., 1866), p. 40; JRC: Evidence of Brigadier-General Nelson, p. 625; Evidence of Lt Herbert Brand, p. 661.

6 JRC, Trial of George W. Gordon, p. 1050.

7 Noel, *The Case of George William Gordon,* p. 41; JRC: Trial of George W. Gordon, p. 1051; Evidence of Augustus Lake, Trial of George William Gordon, p. 277.

8 JRC: Evidence of Augustus Lake, Trial of George William Gordon, p. 277; Trial of George W. Gordon, p. 1051.

9 JRC, Trial of George W. Gordon, p. 1052.

10 *Ibid.*; JRC, Evidence of Augustus Lake, Trial of George William Gordon, p. 277.

11 JRC, Trial of George W. Gordon, p. 1052.

12 JRC: Evidence of Lt Herbert Brand, p. 655; Trial of George W. Gordon, p. 1052; Evidence of Augustus Lake, p. 280.

13 JRC: Evidence of Dr E.W. Major, p. 27; Evidence of Augustus Lake, p. 281.

14 John Gorrie, *Illustrations of Martial Law in Jamaica. Compiled from the Report of the Royal Commissioners, and Other Blue Books Laide Before Parliament*, Jamaica Papers, no. 6 (London: Jamaica Committee, 1867), p. 46; Report, pp. 36–7.

15 *Ibid.*, p. 37.

16 JRC, Nelson to Eyre, 23 Oct 1865, p. 621.

17 *Ibid.*; JRC: Evidence of George Clarke, p. 129; Evidence of Gordon Ramsay, p. 636; Evidence of Augustus Lake, p. 282.

18 JRC, Evidence of Mrs Maria J. Gordon, pp. 722–3.

19 CO 137/395, Eyre to Cardwell, 20 November 1865, no. 291.

20 JRC: Evidence of Edward Eyre, p. 90; Evidence of Dr Robert Bruce, p. 303.

21 BMS, 'Jamaica Affairs', vol. 1, p. 135, The Arrest of Dr Bruce; CO 137/427, Grant to Duke of Buckingham, 9 October 1867, no. 200, enclosure: Levien to Irving, 7 October 1867.

22 JRC, Evidence of Edward Eyre, p. 89.

23 JRC, Evidence of Sidney Levien, p. 199–200: *County Union*, 17 October 1865; *Ibid.*, p. 200.

24 *Ibid.*, p. 198.

25 CO 137/427, Grant to Duke of Buckingham, 9 October 1867, no. 200, enclosure: Levien to Irving, 7 October 1867.

26 *Ibid.*; JRC, Evidence of Sidney Levien, p. 198.

27 CO 137/403, Storks to Cardwell, 24 March 1866, no. 73, Enclosure: Return of Convictions, Acquittals, etc. of Persons tried under the Special Commission of Oyer and Terminer at Kingston, between 24 January and 9 March 1866. Sir John Peter Grant, the Governor of Jamaica, ordered Levien to be released from prison early, in August, 1865; see CO 137/407, Grant to Carnarvon, 6 September 1866, no. 6; *The Colonial Standard and Jamaica Despatch*, 25 August 1866.

28 The Provost-Marshal of Up Park Camp, Major J.H. Prenderville, dealt with 200 prisoners at the base during martial law. Most of the prisoners were sent on to Morant Bay for trial, flogged or released, but three were executed. See JRC, Evidence of Major J.H. Prenderville, p. 818.

29 JRC, Evidence of William Kelly Smith, p. 195.

30   *Ibid.*, pp. 195–6.

31   JRC, Evidence of Emanuel Joseph Goldson, pp. 309–11.

32   JRC: Evidence of William Payne Georges, pp. 891–3; Evidence of William Kelly Smith, p. 196; Appendix, Official Proceedings of Courts Martial: Case of Samuel Clarke, p. 1149.

33   JRC, Appendix, Official Proceedings of Courts Martial: Case of Samuel Clarke, p. 1149; Gorrie, *Illustrations of Martial Law*, p. 67; BMS, 'Jamaica Affairs', vol. 2, p. 8, Clipping from *Daily News*, 1 August 1866, Report of the House of Commons.

34   JRC, Evidence of George Clarke, pp. 124, 131.

35   *Ibid.*, pp. 125–7.

36   *Ibid.*, pp. 127–9.

37   *Ibid.*, p. 130.

38   CO 137/394, Eyre to Cardwell, 8 November 1865, no. 275: Nelson to O'Connor, 4 November; Eyre to O'Connor, 6 November.

39   Swithin Wilmot, 'From Falmouth to Morant Bay: Religion and Politics in Jamaica, 1838–1865', Paper presented at the Association of Caribbean Historians' Conference, Havana, April, 1985, pp. 7, 13–14.

40   JRC, Evidence of Rev. Edwin Palmer, p. 304.

41   CO 137/409, no. 7, 'A Narrative of the Arrest and Imprisonment of the Rev. E. Palmer'.

42   *Ibid.*

43   CO 137/403, Storks to Cardwell, 24 March 1866, no. 73, Enclosure: Return of Convictions, Acquittals, etc. of Persons tried under the Special Commission of Oyer and Terminer at Kingston, between 24 January and 9 March 1866. But Harry and Crole were convicted of uttering seditious language and sentenced to six weeks' imprisonment. Goldson was found guilty of the same offence and imprisoned for twenty days; see *The Colonial Standard and Jamaica Despatch*: 17 February 1866, 24 February 1866. In addition, twenty-nine people were found guilty of felonious riot at these trials and sentenced to periods of imprisonment ranging from life to two years; see JRC, Evidence of William March, p. 856.

44   JRC, Evidence of Alexander Phillips, p. 346.

45   JRC, Evidence of William Foster March, p. 890. See also March's application for an appointment in the public service: CO 137/408, Grant to Carnarvon, 21 November 1866, no. 45, Enclosure: W. Foster March to Grant, 8 November 1866.

46   CO 137/425, Grant to Duke of Buckingham, 4 July 1867, no. 116: Enclosures, Bowerbank to Irving, 17 July 1867 and Nairne to Bowerbank, 12 November 1867; JRC: Evidence of Maximillian Benuzzi, p. 929; Evidence of Rev. George Truman, p. 415.

47   CO 137/424, Grant to Buckingham, 23 May 1867, no 97, Enclosure: Kemble to Myers, 2 November 1865; US Consular Reports T31, vol. 22, Gregg to Seward, 1 March 1866, no. 18.

48   CO 137/394, Eyre to Cardwell, 8 November, 1865, no. 273, Luke to Nelson, 24 October.

49   *Ibid.*, Bowerbank to Jordon, 30 Sept 65.

50   CO 137/399, Storks to Cardwell, 20 February 1866, no. 32, memorandum from Eyre, 12 February; CO 137/394, Eyre to Cardwell, 8 November, 1865, no. 273, minute by the executive committee, n.d. In May, 1866, Sir Henry Storks granted Crosswell permission to return to Jamaica; see CO 137/404, Storks to Cardwell, 2 May 1866, no. 102.

51   PRO 30/48/44, Cardwell Papers, 'Jamaica' by Lewis Q. Bowerbank; CO 137/391, Eyre to Cardwell, 6 June 1865, no. 137, Taylor's minute.

52   PRO 30/48/42, Cardwell Papers, Eyre to Cardwell, private and confidential, 23 October 1865.

53   CO 137/393, Eyre to Cardwell, 24 October 1865, confidential; Gad J. Heuman, *Between Black and White: Race, Politics, and the Free Coloreds in Jamaica, 1792–1865* (Westport, Conn.: Greenwood Press, 1981), p. 191–3.

54 CO 137/393, Eyre to Cardwell, 23 October 1865, no. 253.

55 MMS 199: Letter of J. Mearns, 23 December 1865; Edmondson to the Gen. Sec., November, 1865.

56 *Ibid.*, Murray to Hoole, 23 December 1865; JRC, Evidence of Samuel Constantine Burke, p. 1021.

CHAPTER 11 | The aftermath

The Royal Commission and Eyre's removal from office

News of the rebellion reached London ahead of Governor Eyre's report of the events at Morant Bay. Jamaican newspapers as well as passengers on an earlier ship had already publicized the rebellion, and the British press had reprinted some of the stories emanating from Jamaica. When Eyre's dispatch arrived on 16 November, the reaction in the Colonial Office was one of relief that the insurrection had been suppressed. However, there was also concern about the manner in which the rebellion had been put down.[1]

The Colonial Secretary, Edward Cardwell, congratulated Eyre on his 'spirit, energy and judgment' and on the 'effectual measures for the suppression of this horrible rebellion'. At the same time Cardwell wrote privately to the Governor pointing out that he had thus far only seen extracts of the military reports accompanying Eyre's dispatch. Yet Cardwell was very clear that these were not sufficient: more information would be needed to justify the military actions which had been taken. In the meantime, Cardwell intended to publish Eyre's dispatches to counteract some of the negative reports in the British press.[2]

Almost immediately Cardwell came under pressure to withhold support for the actions of the authorities in Jamaica. Louis Chamerovzow, the secretary of the British and Foreign Anti-Slavery Society, wrote to Cardwell suggesting that the committee had information about the events at Morant Bay which justified this caution. In the next few weeks the tone of Cardwell's letters to Eyre became more questioning. Writing privately to the Governor on 23 November, Cardwell raised the issue of George William Gordon. Cardwell was very concerned about Gordon's arrest in Kingston and subsequent transfer to an area under martial law. As Colonial Secretary, he expected questions on this matter and needed satisfactory answers.[3]

A week later Cardwell again expressed his uneasiness to Eyre about the situation. Cardwell had expected that martial law would have ceased much earlier, and he continued to express doubt about removing an individual from civil jurisdiction to try him by a military court. Cardwell recognized that Eyre and the authorities had acted because of a belief in a 'systematic conspiracy', but there was 'no proof yet given to us that the conspiracy itself exists. On the contrary, it appears that there has been no resistance in any case even to the smallest bodies of troops. . . .'[4]

Cardwell was coming under increasing pressure from individuals and groups calling for Eyre's removal from office. One of the delegations which called at the Colonial Office in early December consisted of 250 members of the British and Foreign Anti-Slavery Society. When Charles Buxton, an MP and the son of the abolitionist Thomas Fowell Buxton, asked Cardwell during the meeting to suspend Eyre immediately, a member of the delegation shouted, 'Yes, by the neck'. Other petitions were less graphic but also very pointed. For example, a memorial from the citizens of Canterbury argued that Eyre 'judged by his own Official reports. . . is totally unfit for the discharge of the duties entrusted to him by the British government'. Like the members of the Anti-Slavery Society, the citizens of Canterbury wanted Eyre removed from office.[5]

Sentiment against Eyre was strong enough to lead to the formation of the Jamaica Committee. This consisted of defenders of the West Indian blacks, representatives of the dissenting churches associated with Exeter Hall, and parliamentary radicals. The chairman of the committee was Charles Buxton, and among its more well known members was John Stuart Mill, the economist and philosopher and recently elected MP for Westminster. Another prominent supporter was John Bright, the Reform leader in the House of Commons and formerly an opponent of the Corn Laws and of the Crimean War. In addition, there were seventeen other members of Parliament on the committee. Summarizing the character of the committee, Bernard Semmel described its members as 'radical in politics, non-conformist in religion, men whose ties were to middle-class business enterprise, rather than to the land; professors, journalists, political economists, non-conformist ministers'. This committee would become significant in the attempt to try Governor Eyre for his part in the suppression of the rebellion.[6]

By December it was becoming clear to the Colonial Office that an inquiry into the events at Morant Bay would prove necessary. Friends as well as opponents of Governor Eyre were concluding the same. For example, a group of missionaries working in Jamaica whom Eyre regarded as hostile believed that a commission of inquiry was essential. Although the missionaries were unsure about the nature of the suppression, they believed that 'in order that the truth may be discovered, and that, for the satisfaction of the public mind and the safety of the public interests, the causes and consequences of the outbreak may be duly and accurately ascertained.' The best means of accomplishing this was through an 'impartial investigation, by a special Commission from England. . . .' In England, Eyre's supporters also agreed that such an investigation was needed, although their aim was to counter the increasing invective directed against Eyre, especially in the British press.[7]

When Cardwell informed Eyre of the decision to proceed with a commission of inquiry, the Colonial Secretary pointed out that the government was not prejudging the result. As Cardwell explained, it was necessary to relieve Eyre of his authority temporarily while the commission was in progress. The government believed that Eyre should not be 'responsible for the safety of the colony, and at the same time subject to an Inquiry by independent persons into acts done in repression of the recent outbreak'. Accordingly, the government appointed Sir Henry Storks, the Governor and commander of the forces in Malta, to preside as Governor of Jamaica during the investigation. Storks was also to lead the commission of inquiry as well as head the forces in Jamaica during his stay in the colony.[8]

Eyre appears to have been surprised by this development but continued to believe in the rectitude of his own actions. When he received the dispatch informing him of Storks' appointment, Eyre reportedly told his wife, ' "Would you believe it, Ada! they have suspended me – actually suspended me. But never mind, darling, I have done my duty," and he said no more that day on the subject.'[9]

Storks arrived in early January. Apart from the Royal Commission, one of his earliest problems was the large number of prisoners who had been sentenced to gaol during the period of martial law. There were over 100 men and women, serving terms ranging from six months to twelve years. Storks doubted the legality of these sentences and also his powers to keep the prisoners in gaol after martial law had ceased. One remedy was to make use of the Governor's prerogative of pardon.

> But such a course would have confirmed the reports in circulation amongst the Negroes as to the general disapproval of Mr Eyre's acts, and as to the instructions, it was said, I had received to espouse the cause of the Negro.

In the end, Storks moved writs of *habeas corpus* before the Chief Justice; these were granted, and Storks confirmed that the prisoners would be discharged gradually.[10]

But Storks' principal concern was the Royal Commission. Although he reported that the establishment of the Commission had been well received in the island, he did note that there were problems. In Storks' view the Commission 'will make [the blacks] stubborn and impress them with the opinion, that they have been badly treated'. This observation was reinforced by a magistrate in St George, Edward Skyers, who recalled the rumours which were circulating in the parish after the appointment of the Royal Commission. According to Skyers, blacks believed Eyre would be hanged and that 'a new Governor had come out with new laws from the Queen to give them rent free land and land free'. Similarly, the Rev. George R. Brain confirmed that many blacks believed that the Queen had sent for Storks to bring Eyre to trial; Brain concluded that 'their feeling towards His Excellency [Eyre] and the Executive [was one of] ineffable contempt'. As a result of these reports, Storks issued a statement which was designed to calm the situation.[11]

But the Commission continued to have an unsettling effect for many blacks in the island. Planters from at least two parishes reported problems with labour because of the hearings. For example, a planter in St Andrew, A. Miles, complained at the end of February that 'up to this last fortnight, in consequence of this Commission coming out, the people had retired from labour almost entirely'. For Miles it was not simply a problem of labour; the people also refused to pay any rent for their land since they believed that the Queen had said they were to live rent-free. A planter in St Thomas in the East, Plato Elphick, had similar problems. He observed that since the arrival of the Commission, his workers 'seem to be expecting some great thing, and they had struck work with me some two or three times'.[12]

The Royal Commission held its first meeting on 20 January. In addition to the president of the Commission, Sir Henry Storks, there were two other members, the Recorder for Leeds, J.B. Maule and the Recorder of the City of London, Russell Gurney. Storks outlined the aims of the Commission at the outset of the proceedings:

> The royal commissioners, in obedience to Her Majesty's commands, are anxious to obtain the fullest information touching the origin, nature, and circumstances of the late disturbances, and the means adopted in the course of their suppression. With this view they will summon such witnesses as appear to them likely to afford information on these points and they will be glad to receive information from others as to any person who will be able to throw light upon these transactions.[13]

The Commission generally met in Spanish Town, although there were also sittings in St Thomas in the East. In all, 730 witnesses appeared before the Commission over a period of fifty-one days. Witnesses included senior members of the government, such as Eyre and members of his executive committee as well as black peasants whose creole sometimes had to be translated for the commissioners.[14]

Inevitably, the commissioners found themselves confronting people whose language or culture they did not understand. In their examination of Thomas McFarlane, for example, who was a black labourer, the commissioners had difficulty ascertaining McFarlane's occupation:

> 42,279.   Do you live at Coley? – Yes.
> 42,280.   What are you; what do you do when you are at home?
> – I don't do nothing.

42.281. How do you get your clothes; how do you live? – I don't do nothing.

42,282. Do you live on air, and do nothing? – Yes.

42,283. Have you got a father or mother alive? – Yes; father dead, only a mother.

42,284. Does she keep you? – Yes.

42,285. What is your age; how old are you? – That I can't tell.

42,286. You haven't the slightest idea how long you have been alive? – No.

42,287. Don't you work in the fields? – Yes; I work in the fields.[15]

But it was not only linguistic or cultural misconceptions which confronted the commissioners. They sometimes had to deal with awkward witnesses.

One of them was Major-General Forbes Jackson, a former officer in the East India Company who had retired to Jamaica. As a magistrate living in the north-east of St Thomas in the East, he had accompanied the first detachment of troops which had arrived from Newcastle. During his testimony, Jackson had to be rebuked on several occasions by the commissioners 'for the intemperance of his language'. At one point in his examination, Jackson angrily declared to one of the commissioners, Russell Gurney, 'Don't threaten me, I will answer the question in my own way, or I will leave the court.' Asked to restrain himself, he none the less attacked Gurney, suggesting that the commissioner knew nothing about the matter under investigation since he was a 'mere drawing-room man'.[16]

Jackson proved to be a difficult witness, but others could not deal with some of the Commission's persistent questioning. This was particularly the case over the court martial of George William Gordon. One of the most important witnesses who appeared before the Commission was the president of the court martial, Lt Herbert Brand. Brand was unable to explain some of his lapses to the Commission. For instance, the commissioners asked him whether he thought it necessary to examine three witnesses who could attest to George William Gordon's state of health. This was significant since Gordon's ill-health might explain why he did not attend the meeting of the vestry on 11 October:

32,560 . . . after the prisoner made that statement [about the witnesses] did not you consider it necessary to examine those three persons? – Of course we did not, or we should have examined them.

32,561. After the prisoner made that statement did you make any inquiry as to any of those parties, whether they could be obtained? – That I cannot say.[17]

Earlier in the questioning Brand had denied that Gordon had asked his doctor, Dr Major, to appear on his behalf. Yet the Provost-Marshall, Gordon Ramsay, flatly contradicted Brand's statement. Ramsay indicated that he had searched for Dr Major, after Gordon had made the request. By careful questioning, then, the commissioners were able to undermine much of Brand's testimony and, consequently, the conduct of the court martial itself. But the commissioners were not alone in their scrutiny of the evidence: the Jamaica Committee had two representatives at the Commission who also had an impact on the proceedings.[18]

The two barristers were John Gorrie and John Horne Payne. Both men also acted on behalf of people who had suffered under martial law. For example, Gorrie represented the widow of George William Gordon as well as 'numerous other parties who allege themselves to be sufferers by the measures used for the suppression of the disturbances. . . .' When Payne appeared before the Commission on 27 January, he declared that he was acting on behalf of more than 100 people, many of whom were relatives of those alleged to have been shot without trial during martial law. The two barristers were not allowed to cross-examine witnesses, but could ask 'questions which would test the evidence or throw light on the occurrences'. This was also the case for barristers who were present to defend the government or to represent the interests of Edward Underhill and the Baptist missionaries.[19]

Gorrie worked especially hard to weaken testimony implicating George William Gordon in the rebellion. For example, during the examination of Lt Brand, Gorrie asked him several questions specifically about a document addressed 'To the poor people of St Ann' and alleged to have been written by Gordon.

> 32,541.   What steps were taken either by the prosecutor or by you, as President of the Court martial, which led you to believe it [the document] was issued by Mr Gordon? – I forget now what led us to believe it. I forget now what led us to any of our conclusions, it is so long ago.
> . . . 32,544.   I wish to know what led you to the belief that the printed document was issued by Gordon. – I do not know that I ever had that belief.
> 32,545.   I wish to know whether you had or not? – That I cannot remember.[20]

Gorrie also questioned Brand about the guilt of Samuel Clarke, who was hanged after a court martial headed by Brand. As in the case of George William Gordon, Gorrie was seeking to show that Clarke had no direct involvement in the rebellion:

33,381. . . . Is there anything in the evidence to prove any complicity on the part of Samuel Clarke with the disturbances at Morant Bay? – The Court must have thought so, I presume. 33,382. Is there anything in these records of evidence more than proofs of a statement made by Clarke several months before martial law was proclaimed? – I cannot answer those questions, I cannot tell; you do not know how I voted on the Court martial. . . . 33,383. Tell us whether any charge was proved against Samuel Clarke during martial law – that is, for acts done during martial law? –I do not know.[21]

Gorrie and Payne not only sought to weaken the case against George William Gordon and Samuel Clarke; they also attempted to cast doubt on the nature of the rebellion itself.

When the Commission concluded its efforts on 9 April there was a great deal of conflicting evidence. Moreover, it was not always clear who was telling the truth. Some witnesses lied; as *The Colonial Standard* pointed out, this included men and women who exaggerated the flogging they had received. One woman, Sarah Robinson, wrongly claimed that soldiers had killed a woman in childbirth as well as the midwife who was assisting the delivery. The testimony of some witnesses may have been affected by the hope of compensation. Others contradicted themselves: a labourer who lived on Holland Estate, Alexander Paul, testified before the Commission that he was tried and heavily flogged but that there were no witnesses brought against him. Yet during questioning about these witnesses in advance of his testimony to the Commission, Paul stated just the opposite. Despite these problems, the commissioners were able to sift through the evidence and produce a report of just over forty pages.[22]

In their conclusion the commissioners praised Governor Eyre for his 'skill, promptitude and vigour' in quickly dealing with the rebellion. In addition, they found that the military and naval operations were 'prompt and judicious'. However, there was concern about the length of martial law and about the punishments which the commissioners regarded as 'excessive'. Specifically the report found:

1 That the punishment of death was unnecessarily frequent.
2 That the floggings were reckless and at Bath positively barbarous.
3 That the burning of 1,000 homes was wanton and cruel.[23]

Once the report reached England the effects were dramatic. Meetings were again held denouncing Eyre and the authorities in Jamaica. Even some of the Governor's supporters found it difficult to defend the atrocities committed by the troops and the Maroons in St Thomas in the East. Those who had condemned the suppression, such as the Jamaica Committee, were vindicated by the Commission's report. It was clear, for example, that Eyre would have to be recalled and a new Governor sent to the colony. For many members of the Committee, however, this was not sufficient. They not only wished to see Eyre suspended but also wanted him tried for murder.[24]

John Stuart Mill was the most vocal advocate for prosecuting Governor Eyre. During a heated meeting of the Jamaica Committee, Mill argued forcefully that if Eyre escaped trial, 'every rascally colonial official would be given a free hand to perform mischief, and a horrible precedent affecting the liberties of Englishmen would be set'. The head of the Jamaica Committee, Charles Buxton, maintained that prosecuting Eyre would be an enormous blunder. But Mill carried the meeting.[25]

Back in Jamaica Eyre was preparing to leave the colony. He had been informed of his dismissal as Governor of Jamaica, and it seemed likely that his career in the colonial service was over. In responding to the dispatch also censuring him for his action in the suppression of the rebellion, Eyre continued to defend his actions. Although he was retiring to private life, he maintained that he had 'always endeavoured to do [his] duty faithfully as a servant of the Crown, and the conviction that in doing it on the late occasion [he] saved a noble colony from anarchy and ruin'.[26]

There was little doubt that many people in Jamaica agreed with Eyre's assessment. As he left the island for the last time and his carriage made its way to the wharf in Kingston, people lined the streets waving and cheering. Others were at the wharf to bid him farewell. Once on board ship, Eyre met a group representing 1,200 signers of a memorial to him. Composed of the leading planters and merchants in the colony, the delegation praised Eyre for having put down the rebellion and expressed their sympathy to the Governor for the attacks against him. In replying, Eyre repeated his view that, although he was being dismissed from public service, 'there has been nothing in [his] conduct to merit it, nothing to occasion self-reproach, nothing to regret'.[27]

Eyre's departure from Jamaica did not end the controversy over the suppression of the rebellion. Landing in Southampton on 12 August, Eyre was invited to attend a banquet to be held the following week and organized by some of the leading citizens of the town. Once news of this dinner became known, others opposed to Eyre decided to arrange a counter-meeting, denouncing the organizers of the dinner for their 'feast of blood'. On 21 August the separate events were held, the first attended by luminaries such as the Earl of Cardigan, the commander of the Light Brigade during the Crimean War, the Earl of Shrewsbury and Talbott, and the noted poet and historian, Rev. Charles Kingsley. Outside, a crowd formed, many of whom actively denounced the diners and called for Eyre to be handed over to them. When the dinner was over many of the participants had to confront the crowd, and there were angry scenes outside the banquet hall. In another part of town the counter-meeting was also well-attended: some newspapers described it as the largest working-class meeting the city had known. This gathering adopted resolutions protesting against the defence of Eyre and the disgrace the dinner brought on the town of Southampton.[28]

About a week after the dinner at Southampton, friends of Governor Eyre held a meeting to organize a fund-raising committee to support his defence against the threatened prosecution. This was the basis for the Eyre Defence Committee, a group which was very different from its counterpart, the Jamaica Committee. While the Jamaica Committee consisted largely of radicals and members of the scientific establishment, the Eyre Defence Committee drew its members from the literary establishment and also from landed society, the army and the Church establishment. Apart from Charles Kingsley, some of its more famous members included Thomas Carlyle, Charles Dickens and Alfred, Lord Tennyson.[29]

Carlyle was a highly significant recruit to the Defence Committee. The author of an 'Occasional Discourse on the Nigger Question' published in 1849, Carlyle had maintained that emancipation itself was a disaster. For him, blacks were an inferior race and the end of slavery had meant the ruin of the former slave colonies. In 1849 Carlyle was a lone public voice from the intellectual establishment espousing such views. But as Catherine Hall has demonstrated, this was no longer the case by the late 1850s and 1860s. By that time, the movement away from an anti-slavery ideology and to-wards a more overt form of racism was clear. Edward John Eyre shared Carlyle's views about blacks; they were simply 'not up to freedom'. For the Defence Committee and for Eyre and Carlyle, it was therefore ludicrous to compare a rebellion of blacks with one in England, as the Jamaica Commit-tee sought to do.[30]

This was obviously a persuasive argument for many. By the end of 1866 there were reports that the Eyre Defence Committee had already collected £10,000. Although possibly apocryphal, there was no doubting the large numbers of people who supported Eyre. When the committee published the names of its contributors some years later, the list included a significant number of peers, bishops, MPs, generals, admirals as well as 30,000 other individuals.[31]

Like the Eyre Defence Committee, the Jamaica Committee was also active. It not only continued to seek financial support but also to prosecute Governor Eyre. The committee's first attempt in this direction came in March, 1867, when its solicitors sought to obtain a warrant for Eyre's arrest as an accessory to the murder of George William Gordon. Since the former Governor had moved to Shropshire, the committee's barrister, Fitzjames Stephen, appeared before the magistrates of the Market Drayton Petty Sessional Division. Despite a lengthy hearing, however, the magistrates could not find sufficient evidence to commit Eyre for trial. Two weeks later the cases of General Abercrombie Nelson and Lt Herbert Brand came before the Middlesex grand jury; the jury's task was to decide whether the two officers should be placed on trial for the murder of Gordon. Although the Lord Chief Justice was in favour of an indictment, the jury found 'no bill' in the case against Nelson and Brand. The case was dismissed.[32]

Nearly a year later there was an unexpected development in the case against Governor Eyre. Eyre moved from Shropshire to London and therefore came under the jurisdiction of the Middlesex courts. Moreover, he instructed his solicitor to inform the Jamaica Committee of his change of address, clearly wishing to rid himself of any threatened prosecution. In response, the Jamaica Committee applied for a warrant against Eyre, again on the charge of murder. But the chief magistrate denied the request, saying that it was pointless to retry the case.[33]

The Jamaica Committee was not yet ready to give up. The committee decided that it might be more fruitful to try Eyre for high crimes and misdemeanours under the Colonial Governor's Act. Appearing before a different magistrate on 15 May, the new barrister for the Jamaica Committee, Sir Robert Collier, convinced him that Eyre should be committed for trial at the Court of Queen's Bench. When asked whether he had anything to say, Eyre made an impassioned speech:

> I have only this to say, that not upon me, but upon those who brought me here, lies the foul disgrace that a public servant, who has faithfully discharged his duty for upwards of twenty years, has been now, after two years and a half of persecution, brought to a criminal court and committed for trial for having performed his duty at a trying moment, and thereby saved, indubitably, a great British colony from destruction, and its well-disposed inhabitants, white and black, from massacre or worse.

The speech was met with spontaneous applause from the courtroom spectators.[34]

Eyre's trial took place in June, 1868. Once again, the grand jury found that there was insufficient evidence to indict Eyre, this time for high crimes and misdemeanours. The case of the Jamaica Committee was therefore over: it had lost in Shropshire, it had been unsuccessful in prosecuting Nelson and Brand, and now it had failed against Eyre on a reduced charge. This was its final defeat in court.[35]

But Eyre was not yet out of legal trouble. In 1869 he had to face a series of civil suits brought against him by people who had been injured or lost property during the rebellion. Fortunately for the ex-Governor, the Jamaican Legislature had passed an Act of Indemnity which exempted him from financial responsibility relating to the suppression. This act was upheld by the courts in Britain.[36]

It was more difficult for Eyre to get a pension or to be considered for another appointment. Yet the former Governor did not lack supporters. For example, Henry Taylor, a senior figure in the West Indian department at the Colonial Office, commented towards the end of 1867 that there was 'nothing to prevent Mr Eyre's re-employment and that his non-employment would be a loss to the service'. Of course, Taylor recognized that this was a political matter and not one he could influence. The Liberal government under Gladstone did move to defray Eyre's legal expenses in 1872 and, on its return to office two years later, the Conservatives voted to grant him a pension. But Eyre never worked again in the public service, partly due to the pressure of the Jamaica Committee. He eventually moved to a remote house in Devon, where he lived almost anonymously with his family until his death in 1901 at the age of 86.[37]

Prosecutions following the suppression of the rebellion

Eyre was not the only person who had to face prosecution as a result of the rebellion. In Jamaica a number of individuals were also tried for their role in its suppression. The most prominent of these was the Provost-Marshal in Morant Bay, Gordon Ramsay. As the man in charge of martial law in the town, Ramsay's behaviour had clearly been arbitrary. It was over one particular incident, the hanging of a prisoner named George Marshall without trial, that Ramsay was first suspended from office and then brought to trial.[38]

Ramsay's first appearance in court was before a bench of magistrates in St Catherine. The charge was murder and the magistrates decided to dismiss it on a vote of five to three. But the three magistrates in the minority registered a protest against discharging Ramsay. Moreover, on examining the depositions, the Attorney-General issued a warrant for Ramsay's arrest, again on a charge of murder.

The case was heard at the circuit court at Morant Bay in October, 1866. Because of rumours of a possible disturbance at the court, the government took precautions to preserve the peace. Several government ships were in the vicinity, a detachment of armed police was sent from Kingston, and troops in Morant Bay were alerted. The day passed peacefully, but the grand jury ignored the charge of the presiding judge. Although the judge directed them to find a true bill against Ramsay, the jury threw out the case against him. In spite of uncontradicted evidence implicating Ramsay for the murder of Marshall, Ramsay was released. Writing to the Colonial Office after the case was over, the Governor of Jamaica, Sir John Peter Grant, reported the Attorney-General's view that 'no Grand Jury in the Island will find a true Bill against Mr Ramsay and that any further proceedings here would be useless'. The Governor's only recourse was to refuse to reinstate Ramsay as an inspector of police.[39]

This pattern was repeated in the case of John Woodrow who was accused of excessively flogging certain women in St Thomas in the East during the suppression of the rebellion. Believing that there was a strong case against Woodrow, the Attorney-General brought it before the grand jury which also heard Ramsay's case. However, the grand jury refused to indict Woodrow, in spite of the Attorney-General's view that it 'was one of the best supported of the flogging cases'.[40]

In at least one instance the Governor was able to dismiss a magistrate, William Pitt Kirkland, who had authorized extreme flogging. The evidence taken before the Royal Commission showed that Bath had been the scene of what Governor Storks called 'great barbarity'. Men had been whipped with wire cats, and women had also been the victims of corporal punishment. Although it was true that Kirkland's stores in various parts of the parish had been plundered, this did not excuse his actions. Storks had not only removed Kirkland from the magistracy but also from his appointment as collector of dues in the parish.[41]

Civilians were not alone in facing criticism for their actions in quelling the rebellion. Members of the armed forces also came under attack. As we have seen, General Nelson and Lieutenant Brand were both put on trial in London; in Jamaica, Ensign Cullen and Surgeon Morris faced extensive questioning by the Royal Commission about allegations of their having shot people without trial during the suppression. When the cases of Cullen and Morris were examined further, it was decided that the two men would be tried in Jamaica before a court martial to answer the charges against them. In the end, Cullen as well as Morris were acquitted.[42]

One of the officers who also came under censure was Colonel Thomas Hobbs, the man in charge of the forces based at Monklands in western St Thomas in the East. Even before the report of the Royal Commission, Hobbs was in difficulties with General O'Connor. During the military operations in suppressing the rebellion, it emerged that Hobbs had seized property said to belong to the rebels and had sold it. His intention was to distribute the proceeds among his troops. The items included clothing, books, mules and cattle. In his defence, Hobbs claimed that he had never before been involved in this type of operation. He therefore found 'it exceedingly difficult to know what [his] position was and is, [his] only wish in this, as in all other cases is to do what is right'.[43]

Worse was to follow. The Commission's report suggested that Hobbs had been more severe and cruel than was necessary in putting down the rebellion. Unused to such criticism, Hobbs' mind became unhinged; he was eventually examined by a board of medical officers and declared of unsound mind. Hobbs was ordered home and, in May, 1866, he and his family boarded a ship for the journey to England. Although closely watched and under the supervision of an army surgeon, Hobbs threw himself overboard and drowned soon after leaving Jamaica.[44]

One episode, which occurred a few months after Hobbs' suicide, is revealing about the views of officers involved in the suppression of the rebellion. Lt Herbert Brand was the young naval officer who had presided over the trial of George William Gordon. Since the Commission's report had found that there was insufficient evidence even to indict Gordon, Brand was the object of considerable criticism by the opponents of Governor Eyre. Among this group was the former head of the Jamaica Committee, Charles Buxton, who attacked Brand's conduct during a Parliamentary debate in July, 1866. Brand's response was a letter to Buxton which maintained that:

> You may be a very fine *buckra* among the polished gentlemen at
> Exeter Hall who wanted Mr Eyre suspended with a rope, and the
> old ladies of Clapham; but when you come with your peculiar
> little assertions in print, and such barefaced lies, too, I think it is
> time for the trampled worm to turn.

As a result of this letter, Brand was suspended from his command of a naval ship, sent back to England and placed on half-pay.[45]

The nature of the suppression inevitably led to calls for compensating the victims of the rebellion. Soon after Storks arrived in Jamaica, he appointed a commission to examine the claims for compensation. It was chaired by Alexander Fyfe, the man in charge of the Maroons during the rebellion.[46]

The claims were predictably far-ranging. They included one from a member of the militia who had been wounded at Morant Bay and taken to private lodgings in Kingston rather than the hospital, thereby incurring an enormous bill for medical care. The widow of George W. Gordon sought compensation, as did Sidney Levien who wanted 'vindication from the foul aspersions cast upon me by Mr Eyre [and] for the pecuniary damage I have sustained through the abuse of power with which he was officially invested'.[47] There were rich applicants like the Haitians who had been deported and poor ones such as William Groves: he described himself as 'a poor man with a family paying a considerable amount of Taxes and lost my little all by that disturbance'.[48]

When the compensation commission made its report in 1867, it observed that one category for possible compensation totalled £10,136 for damage done by rioters; another was for damage done by the troops and others in suppressing the rebellion. While the commission rejected any claims for property destroyed by the rioters, it favoured paying for damage done in the suppression of the rebellion to those who had nothing to do with the outbreak. This sum came to £2,426. But the Secretary of State for the colonies made it clear that these funds were to come from Jamaica itself and not from any Imperial sources.[49]

Crown Colony government and the memory of Morant Bay

The claims for compensation as well as the prosecutions and trials in Jamaica and England reflected the gravity of the events at Morant Bay. Yet the political changes which were a direct consequence of the rebellion had a more long-lasting effect. Crown Colony government fundamentally changed the politics of Jamaica. The new system did away with Assembly government and replaced it with a Legislative Council. It consisted of officials in the government, such as the Attorney-General, the Colonial Secretary and the Financial Secretary; in addition, the Governor could nominate up to six individuals, who would always be in a minority to the officials. Since Grant appointed three unofficial members to sit on the Legislative Council, there were eight official votes against the three chosen from outside the government. There was no representative element in the Legislative Council and, effectively, no opposition to the Governor.[50]

The man chosen to inaugurate this system was Sir John Peter Grant, a retired Indian civil servant who had spent thirty-four years in India. A product of Eton and Haileybury, Grant had joined the Bengal civil service at the age of twenty-one. He served in a variety of positions in India, including his last appointment as Lieutenant-Governor of Bengal. He retired from this post in 1862.[51]

Arriving in Jamaica in August, 1866, Grant was able to bring about a significant number of administrative reforms during his term of office. Among the most important was the establishment of new district courts, the creation of a new police force modelled along the lines of the Irish constabulary and the disestablishment of the Church of England in Jamaica. He also had the capital moved from Spanish Town to Kingston and encouraged the immigration of East Indian indentured labourers. Roads were improved, new irrigation schemes were developed and more money was devoted to education. As Roy Augier has argued, Grant effectively put into place the administrative apparatus of a modern state.[52]

These reforms were not without their costs. At the most basic level taxes were increased. There was also a feeling in the colony that too many changes were being enacted without the involvement of the people. For *The Falmouth Post*, the system was one of 'paternal despotism', with little role even for the nominated unofficial members of the Legislative Council. One long-standing resident of the island and a former stipendiary magistrate, Stephen Bourne, had an additional complaint: there were too many continuities from the Eyre period. For Bourne,

> the Attorney-General, however, who advised Governor Eyre is the same; two of the friends of Governor Eyre are members of the Council, and I do not hear that Stipendiary Magistrates have replaced the Local Magistrates. . . . I cannot hear that any compensation has been made to the persons whose Houses were destroyed by the Military, or that any Schools have been set on foot for the poor orphans whose parents were shot or hung during the prevalence of Martial law.[53]

During the 1870s there was increasing dissatisfaction with Crown Colony government. In general terms, the system 'made the society as a whole more dependent, less responsible, less self-directing than it had been'.[54] More specifically, coloureds felt the loss of political offices which had previously been available to them. But this was also the view of many whites. As Graham Knox has observed:

> In the late 70s planter opposition reached serious proportions and their journals lashed out at the government for its financial extravagance, inefficiency, despotism and the arbitrary policy of excluding Jamaicans from the administration.[55]

Yet Crown Colony government ultimately worked in favour of the whites by reinforcing their political and social authority. There was little doubt that the coercive levers of power were under their control. Patrick Bryan has pointed out that coloureds and blacks were removed from the sergeant ranks of the militia after the outbreak of riots in 1894. Thereafter, the militia had be to captained by whites only. Blacks and coloureds could be footsoldiers, but authority was in the hands of the whites.[56]

It was more than a case of dominating the forces of law and order. Despite continuing economic difficulties in the last half of the nineteenth century, whites remained at the top of the social structure and blacks at the bottom. This was reinforced by the emergence of social Darwinism, an ideology which was interpreted as providing support for continuing white social authority. Even liberals in Britain regarded this new ideology as confirming the need for strong government and for a form of trusteeship. For liberals, this system would safeguard the whites but serve the best interests of the blacks.[57]

Whites in Jamaica also sought to maintain control of local politics. The limited franchise under Crown Colony government was directed toward this end. In the wake of the Morant Bay rebellion, black political activity was actively discouraged. It was not until the 1890s that Dr Robert Love, a

Bahamian-born black educated in the United States, was able to establish the *Jamaica Advocate*. A weekly paper, the *Advocate* provided a platform for black Jamaicans. Love was also involved in the formation of the People's Convention, an organization set up to improve the condition of blacks in the island. But as Joy Lumsden has concluded, 'these were the first attempts at black dominated associations since 1865 and the obstacles they faced owed much to the fears generated by the Morant Bay disturbances and their aftermath.'[58]

In varying ways, whites and blacks remembered Morant Bay. For whites, Governor Eyre remained a hero who had saved the colony. As late as 1903 one citizen was still appealing for a statue to be erected in memory of Eyre 'and his heroic act of salvation at Morant Bay'.[59] However, blacks had another way of commemorating the Morant Bay rebellion and were honouring a very different figure: Paul Bogle.

A year after the rebellion, in October 1866, there was a report that there would be an outbreak on the anniversary of the rebellion. Stephen Cooke, the clerk of the peace for St Thomas in the East, had been told that he would be murdered on 11 October, and his brother had learned that a group of people intended to celebrate Paul Bogle's entry into Morant Bay. One account suggested that the inhabitants of Stony Gut were coming to Morant Bay 'for the purpose of *raising the Spirit of Paul Bogle*, and to set fire to the town'. When these reports were investigated there was nothing to substantiate them.[60]

Ten years later there was another threatened rebellion in St Thomas in the East, this time with some striking similarities to the events leading up to 1865. The outbreak was to begin with the burning of several estates in the Plantain Garden River district. Moreover, there were rumours that the Maroons and the 'coolies' would side with the blacks. There was also an increase in revivalist activity, particularly involving Native Baptist leaders. In addition, blacks were complaining about the problem of obtaining justice in the district courts. Just as in St Thomas in the East in the 1860s, the peasantry were again running their own mock courts. The authorities therefore decided to take action: the constabulary in the parish was increased and a gunboat was stationed in the harbour at Port Morant. In the end there was no rebellion.[61]

This was not the last time that the memory of Morant Bay would be invoked. At the end of the nineteenth century there were again rumours that the people were planning another Morant Bay. Although there was no outbreak, the memory of the rebellion and of Paul Bogle has survived. In the Kumina ceremonies of contemporary western Jamaica, an African religion brought to Jamaica by the Central African indentured labourers, Bogle is remembered fondly, and some claim that his spirit pays occasional visits to the services. Kenneth Bilby suggests that Bogle's intention is not to possess the participants, but to enjoy the music and offer his support for the cult, just as some Africans had supported him in the rebellion. An observer in the 1950s also reported that Bogle's memory was very much alive in St Thomas and was associated with protest against unjust living conditions. Some people believed that Bogle would return unless there was real change.[62] Culturally and spiritually, Paul Bogle and the Morant Bay rebellion live on.

Notes

1 Bernard Semmel, *The Governor Eyre Controversy* (London: McKibbon & Kee, 1962), p. 55.
2 Semmel, *Governor Eyre Controversy*, p. 56; PRO 30/48/42, Cardwell Papers, Cardwell to Eyre, 17 November 1865.
3 PRO 30/48/42, Cardwell Papers, Cardwell to Eyre, 23 November 1865.
4 *Ibid.*, 1 December 1865.
5 Semmel, *Governor Eyre Controversy*, p. 22; CO 137/397, Memorial from Citizens of Canterbury for investigation into the circumstances attending the late Insurrection to Cardwell (filed under Miscellaneous Offices).
6 Semmel, *Governor Eyre Controversy*, pp. 60–1, 65–6, 68.
7 CO 137/396, Eyre to Cardwell, 20 December 1865, no. 332; Semmel, *Governor Eyre Controversy*, p. 26.
8 Semmel, *Governor Eyre Controversy*, p. 27; PRO 30/48/42, Cardwell Papers, Cardwell to Eyre, 17 December 1865.
9 Henry Clarke, 'The Journals of Henry Clarke', vol. 2, 16 February 1866.
10 CO 137/401, Storks to Cardwell, 9 March 1866, confidential.
11 PRO 30/48/43, Cardwell Papers, Storks to Cardwell, 8 January 1866, private; JRC, Evidence of Edward Skyers, p. 593; Papers, Brain to Myers, 27 January 1866, p. 190, subenclosure in no. 2; CO 137/399, Storks to Cardwell, 5 February 1866, no. 19.
12 JRC: Evidence of A. Miles, p. 523; Evidence of Plato Elphick, p. 833.
13 *The Morning Journal*, 24 January 1866.
14 Semmel, *Governor Eyre Controversy*, pp. 68–9.
15 JRC, Evidence of Thomas McFarlane, p. 906.
16 BMS, 'Jamaica Affairs', vol. 1, p. 148, Report on Royal Commission.
17 JRC, Evidence of Lt Herbert Brand, p. 660.
18 JRC, Evidence of Gordon Ramsay, p. 635.
19 *The Morning Journal*, 24 January 1866; *The Colonial Standard and Jamaica Despatch*: 27 January 1866, 1 February 1866.
20 JRC, Evidence of Lt Herbert Brand, p. 659.
21 *Ibid.*, p. 676.
22 *The Colonial Standard and Jamaica Despatch*: 24 February 1866; 10 October 1866; JRC: Evidence of Alexander Paul, pp. 227–8; Evidence of Solomon Lindo, p. 228; Report. For a more complex view of the case involving Sarah Robinson, see John Gorrie, *Illustrations of Martial Law in Jamaica. Compiled from the Report of the Royal Commissioners, and Other Blue Books Laide Before Parliament*. Jamaica Papers, no. 6 (London: Jamaica Committee, 1867), p. vi.
23 Report, pp. 40–1.
24 Semmel, *Governor Eyre Controversy*, pp. 71–2.
25 *Ibid.*, pp. 72–3. Buxton resigned over this issue, and Mill replaced him as chairman of the Jamaica Committee.

26 CO 137/406, Storks to Cardwell, 9 July 1866, no. 144.

27 Semmel, *Governor Eyre Controversy*, pp. 92–3. See also the description of Eyre's departure in *The Colonial Standard and Jamaica Despatch*: 25 July 1866, 26 July 1866.

28 *Ibid.*, pp. 92–100.

29 Catherine Hall, 'The Economy of Intellectual Prestige: Thomas Carlyle, John Stuart Mill, and the Case of Governor Eyre', *Cultural Critique* 12 (Spring, 1989), p. 185.

30 *Ibid.*, pp. 178, 182, 190.

31 Semmel, *Governor Eyre Controversy*, p. 122.

32 *Ibid.*, pp. 155–7, 163.

33 *Ibid.*, p. 170.

34 *Ibid.*, pp. 171–3.

35 *Ibid.*, p. 178.

36 *Ibid.*, p. 183.

37 CO 137/429, Eyre to Buckingham, 18 December 1867, Taylor's minute, 22 December; Semmel, *Governor Eyre Controversy*, pp. 183–7; Hall, 'The Economy of Intellectual Prestige', p. 193; James Morris, *Heaven's Command: An Imperial Progress* (London: Faber & Faber, 1973), p. 317; Malcolm Uren and Robert Stephens, *Waterless Horizons: The first full-length study of the extraordinary life-story of Edward John Eyre . . .* (Melbourne: Robertson and Mullens, 1941), p. 25.

38 See chapter 9 for more information about the hanging of George Marshall.

39 CO 137/408, Grant to Carnarvon, 8 November 1866, no. 43, enclosure: Grant's minute of Mr Ramsay's case, 6 November; CO 137/401, Storks to Cardwell, 10 March 1866, confidential; *The Colonial Standard and Jamaica Despatch*: 22 October 1866, 24 October 1866; CO 137/407, Grant to Carvarvon, 24 October 1866, no. 33. According to Olivier, Ramsay subsequently committed suicide; see Lord Olivier [Sydney Haldane], *The Myth of Governor Eyre* (London: The Hogarth Press, 1933), p. 257.

40 CO 137/407, Grant to Carnarvon, 24 October 1866, no. 34.

41 CO 137/404, Storks to Cardwell, 20 April 1866, no. 94.

42 CO 137/404, Rogers to the Under Secretary of State, War Office, 30 May 1866; CO 137/409, War Office: Carvarvon to Grant, 31 August 1866; CO 137/428, War Office: Lugard to Rogers, 26 March 1867.

43 CO 137/403, Storks to Cardwell, 24 March 1866, no. 71, enclosures: O'Connor to Hobbs, 6 November 1865; Hobbs to O'Connor, 9 November 1865; Hobbs to O'Connor, 16 November 1865. The plundering by the soldiers was significant. Olivier claimed that it amounted to £700; this did not include the horses, mules and donkeys which Hobbs expropriated, some of which were taken to Up Park Camp to be sold. See Olivier, *Governor Eyre*, p. 280.

44 Semmel, *Governor Eyre Controversy*, p. 90; *The Falmouth Post*, 8 May 1866.

45 Semmel, *Governor Eyre Controversy*, p. 150; CO 137/428, Admiralty to Rogers, 1 February 1867.

46 CO 137/427, Grant to Buckingham, 8 October 1867, no. 196, enclosure: The Commission to the Hon. Alexander Fyfe, David Ewart and Daniel Trench, 10 January 1866.

47 CO 137/423, Grant to Buckingham, 15 April 1867, no. 76, enclosure: Ross to Carnarvon, 23 March 1867; CO 137/444, Grant to Granville, 3 December 1869, no. 275; CO 137/427, Grant to Buckingham, 9 October 1867, no. 200, enclosure: Levien to Irving, 7 October 1867.

48 CO 137/428, Foreign Office to Colonial Office, 6 December 1867, enclosures; CO 137/429, Bischoff, Coxe and Bompers to Cardwell, 14 February 1867; CO 137/430, Grant to Buckingham, 10 February 1868, no. 18, enclosure: Groves to Grant, 13 January 1868.

49 CO 137/427, Grant to Buckingham, 8 October 1867, no. 196; *Ibid.*, enclosure: Buckingham to Grant, 16 December 1867, no. 167.

50 Vincent John Marsala, *Sir John Peter Grant, Governor of Jamaica, 1866–1874* (Kingston: Institute of Jamaica, 1972), p. 35.

51 *Ibid.*, pp. 29–31.

52 *Ibid.*, chapters 3–5; Robert J. Stewart, *Religion and Society in Post-Emancipation Jamaica* (Knoxville: University of Tennessee Press, 1992), p. 174; Roy Augier, 'Before and After 1865', *New World Quarterly* 2 (1966), p. 35.

53 CO 137/429, Bourne to Buckingham, 25 June 1867.

54 Augier, '1865', p. 22.

55 Graham Knox, 'Political Change in Jamaica (1866–1906) and the Local Reaction to the Policies of the Crown Colony Government', in *The Caribbean in Transition: Papers on Social, Political, and Economic Development*, edited by F.M. Andic and T.G. Mathews (Río Piedras: Institute of Caribbean Studies, University of Puerto Rico, 1965), pp. 142–3.

56 Patrick Bryan, *The Jamaican People, 1880–1902* (London: Macmillan Caribbean, 1991), p. 30.

57 *Ibid.*, p. 49; Christine Bolt, *Victorian Attitudes to Race* (London: Routledge & Kegan Paul, 1971), p. 91.

58 Bryan, *The Jamaican People*, pp. 14, 261; Joyce Mary Lumsden, 'Robert Love and Jamaican Politics', (Ph.D. thesis, University of the West Indies, 1987), p. 329.

59 Bryan, *The Jamaican People*, p. 11.

60 CO 137/407, Grant to Carnarvon, 23 October 1866, no. 29; *The Falmouth Post*, 19 October 1866.

61 Stewart, *Religion and Society*, pp. 184, 186–7; Lumsden, 'Robert Love', p. 149; *The Falmouth Post*, 2 April 1875.

62 Knox, 'Jamaica', p. 145; Kenneth M. Bilby and Kia Bunseki Fu-Kiau, 'Kumina: A Kongo-Based Tradition in the New World', *Cahiers du CEDAF*, vol, 8, no. 4 (1983), pp. 29, 104, n. 23.

Epilogue

When Thomas Harvey and William Brewin visited Jamaica in 1866 they travelled to Morant Bay. There they found a small town beautifully situated in the foothills of the Blue Mountains. As they described it, the town bore evidence of 'decaying prosperity'; more significantly, however, they found graphic testimony of what had transpired in October, 1865:

> [Morant Bay] will long carry the tokens of the sad events which have made it notorious; the roofless and ruined Court-house, with its marks of fire and violence [and] the five or six long mounds covering the remains of the dead, several of which are conspicuously placed near the entrances to the town. . . .[1]

These images, especially the burnt-out court house and the mounds of the dead, help to illustrate the causes and consequences of the Morant Bay rebellion.

One of the most significant issues in the rebellion was land. In the aftermath of emancipation, ex-slaves equated freedom with the ownership of land as well as with the legal end of slavery. Land was of obvious economic importance to the blacks; it provided them with independence from the plantations and a bargaining tool for higher wages. But land was also meaningful in other ways. As Jean Besson has suggested, it 'had considerable symbolic significance to a people who had not only once been landless, but property themselves'.[2] It was not simply a question of economic security; owning land meant

> a religious respect for the earth, for a piece of ground where the living could settle, the unborn enter, the dead could be buried, the deities could descend, and the ancestors could be venerated locally.[3]

One of the rebel leaders, James Bowie, voiced a commonly-held view that the Queen would not have freed the people without giving them their provision grounds. As Bowie put it, 'the rent too heavy and the back land [the provision grounds] was given up to the island from our Queen to the black people'. By 1865 many blacks were no longer willing to pay this rent.[4]

The issue of the backlands was compounded by the one-sided administration of justice in Jamaica. This was especially the case in St Thomas in the East, where planters dominated the magistracy. The situation was made worse by the exorbitant fees imposed by the courts. When the one neutral magistrate in the parish, T. Witter Jackson, was removed from St Thomas in the East, blacks lost all hope of justice. The development of alternative courts, controlled by blacks, was an expression of the people's frustration with the established judicial system.

The black courts in the Blue Mountain district centred around Paul Bogle and the Native Baptists. For the Native Baptists, religion contained a significant political dimension. Bogle also made use of the Native Baptists to support his political and religious ally, George William Gordon, who was the representative to the House of Assembly from St Thomas in the East. Gordon was a spokesman for the ex-slaves and a thorn in the side of the hierarchy in the island, led by the Governor, Edward Eyre. When the custos of St Thomas in the East removed Gordon from his place on the parish vestry, ostensibly because he was a Native Baptist, blacks in the parish were furious. This was especially the case in the communities led by Paul Bogle.

The political temperature in Jamaica rose considerably during 1865. The Underhill meetings across the island were highly critical of the government and of the House of Assembly. These meetings were one form of dissent; in St Thomas in the East, Paul Bogle and his associates were organizing gatherings of a very different kind. At these meetings, held in September and October, the grievances about land and justice were again aired. James McLaren, one of the rebel leaders, also protested about the level of wages, comparing them to slavery:

> Why cause me to hold this meeting; myself was born free, but my mother and father was slave; but now I am still a slave by working from days to days. I cannot get money to feed my family, and I working at Coley estate for 35 chains for 1s., and after five days' working I get 2s.6d. for my family. Is that able to sustain a house full of family?[5]

At these meetings oaths were taken, some of which contained threats to kill the whites and pay no rent for the backlands. Violence at Morant Bay was now on the agenda. Bogle therefore attempted to placate the Maroons; he wished to ensure that they would support his cause. He believed that there was a possibility of success against the authorities if he had the backing of the Maroons; without them, he was aware of imminent defeat.

When the rebels marched to Morant Bay on 11 October, their first target was the police station. Since their aim was to use the weapons stored there, it soon became clear that this was no ordinary demonstration. The marchers were drilled, and there were captains in charge of them. Shouts from the crowd of 'Colour for Colour' and 'War, War' were also significant; the crowd chose its targets carefully. For the crowd, the colour of its victims mattered, but so did class and political allegiance. A leading black, Charles Price, was killed at Morant Bay, in part because his loyalties were with the custos and the curate of the parish. The massacre at Morant Bay, the release of prisoners from the gaol and the subsequent attacks on outlying plantations and estates were further evidence of organization and planning.

Women had a prominent role in the rebellion. At Morant Bay they threw stones at the volunteers, encouraged the men to continue fighting and were responsible for the burning down of the court house. Some had scores to settle: Elizabeth Faulkner wanted to kill a black shopkeeper 'because of his dishonest business practices'. Mary Ward and other women implicated in the killing of Charles Price complained that he had not paid them for their work. Swithin Wilmot has suggested that 'women may have had their own agenda in addition to the general ones relating to land, low wages and oppressive and partial administration of the law'.[6]

Once news of the outbreak reached the authorities they reacted quickly and with overwhelming force. Eyre, until then a discredited Governor, travelled to St Thomas in the East, helping to direct operations against the rebels. Using a combination of imperial and local forces, the authorities violently suppressed the rebellion. The brutalities associated with the suppression recalled the horrors of the Indian Mutiny eight years earlier, and the overwhelming violence toward the black population is partly explicable by the hardening racial attitudes of the mid-nineteenth century. But it was also a result of a belief that blacks were intent on ousting whites and browns from the island.

The government made use of the outbreak to execute leading political dissidents in the island, including George William Gordon. In addition, Governor Eyre was able to convince a largely cowed House of Assembly to abolish the constitution and to institute Crown Colony rule from London. In the process, representative government, however flawed, was destroyed for nearly another century.

It soon became apparent that the authorities had overreacted to events in Jamaica. Although the outbreak in St Thomas in the East was serious, there was no proof of an island-wide conspiracy. No doubt there were threats of arson against court houses and of rebellion elsewhere in the island. But these warnings were evidence of shared grievances across the island rather than of plans for an island-wide revolt.

When a Royal Commission investigated the rebellion, it criticized Eyre and the government for their barbarous use of force. Eyre resigned. But George William Gordon, Paul Bogle and nearly 500 others had been killed. Ironically, although Eyre was regarded as a hero by many of the whites and browns in Jamaica for suppressing the rebellion, he is now nearly forgotten. Instead, Paul Bogle and George William Gordon are Jamaican National

Heroes, and it is the rebels at Morant Bay who are immortalized in the lyrics of the Jamaican group, Third World:

96° in the Shade
Real hot in the Shade

Said it was 96° in the Shade
Ten Thousand Soldiers on Parade
Taking I and I to meet a Big Fat Boy
Sent from Overseas
The Queen Employ
Excellency before you I come
With my Representation
You know where I'm coming from.

You caught me on the loose
Fighting to be Free
Now you show me a Noose
On the Cotton Tree
Entertainment for you
Martyrdom for me.[7]

Notes

1   Thomas Harvey and William Brewin, *Jamaica in 1866: A Narrative of a Tour Through the Island, with Remarks on its Social, Educational and Industrial Condition* (London: A.W. Bennett, 1867), p. 11.

2   Jean Besson, 'A paradox in Caribbean attitudes to land', in *Land and Development in the Caribbean*, edited by Jean Besson and Janet Momsen (London: Macmillan Caribbean, 1987), p. 18. Sidney W. Mintz reinforces this point in his *Caribbean Transformations* (Chicago: Aldine Publishing Co., 1974), p. 155.

3   Robert J. Stewart, *Religion and Society in Post-Emancipation Jamaica* (Knoxville: University of Tennessee Press, 1992), p. 197.

4   JRC, Evidence of John Williams, p. 167; Veront M. Satchell, *From Plots to Plantations: Land Transactions in Jamaica, 1866–1900* (Mona, Jamaica: Institute of Social and Economic Research, 1990), p. 64.

5   JRC, Evidence of William Anderson, p. 165.

6   Swithin Wilmot, 'Women and Protest in Jamaica, 1838–1865', Paper presented at the Nineteenth Annual Conference of Caribbean Historians, Martinique, April, 1987, pp. 17–18.

7   Third World, '1865', in the tape '96° in the Shade' (Island Records, 1977). For a different kind of historical echo, that reflected by the novelist V.S. Reid, in his novels on the Morant Bay rebellion, see Nana Wilson-Tagoe, *The Historical Imagination in West Indian Literature* (Macmillan Caribbean, forthcoming), ch. 2.

Bibliography

Manuscript sources
Jamaica

Archives of Jamaica
Private Diary of Thomas Witter Jackson, Stipendiary Magistrate in St Thomas-in-the-East: April, 1863–January, 1865.

National Library of Jamaica
B/N. Biographical Files.
MS 894. Thomas Carlyle petition in defence of Eyre.
MS 900, MS 927. Gov. Edward Eyre correspondence.
MS 892a. George William Gordon: Last letter.
MS 892b. George William Gordon: Business Papers.
MS 881, MS15. Jamaica Baptist Union.
MS 1685. Jamaica Riots, 1865: Reminiscences by the Right Hon. Elibank, Retired Command, Royal Navy.
MS 74. Morant Bay Rebellion: Contemporary Newspaper Cuttings.
MS 1828. The Negro Riot in St Thomas in the East.
MS 895. Henry Taylor correspondence.
MS 885/886. E.B. Underhill correspondence.

Private Papers
Henry Clarke, 'The Journals of Henry Clarke' (in possession of Mr Oliver Clarke, Kingston).

England

Baptist Missionary Society Archives, London
WI/5. Jamaica correspondence.
H14. E.B. Underhill Papers.
E.B. Underhill: 'Extracts from Correspondence with Missionaries in Jamaica on the Disturbances – 1864–66'.
H14/7. Morant Bay Disturbances.
'Jamaica Sundries': Cuttings from *The Missionary Herald*, 1858–62.
'Jamaica Affairs', 3 volumes.

Public Record Office, London
CO 137. Original Correspondence of Jamaican Governors.
CO 138. Letters from the Secretary of State.

CO 884/2. Confidential Print, no. 2: Papers Relating to the Insurrection in Jamaica, October, 1865, Printed for the Use of the Cabinet, December, 1865.

PRO 30/48/42. Edward Cardwell Papers: August–December, 1865, Correspondence with Governor Eyre.

PRO 30/48/43. Edward Cardwell Papers: December. 1865–October, 1867, Correspondence with Governor Eyre, Sir H Storks, Sir J.P. Grant and others.

PRO 30/48/44. Edward Cardwell Papers: 1865–66, Extracts from Colonial Office Confidential Prints, Proceedings of the Jamaica Royal Commission of Enquiry, press cuttings, draft manuscript reports.

Rhodes House, Oxford
Anti-Slavery Society Papers. BWI, Jamaica General, 1860–69, S22 G64, Correspondence.

School of Oriental and African Studies, University of London
Methodist Missionary Society, MMS 199: Jamaica Correspondence, 1858–1865.

United States

National Archives, Washington, D.C.
Dispatches from US Consuls in Kingston, Jamaica, 1796–1906: vol. 21, 5 March 1864–6 December 1868.

Newspapers

Jamaican
The Colonial Standard and Jamaica Despatch
The County Union and Anglo-Jamaican Advertiser
The Falmouth Post
The Jamaica Guardian
The Jamaica Watchman and People's Free Press
The Morning Journal
The Sentinel

British
The Baptist Magazine
The Daily News
The Missionary Herald
The Morning Star

Parliamentary materials

Parliamentary Papers [*PP*], 1831/32, (561) XLVII, Report from the House of Assembly of Jamaica on the injury sustained during the recent rebellion.

PP, 1840, (212) XXXV, Papers Relative to the West Indies, Part I.

PP, 1847/48, (685) XLIV, Dispatches received from Sir Charles Grey, Governor of Jamaica.

PP, 1849, (280) XXXVII, Correspondence with Governors of Jamaica, Trinidad and Mauritius, relating to the General Condition and Government of those Colonies, Part I: Jamaica.

PP, 1866, (3682) XXX, Papers Laid before the Royal Commission of Inquiry by Governor Eyre.

PP, 1866, (3683) XXX, Report of the Jamaica Royal Commission.

PP, 1866, (3683–1), XXXI, Report of the Jamaica Royal Commission, Part II, Minutes of Evidence and Appendix.

Printed primary sources

Anon., *Address to His Excellency Edward John Eyre, Esquire, 1865,1866.* (Kingston: M. DeCordova & Co., 1866).

Anon., *The Florence Hall Controversy and the Falmouth Riots* (Falmouth, Jamaica: James Mockler, [1859]).

Anon., *Observations on the Royal Commission and the Disturbances in Jamaica* (London: Robert Hardwicke, 1866).

Bleby, Henry, *Death Struggles of Slavery: Being a Narrative of Facts and Incidents which Occurred in a British Colony during the Two Years Immediately Preceding Negro Emancipation* (London: Hamilton, Adams and Co., 1853).

_____, *The Reign of Terror: A Narrative of Facts Concerning Ex-Governor Eyre, George William Gordon and the Jamaica Atrocities* (London: William Nichols, 1868).

[Carlyle, Thomas], 'Occasional Discourse on the Negro Question', *Frasers Magazine*, 40 (December 1849), pp. 670–9.

Finlason, W.F., *The History of the Jamaica Case: Being an Account of the Rebellion of the Negroes in Jamaica: The Causes which led to it, and the Measures taken for its Suppression; The Agitation Excited on the Subject, its Causes and its Character; and the Debates in Parliament, and the Criminal Prosecutions, arising out of it,* 2nd ed., (London: Chapman & Hall, 1869).

_____, *Justice to a Colonial Governor; or Some Considerations on the Case of Mr Eyre: Containing the substance of all the documents and discussions, and proceedings relating thereto* (London: Chapman & Hall, 1868).

_____, *A Review of the Authorities as to the repression of Riot or Rebellion with special reference to Criminal or Civil Liability* (London: Stevens & Sons and Chapman & Hall, 1868).

Fletcher, Rev. Duncan, *The Life of the Honourable George W. Gordon, The Martyr of Jamaica.* 2nd ed. (London: Elliot Stock, 1867).

_____, *Personal Recollections of the Honourable George W. Gordon, Late of Jamaica* (London: Elliot Stock, 1867).

Gardner, William James, *A History of Jamaica from Its Discovery by Christopher Columbus to the Year 1872* (London: Elliot Stock, 1873).

Gorrie, John, *Illustrations of Martial Law in Jamaica: Compiled from the Report of the Royal Commissioners, and Other Blue Books Laid Before Parliament,* Jamaica Papers no. 6. (London: Jamaica Committee, 1867).

Harvey, Thomas and Brewin, William, *Jamaica in 1866: A Narrative of a Tour Through the Island, with Remarks on its Social, Educational and Industrial Condition* (London: A.W. Bennett, 1867).

Hume, Hamilton, *The Life of Edward John Eyre, late Governor of Jamaica* (London: Richard Bentley, 1867).

Jamaica Committee, *Facts and Documents Relating to the alleged Rebellion in Jamaica and the Measures of Repression; including Notes of the trial of Mr Gordon*, Jamaica Papers, no. 1. (London: The Jamaica Committee, 1866).

King, Rev. David, *A Sketch of the Late Mr G.W. Gordon, Jamaica* (Edinburgh: William Oliphant and Co., 1866).

Lake, A.W.H., *Trial of Mr George William Gordon* (Spanish Town: Robert Osborn, 1866).

[Levien, Sidney], *A Chronicle of the Rebellion in Jamaica in the Year of our Lord 1865* (n.p., n.d.).

Lindo, Abraham, *Dr Underhill's Testimony on the Wrongs of the Negro in Jamaica Examined in a Letter to the Editor of The Times* (London: Effingham Wilson, 1866).

Long, Edward, *The History of Jamaica*, 3 vol. (London: T. Lowndes, 1774).

Noel, Baptist Wriothesley, *The Case of George William Gordon, Esq. of Jamaica* (London: James Nisbet and Co., 1866).

Price, George, *Jamaica and the Colonial Office: Who Caused the Crisis?* (London: Sampson, Low, Son, and Marston, 1866).

Roundell, Charles Savile, *England and her Subject Races, with special reference to Jamaica* (London: Macmillan & Co., 1866).

Underhill, Edward Bean, *A Letter Addressed to the Rt. Honourable E. Cardwell* (London: Arthur Miall, 1865).

———, *The Tragedy of Morant Bay* (London: Alexander and Shepheard, 1895).

———, *The West Indies: Their Social and Religious Condition* (London: Jackson, Walford, and Hodder, 1862).

Ward, Samuel R., *Reflections upon the Gordon Rebellion* (n.p., n.d.).

Williams, B.T., *The Case of George William Gordon, with Preliminary Observations on the Jamaica Riot of October 11th, 1865* (London: Butterworth's, 1866).

Secondary sources

Adas, Michael, *Prophets of Rebellion: Millenarian Protest Movements against the European Colonial Order* (Cambridge: Cambridge University Press, 1987).

Augier, Roy, 'Before and After 1865', *New World Quarterly* 2 (1966), pp. 21–40.

Bakan, Abigail, *Ideology and Class Conflict in Jamaica: The Politics of Rebellion* (Montreal & Kingston: McGill-Queen's University Press, 1990).

Beckles, Hilary and Watson, Karl. 'Social Protest and Labour Bargaining: The Changing Nature of Slaves' Responses to Plantation Life in Eighteenth-Century Barbados', *Slavery and Abolition* 8 (December, 1987), pp. 272–93.

Besson, Jean, 'A paradox in Caribbean attitudes to land', in *Land and Development in the Caribbean*, edited by Jean Besson and Janet Momsen, (London: Macmillan Caribbean, 1987).

Bilby, Kenneth M. and Bunseki Fu-Kiau, Kia, 'Kumina: A Kongo-Based Tradition in the New World', *Cahiers du CEDAF*, vol, 8, no. 4 (1983), pp. 1–114.

Bolland, O. Nigel, 'Systems of Domination after Slavery: The Control of Land and Labor in the British West Indies after 1838', *Comparative Studies in Society and History*, 23 (October, 1981), pp. 591–619.

Brathwaite, Edward Kamau, *The Development of Creole Society in Jamaica, 1770–1820* (Oxford: Clarendon Press, 1971).

———, 'Rebellion: Anatomy of the Slave Revolt of 1831/32 in Jamaica', *The Jamaican Historical Society Bulletin*, 8 (December, 1981), pp. 80–96.

_____, 'The Slave Rebellion in the Great River Valley of St James – 1831/32', *The Jamaican Historical Review*, 13 (1982), pp. 11–30.

Bryan, Patrick, *The Jamaican People, 1880–1902* (London: Macmillan Caribbean, 1991).

Buckley, Roger Norman, *Slaves in Red Coats: The British West India Regiments, 1795–1815* (New Haven: Yale University Press, 1979).

Campbell, Mavis Christine, *The Dynamics of Change in a Slave Society: A Sociopolitical History of the Free Coloreds of Jamaica, 1800–1865* (Rutherford, N.J.: Fairleigh Dickinson University Press, 1976).

_____, *The Maroons of Jamaica, 1655–1796: A History of Resistance, Collaboration and Betrayal* (Granby, Mass.: Bergin & Garvey, 1988).

Chutkan, Noelle, 'The Administration of Justice in Jamaica as a Contributing Factor in the Morant Bay Rebellion of 1865', *Savacou* 11/12 (September, 1975), pp. 78–85.

Craton, Michael, 'Continuity Not Change: The Incidence of Unrest Among Ex-Slaves in the British West Indies, 1838–1876', *Slavery and Abolition: A Journal of Comparative Studies* 9 (September, 1988), pp. 144–70.

_____, *Testing the Chains: Resistance to Slavery in the British West Indies* (Ithaca: Cornell University Press, 1982).

Curtin, Philip D., *Two Jamaicas: The Role of Ideas in a Tropical Colony, 1830–1865* (Cambridge, Mass.: Harvard University Press, 1955).

Dutton, Geoffrey, *The Hero as Murderer: The life of Edward John Eyre, Australian Explorer and Governor of Jamaica, 1815–1901* (Sydney and Melbourne: Collins & Cheshire, 1967).

Eisner, Gisela, *Jamaica, 1830–1930: A Study in Economic Growth* (Manchester: Manchester University Press, 1961).

Gaspar, David Barry, *Bondmen & Rebels: A Study of Master-Slave Relations in Antigua, With Implications for Colonial British America* (Baltimore: The Johns Hopkins University Press, 1985).

Gocking, C.V., 'Constitutional Problems in Jamaica, 1850–1866', (D.Phil. thesis, Oxford University, 1955).

Green, William A., *British Slave Emancipation: The Sugar Colonies and the Great Experiment, 1830–1865* (Oxford: Clarendon Press, 1976).

Hall, Catherine, 'The Economy of Intellectual Prestige: Thomas Carlyle, John Stuart Mill, and the Case of Governor Eyre', *Cultural Critique*, 12 (Spring, 1989), pp. 167–96.

_____, 'Imperial Man: Edward Eyre in Australasia and the West Indies, 1833–1866', in Bill Schwartz, ed., *The Expansion of England: Essays in the Cultural History of Race and Ethnicity* (forthcoming).

Hall, Douglas, *Free Jamaica, 1838–1865: An Economic History* (New Haven: Yale University Press, 1959).

Hart, Ansell, *The Life of George William Gordon* (Kingston, Jamaica: Institute of Jamaica, 1972).

Hart, Richard, *Slaves Who Abolished Slavery*, 2 vols., (Kingston, Jamaica: Institute of Social and Economic Research, 1985).

Heuman, Gad, *Between Black and White: Race, Politics and the Free Coloreds in Jamaica, 1792–1865* (Westport, Conn.: Greenwood Press, 1981).

_____, ed. *Out of the House of Bondage: Runaways, Resistance and Marronage in Africa and the New World* (London: Frank Cass, 1986).

Higman, B.W., *Slave Population and Economy in Jamaica, 1807–1834* (Cambridge: Cambridge University Press, 1976).

Hobsbawm, E.J., 'From Social History to the History of Society', in *Essays in Social History*, ed. by M.W. Flinn and T.C. Smout (Oxford: Clarendon Press, 1974).

———, *Primitive Rebels: Studies in Archaic Forms of Social Movement in the 19th and 20th Centuries* (New York: W.W Norton & Co., 1965).

Holt, Thomas C., *The Problem of Freedom: Race, Labor, and Politics in Jamaica and Britain, 1832–1938* (Baltimore: The Johns Hopkins University Press, 1992).

Jacobs, H.P., *Sixty Years of Change, 1806–1866: Progress and Reaction in Kingston and the countryside* (Kingston, Jamaica: Institute of Jamaica, 1973).

Johnson, Howard, ' "A Modified Form of Slavery": The Credit and Truck Systems in the Bahamas in the Nineteenth and Early Twentieth Centuries', *Comparative Studies in Society and History* 28 (October, 1986), pp. 729–53.

Knox, B.A., 'The British Government and the Governor Eyre Controversy', *The Historical Journal* 19, 4 (1976), pp. 877–900.

Knox, Graham, 'Political Change in Jamaica (1866–1906) and the Local Reaction to the Policies of the Crown Colony Government', in *The Caribbean in Transition: Papers on Social, Political, and Economic Development*, edited by F.M. Andic and T.G. Mathews. (Río Piedras: Institute of Caribbean Studies, University of Puerto Rico, 1965).

Kopytoff, Barbara K., 'The Maroons of Jamaica: An Ethnohistorical Study of Incomplete Polities, 1655–1905', (Ph.D. thesis, U. of Pennsylvania, 1973).

Lee, Sidney, ed., *Dictionary of National Biography* (London: Smith, Elder & Co., 1894).

Lorrimer, Douglas A., *Colour, Class and the Victorians: English attitudes to the Negro in the mid-nineteenth century* (Leicester: Leicester University Press, 1978).

Lumsden, Joyce Mary, 'Robert Love and Jamaican Politics', (Ph.D. thesis, University of the West Indies, 1987).

Marsala, Vincent John, *Sir John Peter Grant, Governor of Jamaica, 1866–1874* (Kingston, Jamaica: Institute of Jamaica, 1972).

Marshall, Woodville K., ' "Vox Populi": The St Vincent Riots and Disturbances of 1862', in *Trade, Government and Society in Caribbean History, 1700–1920*, edited by B.W. Higman. (Kingston, Jamaica: Heinemann Educational Books, 1983).

Mathieson, William Law, *The Sugar Colonies and Governor Eyre, 1849–1866* (London: Longmans, Green & Co., 1936).

Mintz, Sidney W., *Caribbean Transformations* (Chicago: Aldine Publishing Co., 1974).

Morris, James, *Heaven's Command: An Imperial Progress* (London: Faber & Faber, 1973).

Paquette, Robert L., *Sugar Is Made with Blood: The Conspiracy of La Escalera and the Conflict between Empires over Slavery in Cuba* (Middletown, Conn.: Wesleyan University Press, 1988).

Porter, Bernard, *The Lion's Share: A Short History of British Imperialism, 1850–1970* (London: Longman, 1975).

Olivier, Lord [Haldane, Sydney], *Jamaica, The Blessed Island* (London: Faber & Faber, 1936).

———, *The Myth of Governor Eyre* (London: The Hogarth Press, 1933).

Patterson, Orlando, *The Sociology of Slavery: An Analysis of the Origins, Development and Structure of Negro Slave Society in Jamaica* (London: McGibbon & Kee, 1967).

Price, Richard, ed., *Maroon Societies: Rebel Slave Communities in the Americas* (Garden City, N.Y.: Anchor Books, 1973).

Reckord (née Turner), Mary, 'The Jamaica Slave Rebellion of 1831', *Past and Present*, 40 (July, 1968), pp. 108–25.

Roberts, W. Adolphe, *Six Great Jamaicans: Biographical Sketches* (Kingston: The Pioneer Press, 1952).

Robotham, Don, *'The Notorious Riot': The Socio-Economic and Political Bases of Paul Bogle's Revolt* (Kingston, Jamaica: Institute of Social and Economic Research, 1981).

Satchell, Veront M., *From Plots to Plantations: Land Transactions in Jamaica, 1866–1900* (Mona, Jamaica; Institute of Social and Economic Research, 1990).

Schuler, Monica, *'Alas, Alas, Kongo': A Social History of Indentured African Immigration into Jamaica, 1841–1865* (Baltimore: The Johns Hopkins University Press, 1980).

Semmel, Bernard, *The Governor Eyre Controversy* (London: McKibbon & Kee, 1962).

Simmonds, Lorna Elaine, ' "The Spirit of Disaffection": Civil Disturbances in Jamaica, 1838–1865' (M.A. thesis, University of Waterloo, 1982).

Simpson, George Eaton, *Religious Cults of the Caribbean: Trinidad, Jamaica and Haiti* (Río Piedras, Puerto Rico: Institute of Caribbean Studies, University of Puerto Rico, 1980 [orig. pub. 1965]).

Stewart, Robert J., *Religion and Society in Post-Emancipation Jamaica* (Knoxville: University of Tennessee Press, 1992).

Third World, '1865', in the tape '96° in the Shade' (Island Records, 1977).

Thompson, E.P., 'The Crime of Anonymity', in Douglas Hay *et al.*, *Albion's Fatal Tree: Crime and Society in Eighteenth-Century England* (London: Allen Lane Press, 1975).

_____, 'The Moral Economy of the English Crowd in the Eighteenth Century', *Past & Present*, 51 (1971), pp. 76–136.

Turner, Mary. 'Chattel slaves into wage slaves: A Jamaican case study', in *Labour in the Caribbean: From emancipation to independence*, edited by Malcolm Cross and Gad Heuman, (London: Macmillan Caribbean, 1988).

_____, *Slaves and Missionaries: The Disintegration of Jamaican Slave Society, 1787–1834* (Urbana: University of Illinois Press, 1982).

Uren, Malcolm and Stephens, Robert, *Waterless Horizons: The first full-length study of the extraordinary life-story of Edward John Eyre . . .* (Melbourne: Robertson and Mullens, 1941).

Wilmot, Swithin, 'Emancipation in Action: Workers and Wage Conflict in Jamaica, 1838–40', *Jamaica Journal*, 19 (August–October, 1986), pp. 55–62.

_____, 'From Falmouth to Morant Bay: Religion and Politics in Jamaica, 1838–1865', Paper presented at the Association of Caribbean Historians' Conference, Havana, April, 1985.

_____, 'Women and Protest in Jamaica, 1838–1865', Paper presented at the Association of Caribbean Historians' Conference, Martinique, April, 1987.

Wilson-Tagoe, Nana, *The Historical Imagination in West Indian Literature* (London: Macmillan Caribbean, forthcoming).

Index

(Page numbers in *italics* refer to illustrations)